The Human Traditio.

CHARLES W. CALHOUN
Series Editor
Department of History, East Carolina University

The nineteenth-century English author Thomas Carlyle once remarked that "the history of the world is but the biography of great men." This approach to the study of the human past had existed for centuries before Carlyle wrote, and it continued to hold sway among many scholars well into the twentieth century. In more recent times, however, historians have recognized and examined the impact of large, seemingly impersonal forces in the evolution of human history—social and economic developments such as industrialization and urbanization as well as political movements such as nationalism, militarism, and socialism. Yet even as modern scholars seek to explain these wider currents, they have come more and more to realize that such phenomena represent the composite result of countless actions and decisions by untold numbers of individual actors. On another occasion, Carlyle said that "history is the essence of innumerable biographies." In this conception of the past, Carlyle came closer to modern notions that see the lives of all kinds of people, high and low, powerful and weak, known and unknown, as part of the mosaic of human history, each contributing in a large or small way to the unfolding of the human tradition.

This latter idea forms the foundation for this series of books on the human tradition in America. Each volume is devoted to a particular period or topic in American history and each consists of minibiographies of persons whose lives shed light on that period or topic. Well-known figures are not altogether absent, but more often the chapters explore a variety of individuals who may be less conspicuous but whose stories, nonetheless, offer us a window on some aspect of the nation's past.

By bringing the study of history down to the level of the individual, these sketches reveal not only the diversity of the American people and the complexity of their interaction but also some of the commonalities of sentiment and experience that Americans have shared in the evolution of their culture. Our hope is that these explorations of the lives of "real people" will give readers a deeper understanding of the human tradition in America.

Volumes in the Human Tradition in America series:

THE HUMAN TRADITION IN

THE CIVIL WAR

AND

RECONSTRUCTION

THE HUMAN TRADITION IN
THE CIVIL WAR
AND
RECONSTRUCTION

No. 4
The Human Tradition in America

Edited by
Steven E. Woodworth

A Scholarly Resources Inc. Imprint
Wilmington, Delaware

Scholarly Resources Inc.
104 Greenhill Avenue
Wilmington, DE 19805-1897
www.scholarly.com

Library of Congress Cataloging-in-Publication Data

The human tradition in the Civil War and Reconstruction / edited by
  Steven E. Woodworth
    p. cm. — (The human tradition in America : no. 4)
    Includes bibliographical references and index.
    ISBN 0-8420-2726-2 (cl. : alk. paper). — ISBN 0-8420-2727-0 (pa. :
    alk. paper)
    1. United States—History—Civil War, 1861–1865 Biography.
  2. Reconstruction Biography. I. Woodworth, Steven E. II. Series.
  E467.H888 2000
  973.7'092'2—dc21
  [B]   99-39902
                                                                    CIP

To the students of the Historians'
Brown-Bag-Lunch Discussion Group,
Toccoa Falls College, 1995–1997

To God Alone Be the Glory

About the Editor

STEVEN E. WOODWORTH is a graduate of Southern Illinois University–Carbondale and Rice University in Houston, Texas. He is the author of numerous books about the Civil War, including *Jefferson Davis and His Generals* (1990) and *Davis and Lee at War* (1995). He teaches history at Texas Christian University in Fort Worth, Texas.

I believe in aristocracy, though—if that is the right word, and if a democrat may use it. Not an aristocracy of power, based upon rank and influence, but an aristocracy of the sensitive, the considerate, and the plucky. Its members are to be found in all nations and classes, and all through the ages, and there is a secret understanding between them when they meet. They represent the true human tradition, the one permanent victory of our queer race over cruelty and chaos. Thousands of them perish in obscurity, a few are great names. They are sensitive for others as well as for themselves, they are considerate without being fussy, their pluck is not swankiness but the power to endure, and they can take a joke.

—E. M. Forster, *Two Cheers for Democracy* (1951)

Contents

Acknowledgments

I take pleasure in acknowledging the kind assistance and valuable advice of Matthew R. Hershey, acquisitions editor at Scholarly Resources, and Prof. Charles Calhoun of East Carolina University, editor of the series of which this book is a part. I am also indebted to Thomas A. Duncan, technical writer for Abbott Laboratories; A. Philip Brown, of Bob Jones University; Christopher Vena, of Bethel Theological Seminary; David Monreal, of Trinity Evangelical Divinity School; Matthew Pinson, of Florida State University; Ens. Matthew Crump, USN; and Paul Davis of Iva, South Carolina, for their friendly advice on parts of the manuscript.

Finally, I can sometimes be quite stubborn about what I want to say, so any errors or problems in the final product are to be attributed to me alone.

Introduction

Steven E. Woodworth

The Civil War shook the American Republic to its foundations. Along with Reconstruction, which occurred alongside it and continued beyond it, the conflict of the 1860s changed the country forever. Its painful cost surpassed anything else Americans have ever suffered. Some 620,000 young men perished on its battlefields, in its camps, and in the squalid wards of its hospitals. At least as many more came home again maimed for life, health ruined and perhaps missing a limb or two. And those who in most cases never left home—the women, the children, the aged, and other noncombatants—felt the effects of the war to greater or lesser extents in the economic dislocation it caused and the anxiety or loss they felt for loved ones in the military. Some of them lost their homes to the destruction wrought by the passing armies. Others lived in fear of bandits who roved in the lawless areas of no-man's-land, where neither side exercised solid authority.

With all its misery and loss, the war was not without its positive effects. Most striking of these was the freedom it gave to 3.5 million slaves in the South. The victorious North also made a halting and ultimately unsuccessful attempt to secure equal treatment in society for former slaves, but that proved more than could be done. The United States survived as a nation and demonstrated to the world that a free republic could indeed govern itself and avoid disintegration into anarchy, as aristocrats and monarchists the world over had been confidently—and gleefully—suggesting would be the case. The war preserved the Constitution and the rule of law, though it badly strained the Constitution's limitations on government power and undermined the role of the states within the federal system. When Reconstruction was over, the government in Washington returned to its accustomed ways like a river returning to its banks after a flood. Yet the new channels carved by the surging floodwaters of government power remained as lurking hazards when future generations would feel the rising tide of temptation to turn to an all-providing, all-powerful government.

In short, the Civil War and Reconstruction era featured a huge and complicated set of events that changed America in many ways, small and large, good and bad. There is good reason to study them carefully and well. In so doing, we should remember that these events happened to individual people and consisted of the actions taken by individual people. Even seemingly huge and impersonal forces were, in fact, the sum and product of myriad choices made by individuals, each with his own goals and problems, each making decisions—with or without realizing their contribution to the sum total—on the basis of his own view of himself and the world. The lives of people, after all, are what history is made of, and the "big story" is always the sum of all the little stories, in which individuals, under the providence of God, make their decisions for good or ill.

Not coincidentally, this book is made of just that: stories of the lives of people, all of whom lived during all or part of the years 1861 to 1877, who played a role, large or small, in the events of that momentous epoch and felt its impact in one way or another. The fourteen subjects covered in the chapters that follow are not by any means a representative sample of the U.S. population at that time. Instead, they are as varied a lot as could well be selected from that era. In many cases either I or the author of an individual chapter selected subjects not because they were like most Americans of the time but because they were not and thus would give readers an idea of some of the different sorts of people who had a hand in the Civil War. The individuals covered range from generals to lower-ranking army officers to a private in the ranks, as well as naval captains, slaves, politicians, and several remarkable women. They include blacks and whites. Among the whites, two were recent immigrants (from Germany and Ireland). Of course, some were Confederate and some were Union. Taken as a whole, they were different in many ways—almost as different as the various authors of these chapters, both in experience, outlook, and interpretation of events. But they were caught up together in one of the great stories of America's past. On behalf of my thirteen fellow contributors to this volume, I invite you to explore and reflect on that story as seen from the diverse perspectives of fourteen unique participants and their fourteen very different modern biographers.

1

Sgt. Peter Welsh

"Is That Not Worth Fiting For?"

Steven E. Woodworth

The story of Peter Welsh, a common soldier of the Civil War, illustrates the experience of the more than one million Northern men who went off to fight for the Union. Welsh was also an Irish immigrant, and he faced difficulties in a new land that at times received this culturally and religiously alien population with something less than open arms. Indeed, the Irish presented the primary ethnic problem of pre–Civil War Northern cities.

In this chapter, historian Steven E. Woodworth incorporates vivid excerpts from Welsh's letters home in depicting what life was like for those in the lower tiers of American Society—and the military—during the Civil War period. Woodworth is an assistant professor of history at Texas Christian University, Fort Worth, Texas, and the author of *Jefferson Davis and His Generals* (1990) and *Davis and Lee at War* (1995).

Although business leaders produced and profited, politicians talked, and generals planned and tried to lead, private soldiers actually fought the Civil War. Some two million of them served before the conflict was over. Their motivations varied yet remained strong enough to keep them in the ranks through times when those who really wanted to desert usually succeeded in doing so. They found war a far cry from the romantic pictures of waving flags and battlefield glory most of them had envisioned at the time of enlistment. It was instead a cold, wet, muddy, filthy, boring, hungry, and often sickening business, but, for whatever reasons, most stuck it out. "A soldier is not a hero in fighting alone," observed one of their officers, "his patience under hardship, privation and sickness is equally heroic; sometimes I feel disposed to put him on a level with the martyrs."[1] The great masses that filled the ranks of both sides were made up of individuals with hopes, dreams, families, and life stories of their own—stories that are often overlooked in the discussion of the great events of the war.

Among the soldiers of both sides were Irish Americans. Large numbers of them had come to America during the late 1840s and throughout the 1850s, driven by famine and a certain degree of oppression in their homeland. They were poor peasants for the most

1

part, unacquainted with American ways, and they were not always welcome. Their poverty and their different customs led many native-born Americans to think them dirty, fractious, and ill mannered, and their Roman Catholicism worried many Protestants who wondered about the "foreign" religion's effect on the body politic. Such concerns sparked the creation of the short-lived Know-Nothing Party during the 1850s, with its anti-immigrant agenda. In the large urban areas where the Irish tended to settle, they occupied the bottom rung of the socioeconomic ladder, had the least money, and did the most undesirable jobs.

When the Civil War began in April 1861, most Irishmen felt no particular call to fight for the Union. They had had little time and, it would seem, less motivation to develop much in the way of abstract patriotism. Beyond that, many of them tended to be racist in their view of blacks, for unlike many residents of the North, they were in direct competition with the free blacks in the job markets of Northern cities. The economic rivalry brought bitter feelings, and the more the war looked like something done on behalf of the African Americans, the less the Irish Americans wanted anything to do with it. The prospect that the conflict might even free substantial portions of the slaves—to migrate to Northern cities, perhaps, and increase the already tough economic competition—was still less welcome. Yet despite all this, many Irishmen did fight for the Union, raising interesting questions of motivation. This is the story of one of those men.

Peter Welsh was born June 29, 1830, in Charlottetown, Prince Edward Island, to Irish immigrant parents. Some years later his family migrated to the United States and settled near Boston, Massachusetts. We know little of his youth, but we do know that in 1857, he and Margaret Prendergast were married at Saint Mary's Church in Charlestown, Massachusetts, with the Reverend Aloysius Janalick presiding. Margaret was as Irish as Peter. Indeed, she had been born in the Emerald Isle, in Athy, county Kildare, one of seven children of Patrick and Margaret O'Toole Prendergast.

Not long after their wedding, the young couple moved to New York City. Peter was a carpenter but found it hard to make a living in the great city, for times were hard after the financial panic of 1857 and work was scarce. As he later admitted, it was not a happy time in their marriage, at least partially because Peter sometimes went on binges of heavy drinking.

By the summer of 1862, with the war already more than a year old, Peter Welsh was still trying to make a hardscrabble living as a carpenter in New York and letting others handle the fighting. About that time, however, a dispute arose among various members of his family still living in Boston, and Peter traveled there to see if he could help them work things out. However, both of the squabbling factions turned on him instead, and he became depressed and began drinking again, using up every cent he had brought with him. When the spree ended, Peter was deeply ashamed of his lack of self-control as well as the fact that he had squandered what little money he and Margaret could spare. In his humiliation, he felt he could not face his family again, much less ask them for money to get back to New York. So in nearby Charlestown, where Company K of the Twenty-eighth Massachusetts Volunteer Infantry Regiment was recruiting, Peter rather impulsively decided to enlist.

The Twenty-eighth Massachusetts was a virtually all-Irish outfit. In the early months of the war, Thomas Francis Meagher, a fiery Irish nationalist forced into exile a decade and a half before by the British authorities in his homeland, had set out to raise a brigade of his fellow Irish Americans to fight for the Union. As unlikely as that prospect seemed, Meagher's own participation seemed stranger still because his previous pro-Southern proclivities were fairly well known. Still, there was a great rush to the colors in the immediate aftermath of the Confederate firing on Fort Sumter, and going to war was the manly thing to do. There were a great many Irishmen in the United States, times were hard, and—at least as stereotype would have it—the Irish needed no special cause to draw them into such a purely enjoyable recreation as fighting. Fighting—for whatever cause—was said by some to have appeal enough. Such was the way Anglo society thought about them in that age and indeed the way many of them thought about themselves. In fact, some of the Irishmen who enlisted did so to gain military training and experience for possible future use against the hated British in Ireland.

Whatever the motivation of the recruits, Meagher succeeded in raising three regiments in New York City—the Sixty-third, Sixty-ninth, and Eighty-eighth New York. He had plans to enlist two other regiments, one from Philadelphia and the other from Boston, but those goals were not immediately realized. The latter two regiments did not join what was then known as the Irish Brigade until the fall of 1862. The Boston regiment was the Twenty-eighth Massachusetts, in which Peter Welsh would soon march as a private in Company K.

It was September 3, 1862, when Welsh enlisted, and he and his new comrades were soon trained and on their way to Washington. By the time they arrived there, the rest of the regiment had already departed for the front. Things were not going particularly well for the Union in Virginia at that time. Four days before Welsh's enlistment, Federal forces under Maj. Gen. John Pope had suffered a severe defeat at the hands of Confederate general Robert E. Lee and his trusty lieutenant Thomas J. "Stonewall" Jackson at the

Second Battle of Bull Run. Lee had then decided to follow up his advantage and cross the Potomac River into Union-held Maryland, seriously threatening both Washington, DC, and Baltimore. In response, Union authorities had rushed every possible reinforcement to the army, now commanded by George B. McClellan in place of the disgraced Pope. Among those who went were the soldiers of the Twenty-eighth Massachusetts, currently attached to Maj. Gen. Ambrose Burnside's Ninth Corps rather than the intended parent unit, the Irish Brigade of Maj. Gen. Edwin V. Sumner's Second Corps.

Welsh and his batch of fellow recruits caught up with the regiment September 13, near Frederick, Maryland. He was pleased that he had been able to stand the long, hard marches of the previous week and felt stronger than ever, though many of his comrades had given out along the way.

The next day the new men had their baptism of fire as the regiment went into action at the Battle of South Mountain. Three days later an even more stern encounter awaited them on the banks of Antietam Creek in a struggle that was the bloodiest single day of the war. Peter never said much of what he saw there, but it must have been a harrowing experience. One of the recruits who had come down with him from Boston less than two weeks before fell dead nearby, and Peter's tentmate (Civil War soldiers usually lived two to a tent while in the field), "a very nice man with a wife and famely," lost his right arm.[2]

After the battle, Peter continued to enjoy good health: "Never was so hearty in my life," he wrote his wife, "exercise in the open air agrees with me better then anything else."[3] He did worry, though, about Margaret, especially about her poor health. He wanted to make sure she was getting the small stipend that the state of Massachusetts had authorized for the support of the families of its soldiers and was disappointed to learn that it was only four dollars per week rather than eight dollars as he had thought. He sent her all the money he could from his pay and urged her to keep their furniture so that they would be able to set up housekeeping again more easily when he got out of the army at the end of the war. That, he reckoned, had to be less than six months off. Still, he assured his wife that even if the war lasted another year, he was better off in the army. The pay was more than he could have gotten as a carpenter in New York, even if he could find steady work. Most of all, he admonished her, "do not fret and worry yourself so much."[4]

The Army of the Potomac slowly followed the beaten Confederates back into Virginia. Early in November, Peter proudly reported to Margaret that he had been promoted to corporal. Later that month the Twenty-eighth transferred from the Ninth Corps to the Second Corps's Irish Brigade, for which it had originally been raised, and the troops camped just north of the Rappahannock River, opposite the picturesque little town of Fredericksburg, Virginia. Peter assured Margaret that no battle would be fought in the near future, newspaper reports notwithstanding. The first snow fell on December 5, and he predicted that the army would soon go into winter quarters.

About that he was mistaken. On Thursday, December 11, reveille sounded at 4:00 A.M. in the camps of the Irish Brigade. Their officers had them eat a quick breakfast, pack their things, leave their knapsacks piled in camp with a detail to watch them, and march toward the Rappahannock. They left camp about daybreak to the ominous rumble of distant cannon, but after two hours of marching, they halted along the hills that overlooked the Rappahannock from the north while other Union troops tried to force their way across the river. They were up again the next morning at four and under way at daybreak, this time marching across a pontoon bridge into Fredericksburg. Throughout the day, they expected to be sent into battle at any moment, but the order never came, though the artillery thundered on. That night, they camped in ankle-deep mud. Peter and some of his comrades succeeded in finding pieces of boards on which to lie, and there he "slept as sound I think as ever I slept in my life."[5]

When the officers awakened them at four the next morning, Saturday, December 13, Peter found a thick layer of frost on the blanket under which he had slept so soundly. After he and his comrades finished their usual breakfast of hardtack, salt pork, and coffee, the officers ordered them into line of battle in one of Fredericksburg's streets, ready for action. There they stood, shoulder to shoulder in two ranks, and waited while Confederate gunners on a ridge called Marye's Heights, about a mile outside town, spotted them from across an open plain and opened fire. The Southern artillerists soon had the range all too well, and Union men started falling. Right beside Peter a shell cut down two men, one standing behind the other.

When the order to advance came, it was almost a relief—until the men saw where they were supposed to advance. Across a wide, smooth plain that sloped very gently upward, they could see that Marye's Heights was crowned with thundering Confederate cannon. At the foot of the ridge, Southern infantrymen, sheltered in a sunken road behind a stone wall, could sweep the plain with their rifle fire. Another Federal brigade had already attempted to storm the ridge, and its dead and wounded littered the ground over which the Irishmen would have to advance. The artillery tore into their ranks at once. "The storm of shell and . . . canister was terrible,"

Peter wrote to Margaret, "mowing whole gaps out of our ranks and we having to march over their dead and wounded bodies." However, he added, "we advanced boldly despite it all."[6] And so they did. The charge of the Irish Brigade was the admiration of both sides that day and one of the war's most amazing displays of raw courage. The five regiments moved forward with steady tread and solid ranks, five U.S. flags flying, one with each regiment. In the center marched the Twenty-eighth Massachusetts, the only unit in the brigade that day to carry its regimental flag into action; it was a green banner displaying a harp as a symbol of Ireland. Terrible and magnificent to those who watched, the charge was only terrible for those who took part. They had hardly cleared the town when Peter's captain, Captain Sanborn, went down, shot in the foot. Then, Company K's only other officer, 2d Lt. John Sullivan, fell dead a few feet from where Peter was marching on the right side of the company. Only Peter and one other man came through unwounded in that part of the line. Overall, 12 of the 37 men the company had taken into battle were killed or wounded. A total of 490 from the Irish Brigade fell that day.

The desperate attack failed, of course, as did the assaults of several other brigades that came soon after. Defeated, Burnside pulled the Army of the Potomac back to the north bank of the Rappahannock. The weeks that followed the lopsided Union defeat at Fredericksburg were a time of discouragement for the men of the Army of the Potomac, just as they were for much of the rest of the nation. The war seemed futile, the expense in blood and treasure enormous. Many, especially among the Irish, hated Lincoln's Emancipation Proclamation and told themselves that most of the nation's troubles were the result of abolitionist "fanatics" and the incompetence—or worse—of the Lincoln administration. Peter thought so too.

In many ways, however, he was a remarkably contented soldier. He lived in a wooden shanty that he and his comrades had built for their winter quarters that year. He had a cracker-box for his writing desk, and writing letters to his beloved Margaret was his favorite occupation when he was not involved in regular drills and other duties. The shanty's chimney, as was typical of such structures, drew very poorly, and the interior was often full of smoke, but Peter minded little. He thrived on the diet of hardtack, salt pork, dried or "dessicated" vegetables, supplemented with beans and rice when available, and he admitted that army regulations banning the sale of liquor to the soldiers were wise. He worked hard and attributed his steady, robust health to all the outdoor exercise and plain food. He even liked his strict but fair commanding officer.

His one grief was Margaret. He missed her terribly, worried often about the health problems of which she complained, and was also pained at her attitude toward the war and, especially, his participation in it. She said she cared nothing for the nation: What had it ever done for her? She objected to Peter's use of soldier's stationery with patriotic pictures and poems on it and to his protest that the Union cause was divinely sanctioned. She replied indignantly that she thought God had nothing to do with the war. Bitterly, she reproached Peter for having caused her little but unhappiness in their married life. Hers were not letters to boost the spirits of a soldier far from home.

Margaret's complaints elicited from the simple Irish American carpenter an eloquent defense of the cause for which he was pledged to fight. True, he admitted, the immediate occasion for his enlistment had been that unfortunate drinking spree in Boston, but he now felt that a larger purpose had brought him to fight for the Union cause. Why must *he* fight for it? What was it to *him*? "This is my country as much as the man that was born on the soil," he explained, "and so it is with every man who comes to this country and becomes a citezen." This he claimed not as a charter of privileges but as a solemn responsibility. "This being the case I have as much interest in the maintenence of the goverment and laws and the integrity of the nation as any other man," he continued.[7]

He then tried to express to his wife the meaning of the war in words that were remarkably similar to those used by the president whose policies he generally opposed. "This war with all its evils with all its errors and missmanagement," he wrote, "is a war in which the people of all nations have a vital interest. This is the first test of a modern free government in the act of sustaining itself against internal enemys and matured rebellion. All men who love free government and equal laws are watching this crisis to see if a republic can sustain itself in such a case. If it fail then the hopes of milions fall and the designs and wishes of all tyrants will suceed. The old cry will be sent forth from the aristocrats of europe that such is the comon end of all republics. . . . The giant republic has fallen."[8]

He admitted to feeling that the Lincoln administration had mismanaged the war, mishandled the army, and, worst of all, freed the slaves, but if slavery was in the way of the Republic's survival, then so much the worse for slavery as far as this Irishman was concerned. Think, he urged Margaret, of what a beacon America was to the oppressed of the world, a place where they could live in freedom and eat the fruit of their labor. "What would be the condition to day of hundreds of thousands of the sons and daughters of poor opressed old erin [Ireland] if they had not a free land like this to emigrate to? . . . The same may be said of thousands from other lands." Though he was a member of a nationality supposedly victimized by severe discrimination in America, Peter Welsh then put the case plainly in terms that still resonate more than a century later: "Contrast the condition of the masses of this with any other country in the world and the advantages we enjoy will stand out boldly so that the blindest can see them. Here there is no bloated peted [petted] rascals or what is called in monarchial countrys the aristocracy. . . . Here the poorest mother may look with joy and satisfaction on her ofspring if she only gives him a proper training in his tender years . . . and from that [he] takes his start with all the honours and the hiest position that a great nation can bestow open before him."[9] Nancy Hanks's son often said the same—and with but little greater eloquence.

"Is this not worth fiting for?" Peter concluded. He answered his own question: "It is our duty to do our share for the comon wellfare not only of the present generation but of future generations. Such being the case it becomes the duty of every one no matter what his position to do all in his power to sustain for the present and to perpetuate for the benefit [of] future generations a government . . . which is superior to any the world has yet known."[10]

Margaret would not be persuaded and continued to complain about the Union cause and Peter's absence. Her husband, still very concerned about her health, offered advice and urged her to see a doctor, avoid overwork, and try not to worry.

On Saint Patrick's Day 1863, General Meagher presided over a full day of festivities in the camps of the Irish Brigade. A good time—and quite a bit of whiskey—was had by all. Festivities stopped abruptly, though, when word came of significant skirmishing several miles up the Rappahannock at Kelly's Ford, and Meagher ordered the brigade into line, ready for battle. Peter's company was now the color company, responsible for bearing the national and regimental banners. The company fell into line, and Captain Sanborn, by now recovered from his Fredericksburg wound, was startled to see that the green flag was missing. Where was it? The bearer could not say. Turning to Welsh, who may have looked more sober than the other noncommissioned officers, Sanborn ordered him to find the colors and get into line with them. When Peter did, Sanborn made him the permanent bearer of the green flag. The next day the decision was made official, and Welsh received the accompanying promotion to the rank of sergeant. "I shall feel proud to bear up that flag of green, the emblem of Ireland and Irish men," he wrote Margaret, "and espesialy having received it on that day dear to every irish heart, the festivel of St Patrick."[11]

The much-depleted size of the Irish Brigade earned it a reserve role at the Battle of Chancellorsville that May, and it saw only brief fighting with few casualties. Still, it had just as much hard marching to do over roads that became bottomless mud when heavy rains came the day after the battle. And the men experienced just as much discouragement when the army retreated after what the soldiers could only conclude had been another defeat. Back on the north side of the Rappahannock, camp life resumed, and Peter, along with Company K's first sergeant, built themselves "the purtyest little shanty in this army."[12] As usual, he was content and healthy.

The quiet routine was broken again on Sunday evening, June 14, 1863, just as the Irish Brigade was coming off a two-day picket-guard detail. Orders came to march immediately, and march they did, all night and most of the next day. Days of long, hard marches followed, now in smothering heat and choking dust, now in torrential rains and calf-deep mud. Lee had slid around the Army of the Potomac's right flank and was racing northward. The Federals followed, keeping themselves between Lee and Washington. Two weeks into the campaign, on Monday, June 29, the Second Corps, of which the Irish Brigade was part, marched thirty-two miles from Frederick to Uniontown, Maryland, "the greatest march ever made by any part of our army," Peter thought.[13] Thousands of exhausted and footsore soldiers fell out along the roads, unable to go on without rest, and later hobbled along to catch up with their regiments as best they could throughout the night. In Company K, Twenty-eighth Massachusetts, Peter was one of the handful who kept up the pace all day, and he was the only man with enough energy left to light a fire and boil a pot of coffee (the soldiers' ubiquitous favorite beverage) before retiring that night.

On Wednesday, July 1, the Second Corps was marching northward again, crossing into "Pencilvenia" while listening to the angry muttering of artillery somewhere off to the north near the town of Gettysburg.[14] The next day, they formed into battle lines near the center of the army. A mile away across rolling farmland, the rebel army remained strangely quiet throughout the morning.

Then, at about four in the afternoon, the Confederates struck hard at the left end of the Union line, and the Irishmen could judge by the gradually approaching roar of battle that things were not going well for the Federals there. Not long after five o'clock, the call for reinforcements came. Among the Second Corps troops sent in response was the Irish Brigade. When the men were ordered to form into line and prepare to march toward the steadily rising crescendo of battle on their left, Catholic chaplain William Corby of the Eighty-eighth New York asked the brigade commander, Patrick Kelly, if he could give the men absolution. Kelly agreed and had the troops called to attention. The chaplain climbed atop a small boulder and told the men his purpose. The soldiers knelt and uncovered their heads while Corby recited in Latin the formula of absolution, then concluded with the reminder that the "Catholic church refuses

Christian burial to the soldier who turns his back upon the foe or deserts his flag."[15] Thus encouraged and challenged, the men rose and took their places in line.

Marching in the center of the division's front line, the Twenty-eighth advanced through a thin skirt of forest called Trostle's Woods, across a farm lane, and out into a field of ripening wheat. On the far side of the field rose a wooded hill that everyone seemed to remember most for the thickly strewn boulders that covered its slope and concealed the Confederate riflemen who blazed away at the advancing Irishmen. On went the Irish Brigade, only some six hundred–strong now, once again making a magnificent charge under their five flags of green—one borne by Peter—and five of red, white, and blue. They pressed in and fought at close quarters with the rebels among the rocks, forcing the Southerners to flee down the back side of the hill. Their success was short-lived, however. New brigades of Confederates came up on both the left and right, the ones in front rallied and came on again, and the Irish Brigade was driven rapidly back across the hotly contested wheat field, barely escaping being surrounded and cut off. A third of their scant numbers had fallen, including half the men of the Twenty-eighth Massachusetts.

The following day brought a noisy artillery bombardment, but its chief aim (and that of the Confederate infantry assault that followed) was another sector of the Union line, and the Twenty-eighth escaped unharmed. Lee retreated, and the Army of the Potomac followed at a far more leisurely pace than when it drove north. Months of desultory and inconsequential camping and campaigning followed in Virginia.

Throughout this period Peter continued to enjoy excellent health, but Margaret's health and state of mind both deteriorated. She was frantic enough in her loneliness to contemplate traveling down to Virginia to visit him, but he had to explain to her that that was simply not possible. Under the steady assault of his wife's complaints, his dedication to the cause began to flag late in 1863. He said that he wished he could be promoted to the rank of commissioned officer so that he could resign and go home. Failing that, he hoped for a furlough—but furloughs could be had only by reenlisting, in effect extending his term of service from the fall of 1865 to early 1867, if he and the war both lasted that long.

In the end, Peter signed on for another term and in exchange took thirty-five days of leave in New York. "The time sliped by on lightning wheels," he later wrote, "it seemed verry short to a man after being a year and a half from home."[16] He returned to the regiment in early April 1864 as the army, now operating under the orders of the more resolute and skillful Ulysses S. Grant, was preparing for its spring offensive against Lee.

"The Twenty-eighth Massachusetts Volunteer Regiment broke camp at Stevensburg, Va., at dark on the evening of May 3, 1864," wrote Capt. James Fleming in his report as senior surviving officer of the regiment several weeks later.[17] They marched all that night and crossed the Rapidan River the next morning, moving into an area of dense woods known as the Wilderness. Battle was joined May 5, but the Twenty-eighth saw mostly skirmishing duties and suffered only a dozen or so casualties. Still, the experience was what Peter called "a prety rough time," with "8 days constantly fighting."[18]

By May 12 the tide of battle had carried the contending armies to a hamlet named Spotsylvania Court House, near the edge of the Wilderness area. There, Lee had succeeded in blocking Grant, and on that morning, Grant made his bid to break Lee's lines in a massive predawn assault spearheaded by the Second Corps. Initial results were good, with Confederate entrenchments overrun and dozens of guns and thousands of soldiers captured, including Confederate general Edward Johnson, taken by one of the Irishmen of the Twenty-eighth.

Somewhere in this first stage of the fighting, Peter Welsh took a bullet in the left arm. "A flesh wound in my left arm," he described it, "just a nice one to keep me from any more fighting or marching this campaign." It had been "the greatest battle of the war," he told Margaret, and "we licked saucepans out of them."[19]

"Slight" was what the doctors at the Second Corps field hospital had called the wound. But on May 14 the surgeon at Carver Hospital in Washington determined that the bullet had shattered the bone in Peter's forearm and was lodged there still. Three days later, doctors operated to remove the bullet, along with some bone fragments. All went well for another three days. Margaret arrived from New York, and was at his bedside well before May 20, when his condition became more serious. The wound hemorrhaged, and although attendants stopped the bleeding, pyemia (blood poisoning) set in within days. Knowledge of antiseptic practices was virtually nil among Civil War surgeons, and infections carried off thousands of soldiers who would otherwise have recovered from their wounds. Now infection went to work on Peter. The wound drained an alarming discharge, nausea and chills set in, and he could no longer eat. By May 28, he was delirious, and before the day was over, the infection had claimed the life of this soldier who had always been so healthy.

"He is dead and will be in New York in morning," Margaret wired her uncle in that city.[20] The army records tell us she took his effects with her—his blanket, cap, two shirts, trousers, and boots. She never remarried.

Peter had once written that the war would be "a powerfull purifier" for the nation. Perhaps, had he been able to see it through to the end, it might have purified him of his racism, as it did at least in part for many Northern soldiers who witnessed the way black troops fought and who came to know some blacks personally. Perhaps he might have seen that the newly freed slave as well as the recent Irish immigrant both had "a stake in America," an interest in the same freedom, and the same chance of bettering himself for which he had fought. For either of them and for the rest of America, that was indeed something "worth fiting for."[21]

Notes

1. John William De Forest, *A Volunteer's Adventures: A Union Captain's Record of the Civil War,* ed. James H. Croushore (New Haven, CT: Yale University Press, 1946), 151.

2. Peter Welsh, *Irish Green and Union Blue: The Civil War Letters of Peter Welsh, Color Sergeant, 28th Regiment Massachusetts Volunteers,* ed. Lawrence Frederick Kohl and Margaret Cosse Richard (New York: Fordham University Press, 1986), 28. For historical accuracy and flavor, Welsh's spelling, punctuation, and syntax have been preserved in this and all succeeding quotes.

3. Ibid., 20–21.

4. Ibid., 24.

5. Ibid., 42.

6. Ibid., 43.

7. Ibid., 65.

8. Ibid., 65–66.

9. Ibid., 66–67.

10. Ibid., 67.

11. Ibid., 80.

12. Ibid., 98.

13. Ibid., 109.

14. Ibid.

15. Harry W. Pfanz, *Gettysburg: The Second Day* (Chapel Hill: University of North Carolina Press, 1987), 268.

16. Welsh, *Irish Green and Union Blue,* 152.

17. U.S. War Department, *The War of the Rebellion: Official Records of the Union and Confederate Armies,* 128 vols. (Washington, DC: U.S. Government Printing Office, 1881–1901), series 1, vol. 35, pt. 1, p. 388.

18. Welsh, *Irish Green and Union Blue,* 156.

19. Ibid.

20. Ibid., 157.

21. Ibid., 67, 70.

2

Winfield Scott Hancock
"The Knightly Corps Commander"

Ethan S. Rafuse

Although it was the private soldiers, such as Peter Welsh, who fought the battles, men of higher rank usually directed their actions and thus exercised an influence on the course of events far out of proportion to their numbers. Those of the highest rank, the great commanders such as Robert E. Lee and Ulysses S. Grant, gained immense fame, becoming well known—if sometimes little understood—by vast numbers of Americans. Yet between army headquarters and the men in the ranks who did the fighting and most of the bleeding were several layers of officers whose job was to turn their commanders' ideas into realities on the battlefield; these were the men who deployed the troops and led them into the zone of danger. The outcome of the battles often hung on the skill, inspirational abilities, and raw courage of such midranking officers.

Winfield Scott Hancock was among the best of these men. In his report on the Battle of Williamsburg in May 1862, Gen. George B. McClellan described Hancock's performance as "superb," and the description became a standard one: In fact, he became known as "Hancock the superb." In presenting Hancock's story, historian Ethan Rafuse, of the University of Missouri–Kansas City and author of several articles on the Civil War as well as a large forthcoming study of Hancock's army commander George McClellan, gives readers a glimpse of the role and importance of midlevel commanders in the Civil War.

The actions of presidents and army commanders have traditionally dominated discussions of the military history of the Civil War. However, the course of military operations was frequently—and often decisively—shaped by decisions made at the corps, division, and brigade levels. The Civil War was the first conflict in which the American people fielded armies of fifty thousand men or more. These armies were too large and conditions in the field changed too rapidly for commanders to exercise close supervision over the entire range of an army's operations. To achieve success on the battlefield, it was therefore essential that leaders in the second echelon possess the character and ability to exercise independent judgment and make sound decisions. Fortunately for its cause, the

13

Union found men equal to the task. This is the story of one of the best of them.

Although he never held a major independent command, few officers were held in higher regard by professional soldiers and the general public by the end of the Civil War than Winfield Scott Hancock. Ulysses S. Grant's postwar relations with Hancock were often strained, yet in his memoirs, Grant wrote: "[Hancock's] name was never mentioned as having committed in battle a blunder . . . his personal courage and his presence with his command in the thickest of the fight won for him the confidence of troops serving under him."[1] On Hancock's death, former New York governor Samuel J. Tilden spoke of "the dashing bravery and consummate abilities of the superb soldier whom the country has lost."[2]

Hancock was one of twin boys born on February 14, 1824, to Benjamin Franklin and Elizabeth Hoxworth Hancock in Montgomery Square, Pennsylvania. The family moved to Norristown, Pennsylvania, three years later, where, after passing the bar in 1828, Benjamin Hancock enjoyed a forty-year career in law and local Democratic politics. From his father, Winfield inherited a powerful respect for the law and for the states' rights and limited-government doctrines of the Democratic Party—qualities that would shape his behavior in war and peace.

Benjamin Hancock hoped his sons would follow in his footsteps and become lawyers. However, it did not take long for the child named after the great soldier of the War of 1812 to exhibit an uncommon fondness for the military. While attending the Norristown Academy, for example, Winfield organized a company of his classmates and led them in drill. In 1840, Benjamin yielded to his son's desire for a military education and secured for him an appointment to the United States Military Academy at West Point, New York. Although he did not devote himself as seriously as he could have to his studies, Hancock nonetheless impressed his fellow cadets; one of them later said Hancock was "as manly a fellow as the Academy ever produced."[3] He completed the program in 1844, graduating eighteenth in a class of twenty-five. When the Mexican War began two years later, Hancock was on recruiting duty and did not reach the theater of operations until midway through the final campaign against Mexico City. He did well in his first battles—at Churubusco on August 20, 1847, and at Chapultepec on September 7—winning a brevet promotion for gallantry.

The benefits of service in Mexico were not limited to the experience Hancock gained managing men in battle. Garrison duty after the fighting ended proved to be a thoroughly pleasant experience for the young officer, who shared a highly congenial mess with Virginians Henry Heth and Lewis Armistead. Together, they toured the magnificent Valley of Mexico, maintained a festive and bountiful table, and enjoyed the company of many attractive young señoritas. "Never," Heth would later recall, "was a mess happier than ours."[4]

Soon after the Treaty of Guadalupe Hidalgo was ratified in March 1848, Hancock and his unit returned to the United States. In June, he was appointed regimental quartermaster for the Sixth Infantry Regiment, a post he held until October 1849, when he was made regimental adjutant. While stationed in Saint Louis, Hancock met and won the hand of Almira Russell, the daughter of a prominent local merchant. They were married on January 24, 1850. The weather on their wedding day was stormy, but the same could never be said of the marriage. During their thirty-six-year union, which produced a son and a daughter, Winfield and Almira Hancock's devotion to one another was unshakable, in good times and bad.

Life in the antebellum army could be hard indeed, not least of all because of the limited opportunities for advancement available to junior officers. In fact, Hancock was not promoted to captain until November 5, 1855. Soon thereafter, he was ordered to Florida and assigned the task of managing the base of supplies for forces operating against the Seminoles. It was a miserable experience, but Hancock's performance impressed his superiors. When William S. Harney, commander of the campaign against the Seminoles, was assigned to duty at Fort Leavenworth, Kansas, in 1857, he secured Hancock's transfer to that post. During his nine months in Kansas, Hancock supported efforts to maintain a truce that had been forged between Free-Soilers and proslavery forces in that troubled territory. He also helped organize Albert Sidney Johnston's expedition to Utah to quell unrest among the Mormons, and he served as quartermaster for a force sent to support Johnston in May 1858.

One year later, Hancock was appointed chief quartermaster for the southern district of California. His duties were not particularly onerous, and he was able to engage in a number of business ventures, none of which were very successful. He also kept an eye on political developments back east. As a states' rights Democrat with many Southern friends, he viewed the prospect of Abraham Lincoln's election to the presidency in 1860 as, in his wife's words, "[a] situation pregnant with danger."[5] He cast his vote for John C. Breckinridge in the November election but did not hesitate to express his determination to stand by the Union when news of the fall of Fort Sumter reached California during the last week of April 1861.

Before Hancock and his Southern colleagues parted company, they gathered at his and Almira's home for one last "never-to-be-forgotten evening." They sang songs, shed tears, and vowed everlasting friendship. But civil war is the cruelest form of war. "Three of the six from whom we parted on that evening in Los Angeles," Almira Hancock would later note, "were killed in front of General Hancock's troops."[6]

On arriving in Washington in September 1861, Hancock received unpleasant news. The army grapevine had it that he was to be assigned to quartermaster duty in Kentucky. Fortunately, George McClellan, commander of the Army of the Potomac, reached Hancock before the War Department did. Horrified at the prospect of his fellow Pennsylvanian's talents being wasted in mundane quartermaster duties, McClellan directed Hancock to maintain a low profile until he could find a brigade for him to command. Hancock did so and was rewarded on September 23 with a commission as a brigadier general of volunteers and a brigade in William F. "Baldy" Smith's division of the Army of the Potomac. He and his wife were delighted, although her enthusiasm was dampened a bit when someone informed her that "if a cannon were fired down Pennsylvania Avenue it would strike a hundred or more newly created brigadiers."[7]

McClellan's regard for Hancock was so high that he probably could have gotten command of a division if he had arrived in Washington sooner, but it was likely for the best in the long run that he did not. Hancock, in the words of staff officer James H. Wilson, became "a warm admirer of McClellan," with whom he shared a keen appreciation of the need to carefully prepare and thoroughly train their volunteer army before operations began.[8] Hancock also shared McClellan's distaste for meddling by politicians in military affairs and those who wanted to make the abolition of slavery a Union war aim. But as the war progressed, officers of prominence in the Army of the Potomac who were loyal to "Little Mac" and his conservative principles came to be viewed with deep distrust by the meddlesome and powerful radical faction of the Republican Party. Starting out as a brigade commander enabled Hancock to steer clear of the open factionalism that distinguished the Army of the Potomac's high command during the first two years of the war; it also allowed him to establish an unimpeachable combat record that somewhat inoculated him from radical criticism when he rose to a level where loyalty to McClellan could be a liability.

Hancock brought an ideal combination of military professionalism and personal magnetism to the task of leading men. Over six feet tall and weighing 170 pounds, with a dark, imperial beard and deep blue eyes, he had a presence that inspired both awe and respect. "Hancock is," proclaimed one soldier, "the tallest, and most shapely, and in many respects . . . the best looking officer of them all . . . dignified, gentlemanly and commanding. I think if he were in civilian clothes, and should give commands in the army to those who did not know him, he would be likely to be obeyed at once, and without any question."[9] Hancock expected much from his men and could be ferocious when they failed to meet his high standards (the art and munificence of his profanity became legendary within the army). But he also recognized that Americans expected their leaders to be democratic as well as heroic, and he endeared himself to his men by sharing their hardships, learning as many of their names as possible, never failing to appear where the fighting was heaviest, and being as lavish in his praise when they did well as he was in his criticism when they did not.

Hancock also mastered the mundane but no less crucial aspects of generalship. During his years as a staff officer he had developed a command of regulations and learned the value of attention to detail, which enabled him to dispose of paperwork and negotiate red tape with alacrity and efficiency. Hancock also did not underestimate the importance of good public relations in what President Abraham Lincoln proclaimed to be "a people's contest."[10] Unlike many of his fellow officers, he made a point of maintaining a good relationship with the reporters who followed the movements of the Army of the Potomac. Moreover, as one fellow officer recalled, "correspondents of the principal journals yielded, like every one else, to his captivating bearing and manners."[11]

On March 23, 1862, after six months of arduous training, Hancock and his brigade boarded ships bound for the peninsula between the York and James Rivers, where McClellan planned to make his grand campaign on Richmond. "I am off at last," Hancock wrote his wife, "and it is a matter of great pain to me that I am unable to see you again before we part—God alone knows for how long."[12]

Unfortunately, the campaign immediately bogged down in front of Confederate works at Yorktown and the Warwick River. Not until after a month-long siege, during which Hancock and his command fought a number of minor skirmishes, did the rebels abandon the lower peninsula. To cover their retreat, they posted a rear guard east of Williamsburg, which the Federal army attacked on May 5. At 11 A.M., Hancock received orders to seize a redoubt at the northern end of the enemy line. The position was unoccupied, and he easily accomplished this task before pushing his men forward to capture a second redoubt and open artillery fire on the Confederate line. When the rebels counterattacked, Hancock pulled his command back slightly. Once the enemy was within thirty paces of the new line, he had his men unleash two volleys that broke the attackers' momentum. He then ordered a bayonet charge that swept the field and turned a stalemated battle into a complete Federal victory. Like a proud father, he beamed with delight over his men's performance. "My men behaved brilliantly, and captured the first color yet taken," he exulted to his wife, "showing hard and determined fighting."[13]

Hancock's superiors were similarly lavish in their praise for *his* performance. General Smith commended him for "the brilliancy of the plan of battle; the coolness of its execution; the seizing of the proper instant for changing from the defensive to the offensive . . . and the completeness of the victory."[14] McClellan's assessment of his performance was more succinct. "Hancock," he wrote his wife, "was superb."[15]

Despite his fine performance at Williamsburg, Hancock remained a relatively minor figure in the Army of the Potomac until the Battle of Antietam on September 17, 1862. During that horrible contest, Israel Richardson, commander of the First Division of the Second Corps, fell mortally wounded, and McClellan personally ordered Hancock to take his place. At the time, the shot-torn division held "Bloody Lane" in the center of the battlefield, which it had captured after a savage struggle. When Hancock reached his new command at 3:00 P.M., the bulk of the fighting in that sector was over. Under orders to hold his ground, he spent the rest of the day shoring up and consolidating his unit's position. The battle was not renewed the following day, and Lee withdrew his army back into Virginia.

McClellan's delay in recrossing the Potomac after Antietam exhausted President Lincoln's patience, and on November 7 the general was replaced as commander of the Army of the Potomac by Ambrose Burnside. Neither McClellan's removal nor Lincoln's Preliminary Emancipation Proclamation, issued on September 22, were popular with Hancock. He respected McClellan and feared that making emancipation a Northern war aim would be counterproductive because it would only induce the South to fight harder. But he refused to join those who spoke of taking the army to Washington to compel a reversal of policy. "We are," he sternly admonished them, "serving no one man; we are serving our country."[16]

Burnside immediately marched the army to Falmouth, Virginia, where he planned to cross the Rappahannock River at Fredericksburg and push on to Richmond. However, by the time he managed to get the troops across the river, the Confederate army was in an impregnable position south of Fredericksburg. Burnside decided to attack it head-on.

The decision was a foolish one, and Hancock knew it, but he was a soldier, and soldiers follow orders. So, on December 13, 1862, he led his three brigades forward. The first advanced to within twenty-five yards of the Confederate position but no further. The second brigade did no better, and neither did the third. The attack cost the division over 40 percent of its manpower. Hancock was unscathed, although a bullet had passed through his overcoat—"just escaping my abdomen," he informed his wife, "one-half inch more and I would have had a fatal wound."[17] The army recrossed the Rappahannock on December 16. On January 25, 1863, Burnside was removed from command, and Joseph "Fighting Joe" Hooker was chosen as his replacement, thanks in part to his ties to the radical Republicans in Congress.

Hooker did a magnificent job reinvigorating the army, and when the time came for operations, he devised a good strategy. But just as he was on the verge of success, Fighting Joe lost his nerve, giving Confederate general Robert E. Lee the opportunity to inflict yet another humiliating defeat on the Army of the Potomac at the Battle of Chancellorsville. For the Federal cause, one of the few bright spots in the battle was Hancock's stellar performance. He and his men fought brilliantly as they covered the army's retreat from the field on May 4. "When all others had left," a staff officer later said, "Hancock held his command in two lines of battle, back to back, one fronting towards Gordonsville, the other towards Fredericksburg, with his artillery firing down the line between; and so kept the enemy at bay until the roads leading to the rear had been cleared . . . and the way was open for his own slow and orderly retreat."[18]

The defeat at Chancellorsville infuriated Hancock. "I cannot stand any more inflictions of this kind," he wrote to his wife, "our last failure . . . should have been a brilliant victory. . . . But it seems that Providence for some wise purpose intended our defeat." If the Lord had, in fact, sided with the rebels at Chancellorsville, Hancock was not surprised. After all, he noted, "the day before the fight Hooker said to a general officer, 'God Almighty could not prevent me from winning a victory to-morrow.'" "Could we," he asked rhetorically, "expect a victory after that?" Hancock did, however, take pleasure in advising his wife that "Hooker's day is over." Like most officers in the Army of the Potomac who strongly identified with McClellan, he never liked Hooker, whom he viewed as a member of "that class of generals who the Republicans care to bolster up." As to whom he hoped would replace Hooker, Hancock did not say, but he knew with certainly it would not be him. "Under no conditions," he assured his wife, "would I accept the command."[19] He did, however, accept promotion to command of the Second Corps on June 10.

Hancock had barely familiarized himself with his new duties before the time came for action. On June 13 the army was once again on the march, this time heading north toward Pennsylvania in pursuit of Lee's army. Hancock pushed his men hard. On June 26, they crossed the Potomac; three days later, they marched thirty hot, dusty miles to Uniontown, Maryland, where they rested before pushing on to Taneytown on the morning of July 1. During the march north, Hancock's wish for a change at the top was fulfilled, for on June 28, Washington gave command of the army to his good friend George Gordon Meade.

As his men were arriving at Taneytown, Hancock rode over to Meade's headquarters, where the two men briefly discussed the situation and Meade's contingency plan to pull the army back to a position several miles to the south, behind Pipe Creek. As they conversed, however, Federal troops were hotly engaged near a small Pennsylvania town called Gettysburg. When news of the battle and the death of John F. Reynolds, commander of the engaged units, reached headquarters, Meade immediately ordered Hancock to Gettysburg to take control of the situation.

Hancock arrived at Gettysburg around four that afternoon and was greeted with a truly depressing sight. Two corps had been overwhelmed north and west of the town, and thousands of Union soldiers could be seen scrambling through the streets and up Cemetery Hill without order or direction. Hancock's arrival turned the tide. The men, recalled one general on the scene, "knew him by fame, and his stalwart figure, his proud mien, and his superb soldierly bearing seemed to verify all the things that fame had told about him. His presence was a reinforcement, and everybody on the field felt stronger for his being there."[20] By nightfall, Hancock had rallied his forces and placed them in a formidable defensive position on the heights south of town. That night, Meade ordered the rest of the army to Gettysburg.

Hancock's heroics at Gettysburg did not end on July 1. The following day his forceful, untiring leadership prevented the folly of Third Corps commander Gen. Daniel Sickles from fatally compromising the Federal position on Cemetery Ridge. On July 3, Hancock and his corps bore the brunt of the famous Pickett-Pettigrew charge; during the preliminary bombardment, he boldly rode the lines through a horrifying rain of shot and shell, encouraging and inspiring his men. Although severely wounded in the groin during the charge, he refused to relinquish command until the enemy attack was repulsed. "I have never seen a more formidable attack," he informed Meade once the rebel tide had ebbed, "and if the Sixth and Fifth Corps have pressed up, the enemy will be destroyed."[21] Although Meade did not "press up," a great victory had been won, and Hancock became a national hero. For his services at Gettysburg, he would receive the thanks of Congress in 1866.

Hancock's wound kept him away from duty for nearly six months. In December, he returned to the army, then in winter quarters near Culpeper, Virginia. His friend Secretary of War Edwin Stanton, however, recognized Hancock was in no condition for the field and ordered him to the less arduous task of raising recruits. (Hancock was one of the few men who maintained cordial relations with both McClellan and Stanton, who despised one another.) Although his recruiting efforts were not particularly successful, a comfortable billet in Harrisburg and the enthusiasm that greeted his public appearances made the assignment rewarding both physically and psychologically.

Hancock returned to Meade's headquarters on March 23, 1864, where he learned of plans to reorganize the army. Two corps, the First and the Third, were to be disbanded, with their units transferred to the Second, Fifth, and Sixth Corps. Hancock formally reassumed command of the Second Corps, now the largest in the army, on March 24, and he threw himself with characteristic energy into the task of organizing and drilling his troops. By the end of April the corps was ready for the campaign being planned by the new general in chief, Ulysses S. Grant.

Hancock's still-painful wound forced him to ride in an ambulance during much of the 1864 Overland campaign, which began on May 4, but when the fighting started, he was back in the saddle, leading and inspiring his men. "I suffer agony on these occasions," he confided to his wife, "but must go into action on horseback."[22] During the Battle of the Wilderness, his sledgehammer attack along Orange Plank Road on May 6 overwhelmed one Confederate corps before the arrival of another, but the failure of other Federal units to come up in support forced the Second Corps back to prepared positions along Brock Road. Hancock rallied his men there and fought off a series of desperate enemy attacks before nightfall put an end to the fighting. A staff officer who encountered him during the battle later remembered being "lost in a contemplation of the dramatic scene presented in the person of the knightly corps commander . . . his right arm was extended to its full length in pointing out certain positions as he gave his orders, and his commanding form towered still higher. . . . It was itself enough to inspire the troops to deeds of unmatched heroism."[23]

At Spotsylvania Hancock's massive assault on the morning of May 12 crushed the "Mule Shoe" salient at the center of Lee's line, and his unit took over twenty-eight hundred prisoners. Included among the prisoners was Gen. Edward Johnson, who, on being brought to Hancock, embraced his old friend from the antebellum army and proclaimed, "This is d - - - d bad fortune; yet I would rather have had this good fortune fall to you than to any other man living."[24]

Despite Hancock's great success on May 12, Lee was not beaten, and fighting continued without letup for several weeks. The low point for the Federals came on June 3 when Hancock and his command joined in an assault on Lee's position at Cold Harbor. The situation was every bit as hopeless as that at Fredericksburg. "The loss in commanders," Hancock wrote afterward, "was unusually severe . . . a blow to the corps from which it did not soon recover."[25]

On June 12, three corps, including Hancock's, were directed to cross the James River to seize Petersburg and the railroads that supplied Richmond. Three days later, when his men arrived in front of the lightly held Confederate works at Petersburg, Hancock deferred to the judgment of his old friend Baldy Smith and did not attack them as vigorously as he could have. A great opportunity was thereby lost, and Grant was forced to resort to siege operations.

On August 21, nine days after receiving word of his promotion to brigadier general in the regular army, Hancock was directed to take his command to Reams' Station to help tear up the railroad on which Lee depended for supplies. Hancock and his troops arrived there on August 24 and were savagely attacked the following day. After a hard fight, the Union troops were driven from the field, with a loss of twenty-seven hundred men and nine guns. In his report, Hancock attributed the defeat to the poor location of "the defensive position at Reams' . . . selected on another occasion by another corps," the fact that the Second Corps had lost twenty thousand men since May, and the poor quality of both the raw recruits and the substitutes Washington had sent to replace them.[26] Years later Hancock's adjutant wrote that, although the men redeemed themselves during an operation along Boydton Plank Road in October, "the agony of that day [at Reams' Station] never passed away from the proud soldier, who, for the first time . . . saw his lines broken and guns taken."[27]

On November 26, Hancock was ordered to Washington to direct the effort to recruit the First Veteran Corps. He remained on this duty until February 1865, when he was named commander of the Middle Military Division and the Department of West Virginia. He spent the rest of the war dealing with guerrillas and preparing for a push southward from Winchester that was never ordered. Then, in the aftermath of Lincoln's assassination, he was called to Washington to oversee the trial and execution of John Wilkes Booth's fellow conspirators.

In August 1866, one month after receiving a promotion to major general in the regular army, Hancock assumed command of the Military Department of the Missouri, where he directed an unsuccessful expedition into western Kansas "to intimidate, and, if necessary," in the words of one participant, "make war on the Indians" in the spring of 1867.[28] The expedition was a complete and utter failure. Hancock's heavy-handed treatment of the Indians with whom he came into contact, which culminated in the destruction of a village in April, provoked a war that would plague the Department of the Missouri for months. By the time a treaty ending the fighting was signed in October 1867, Hancock had left the Great Plains. Two months earlier, he had received orders directing him to replace Phillip H. Sheridan as Reconstruction commander in Louisiana and Texas.

Hancock's appointment was part of President Andrew Johnson's effort to regain control over Reconstruction from the radicals in Congress and their allies in the military. Hancock proved to be everything Johnson hoped he would be. During his own tenure in command, Sheridan had repeatedly antagonized white Southerners by intruding into civil affairs in order to protect the interests of freedmen and the radical party in Louisiana. But Hancock's first action upon arriving in New Orleans in November 1867 was to issue General Orders No. 40, in which he made clear his determination to restrain the influence of the military over civil affairs. "When insurrectionary force has been overthrown . . . and the civil authorities are ready and willing to perform their duties," he declared, "the military power should cease to lead."[29] He had drafted the document while traveling from Saint Louis to New Orleans and first read it to his wife, who approved its sentiments but expressed concern that it might lead the "conscientious reconstructionists" to "use their power against you." Hancock had no doubt that it would. "They will crucify me," he predicted, "I warned the President of my intentions. . . . I shall have his sympathy, but he is powerless to help me."[30]

White Southerners and Northern conservatives cheered the order, its author, and his subsequent efforts to reverse policies put in place by Sheridan. And, as expected, Republicans fumed and pressured the commanding general, Grant, to rein in Hancock. A clash with Grant over the removal of officials appointed by Sheridan led Hancock to request relief from the command in February 1868. On March 16, he was directed to report to Washington; he was placed in charge of the Division of the Atlantic twelve days later.

Hancock's stand against radical rule in Louisiana attracted the attention of Democrats looking for a conservative war hero to nominate for the presidency in 1868. By the time the party's nominating convention met in July, Hancock had a large number of supporters, but they were poorly organized, and the nomination went to Horatio Seymour instead. Although disappointed, Hancock fully supported Seymour's candidacy. After the convention, he wrote to a friend that "the preservation of Constitutional Government eminently depends on the success of the Democratic party in the coming election. . . . Had I been the Presidential nominee I should have considered it a tribute . . . to principles which I had proclaimed and protected; but shall I cease to regard these principles, because by the judgment of mutual political friends another has been appointed to put them in execution? Never!"[31]

On March 5, 1869, Hancock was given command of the Department of Dakota, headquartered at Saint Paul, Minnesota. He remained there until November 1872, when he was put in charge of the Division of the Atlantic, the post he would hold for the rest of his life.

Hancock assumed his new position just before the panic of 1873. Several major railroads responded to the economic depression that followed by ruthlessly slashing wages in an effort to maintain profits, provoking the Great Railroad Strike of 1877. The companies first turned to state and local leaders for assistance in breaking up the strike, but governmental efforts were ineffectual, which compelled President Rutherford B. Hayes to commit Federal troops, under Hancock's direction, to the task. Hancock moved swiftly and surely, and in less than three weeks, the strike was broken. Laurels won in strikebreaking duty and a better-managed campaign enabled him finally to capture the Democratic nomination for president in 1880. Hancock's supporters primarily emphasized his war record in their appeal to the American people. But in the end, that record wasn't enough. In November, James A. Garfield, thanks, in part, to the end of the depression, was elected president by a margin of less than ten thousand votes out of approximately nine million cast.

After attending Garfield's inaugural in March 1881, Hancock returned to his duties as commander of the Division of the Atlantic, which he had performed during his run for the presidency. He spent the remainder of his days administering his command and attending public ceremonies. After a short bout with illness, the old soldier passed away at his home on Governor's Island in New York on February 9, 1886.

News of Hancock's death provoked an outpouring of grief across the nation. To the people of the North, even those with whom he had disagreed politically after the war, he was still and always would be Hancock the Superb, whose consistently magnificent leadership on the field of battle had been critical to the preservation of the Union. And white Southerners mourned the loss of a man whose effort to restore the ascendancy of civil authority in the South and sympathetic attitude toward restoring white Democrats to power had been rays of sunlight in an otherwise dark time.

Hancock's ability to appeal to Americans on both sides of the bloody chasm of war was, in part, due to his selective accommodation to the forces of change that divided the nation between 1850 and 1877. During his lifetime the United States was transformed from a loosely connected society of subsistence farmers and small workshops, where political, economic, and social life revolved around the local community, to an industrial, capitalist nation. Revolutions in transportation and communication and the rise of complex bureaucratic organizations and labor specialization encouraged Americans to view themselves as members of national, professional communities in which a man was defined by what he did rather than where he was born. At the same time, the politics of deference that prevailed early in the nineteenth century, in which government policy making was almost exclusively the concern of elites, was being replaced by mass democratic politics. Now, popular sentiment, even when misguided, had to be taken into account by those who would formulate and implement government agendas. These changes took place much more rapidly in the North than in the South; indeed, the sectional conflict over slavery that produced a civil war was a manifestation of the tension between Northerners who welcomed political, economic, and social modernization and Southerners who wanted to preserve their more traditional society.

As a soldier, Hancock had what it took to perform at a consistently high level in what many historians have labeled the first "modern" war. During his years of service in the antebellum army officer corps, he developed the managerial ability to function effectively in the complex bureaucratic institution that was the Civil War army. Although he practiced an old-fashioned style of battlefield leadership, which demanded conspicuous displays of personal courage from officers, Hancock also recognized that innovations in weapons technology had rendered obsolete the popular notion that war consisted of climactic battles decided by grand assaults on entrenched positions. He appreciated the virtues of well-prepared fortifications and fighting on the tactical defensive, virtues that too few in the Western world would be able or willing to recognize until World War I.

Hancock also understood that in a democracy, the influence of politics, with its petty intrigues and narrow-minded partisanship, could not be ignored in the conduct of military affairs. Politics was a constant concern for him, as it was for the entire Army of the Potomac high command. Yet his unwavering commitment to the modern concept of military professionalism, in which the duties of the soldier and the politician were strictly segregated, led him to focus his energies on the soldier's task of implementing national policy; he resisted the temptation to play the political game to promote his political views or personal interests. Unlike too many of his colleagues, Hancock let his fortunes rest on maneuvers on the battlefield rather than in Washington.

When it came to politics in general, however, Hancock was thoroughly traditional. Although he was a member of the national community of the army officer corps throughout his adult life, he nonetheless embraced the conservative political principles—limited government, states' rights, and a strict construction of the

Constitution—that traditionalist segments of American society espoused in their efforts to resist economic, social, and political change. He was uncomfortable with the tendency toward centralizing political authority that was typical in the modern nation-state and the unprecedented expansion of the power of the Federal government during the Civil War. Furthermore, he was not enthusiastic about the transformation of the war from a struggle to preserve the Union and Constitution "as they were" to one that would alter the nation and provide it with a "new birth of freedom" through the destruction of slavery.

Hancock was able to accept these developments during the Civil War by rationalizing that it was his task to implement, not make, policy and that they were necessitated by wartime exigencies. But the postwar effort by the Radical Republicans to consolidate and build on these changes to ensure that the fruits of victory would not be lost and that justice would be done to the freedmen was too much for Hancock's sensibilities. When finally placed in a position where he had a hand in the formation of policy, his conservatism, lack of sympathy for the plight of the freedmen, and discomfort with the idea of using Federal power to remake the South in the image of the egalitarian, free-labor North pushed him into the often sordid world of Reconstruction and Gilded Age politics, a world for which he was ill suited.

In the end, although Hancock's political endeavors were distinguished primarily by frustration and failure, they did little to diminish the fame he had earned on the battlefields of America's bloodiest war. His consistently stellar service, from the peninsula to Petersburg and particularly at Gettysburg, was critical to the preservation of the Union. For these rather than for his inauspicious efforts in the political arena, Winfield Scott Hancock would be most remembered by the American people.

Notes

1. Ulysses S. Grant, *Personal Memoirs of Ulysses S. Grant,* 2 vols. (New York: Charles L. Webster, 1885), 2:585.
2. Almira R. Hancock, *Reminiscences of Winfield Scott Hancock* (New York: Charles L. Webster and Co., 1887), 259.
3. Ibid., 244.
4. Henry Heth, *The Memoirs of Henry Heth,* ed. James L. Morrison (Westport, CT: Greenwood Press, 1974), 56.
5. Hancock, *Reminiscences of Hancock,* 58.
6. Ibid., 69–70.
7. Ibid., 78.

8. Ibid., 255.

9. Frank L. Byrne and Andrew T. Weaver, eds., *Haskell of Gettysburg: His Life and Civil War Papers* (Madison: State Historical Society of Wisconsin, 1970), 133.

10. Roy P. Bassler, ed., *The Collected Works of Abraham Lincoln,* 9 vols. (New Brunswick, NJ: Rutgers University Press, 1953–1955), 4:438.

11. Phillipe Regis de Trobriand, *Four Years with the Army of the Potomac,* trans. George K. Dauchy (Boston: Ticknor and Co., 1889), 597.

12. Hancock, *Reminiscences of Hancock,* 91.

13. Ibid., 92.

14. U.S. War Department, *The War of the Rebellion: Official Records of the Union and Confederate Armies,* 128 vols. (Washington, DC: U.S. Government Printing Office, 1881–1901) (hereafter cited as *OR*), series 1, vol. 11, pt. 1, p. 528.

15. Stephen W. Sears, ed., *The Civil War Papers of George B. McClellan: Selected Correspondence, 1860–1865* (New York: Ticknor and Fields, 1989), 256.

16. Hancock, *Reminiscences of Hancock,* 92.

17. Ibid., 93.

18. Francis A. Walker, "Hancock in the War of the Rebellion," in *Personal Recollections of the War of the Rebellion: Addresses Delivered before the New York Commandery of the Loyal Legion of the United States,* ed. James Grant Wilson and Titus Munson Coan, 4 vols. (New York: Published by the Commandery, 1891), 1:357.

19. Hancock, *Reminiscences of Hancock,* 94–95.

20. Harry W. Pfanz, *Gettysburg: Culp's Hill and Cemetery Hill* (Chapel Hill: University of North Carolina Press, 1993), 103.

21. *OR,* series 1, vol. 27, pt. 1, p. 73.

22. Hancock, *Reminiscences of Hancock,* 101.

23. Horace Porter, *Campaigning with Grant* (New York: Century, 1897), 57–58.

24. Hancock, *Reminiscences of Hancock,* 104.

25. *OR,* series 1, vol. 36, pt. 1, p. 346.

26. *OR,* series 1, vol. 42, pt. 1, p. 227.

27. Walker, "Hancock in the War of the Rebellion," 363.

28. W. J. D. Kennedy, ed., *On the Plains with Custer and Hancock: The Journal of Isaac Coates, Army Surgeon* (Boulder, CO: Johnson Books, 1997), 58.

29. Hancock, *Reminiscences of Hancock,* 223.

30. Ibid., 124.

31. Ibid., 138–39.

3

Richard S. Ewell
Stonewall's Successor

Peter S. Carmichael

In some ways, Richard S. Ewell was a Confederate counterpart to Winfield Scott Hancock, for both were successful corps commanders who never rose to high levels. But in other, more personal ways, they were very different. The big, handsome, dominant figure of Hancock could never have been mistaken for the slightly built form of Ewell, topped with his bulbous bald pate, nor could the latter's piping, birdlike voice possibly have brought to mind the booming tones of the Union general. Yet by far the greatest differences between the two lay in the very fact that one was a Confederate and the other a Federal. Ewell's lot was to be on the losing side, and thus, his generalship was closely scrutinized and harshly criticized by those lamenting the might-have-beens of the war. He was also attacked for his eccentricities and, above all, for his marriage, relatively late in life and midway through the war, to a first cousin. Finally, although Hancock enjoyed a long career as one of the higher-ranking officers of the post–Civil War U.S. Army (and even a foray into politics highlighted by a respectable run for the presidency), Ewell faced the struggle of putting his life back together in a defeated South; he could never again practice the only profession he had ever known, that of the soldier. Ewell's story is recounted by Peter S. Carmichael, assistant professor of history at Western Carolina University, Cullowhee, North Carolina, and author of *Lee's Young Artillerist: William R. J. Pegram* (1995).

Most Civil War battles were not won by brilliant maneuvers but by generals who avoided egregious mistakes and capitalized on their opponents' errors. Joseph Hooker's negligence enabled Thomas J. "Stonewall" Jackson to launch a devastating flanking attack at Chancellorsville. Confederate James Longstreet exploited a gap in the Federal line at Chickamauga that resulted in the rout of the Union army. And the faulty position of Lee's force at Spotsylvania largely caused the collapse of his lines on May 12. Such errors of judgment have generated tremendous speculation among armchair generals. Unfortunately, what-if scenarios rarely result in meaningful analysis. In many cases, they encourage scholars to look at the outcome of the event first and then work back to consider the circumstances in which the incident developed. This approach does not reveal how the situation unfolded for the men involved.

The legacy of one of Robert E. Lee's corps commanders, Richard Stoddert Ewell, has suffered from such an approach. Ewell's refusal to attack Cemetery Hill at Gettysburg and his failure to strike the Federal flank at the Wilderness has led countless historians and Civil War buffs to speculate about his "lost opportunities." In the process the magnitude of these two miscues has been overstated. Some scholars even contend that Ewell lost the war when he failed to seize Cemetery Hill. The hyperbole surrounding these incidents, as well as Ewell's quirky personality and marriage to an overbearing woman, has made it difficult for historians to evaluate him on his own terms or to understand his perspective and the factors that shaped his decisions.[1]

Ewell was a genuine eccentric, highly excitable, and at times neurotic. He left an indelible impression on Confederate general Richard Taylor when they served together under Stonewall Jackson. Taylor offered a classic description of Ewell as a chirping bird: "Bright, prominent eyes, a bomb-shaped, bald head, and a nose like that of Francis of Valois, gave him a striking resemblance to a woodcock; and this was increased by a bird-like habit of putting his head to one side to utter his quaint speeches." Legends persist that he had mental problems and sometimes hallucinated that he actually *was* a bird. He would chirp softly in his tent for hours at a time, it was said, accepting only sunflower seed or grains of wheat at mealtime. Yet, as Taylor observed, "with all his oddities [and] perhaps in some measure because of them, Ewell was adored by officers and men."[2]

Born in Georgetown, DC, on February 8, 1817, Ewell spent most of his youth on his family's modest farm in Prince William County, Virginia. In July 1836, he accepted an appointment to the United States Military Academy at West Point. Despite the demanding military regimen, Ewell endured cadet life with few demerits or other difficulties, but on the eve of graduation, he did not relish the prospect of a career in the professional army. "I think I have nearly as much aversion to that life as yourself," he wrote his mother, "but you know that the education we get here does not qualify us for any other than a military life, and unless a man has money he is forced to enter the Army to keep from starving."[3] In July 1840, Ewell graduated from West Point, ranking thirteenth out of forty-two cadets, with an officer's commission in the First Dragoons. Leaving his fellow cadets tugged at Ewell's emotions. "It is hard to leave forever those with whom we have shared the hardships of the camp and the terrors of the blackboard," he mused.[4]

As he had predicted, he found army life distasteful. The boredom, loneliness, and primitive conditions of the western frontier left him virtually despondent, but the Mexican War interrupted the tedium. It also provided a new venue for Ewell's wonderful sense of humor. In his correspondence, for example, he recalled when Gen. Winfield Scott approached him and his immediate superior, Maj. Gen. Edwin V. Sumner, and complimented them on "the extraordinary vigilance of our scouts who, as he said, were peering at him from behind every bush as he approached the camp." In fact, tainted drinking water had caused a diarrhea epidemic in the ranks, and Scott had mistaken men who were relieving themselves for scouts. Ewell, who felt the mistake made the general look ludicrous, noted, "When we go to drill, the men have to leave the ranks by dozens and as the Plain is bare as a table, make an exposé of the whole affair. The effect is unique as they squat in rows about a hundred yards from the battalion, and when we deploy as skirmishers, we run right over them."

Although a misstep on the training grounds could prove hazardous, Ewell encountered more serious danger once active campaigning began. He saw plenty of action, the heaviest at Tête de Pont where U.S. forces captured the fortification of Churubusco. Ewell received a brevet for gallantry, but he considered the commendation lacking in distinction. "I wish I had known in time there was to be such an overwhelming quantity of brevets made out," he wrote. "I should certainly have tried hard for another and might have got it."[5]

When Ewell returned to the western frontier for a ten-year tour of duty after the Mexican War, he seemed even less tolerant of and more disgusted with his situation. As with so many other regular army officers, advancement came slowly for him during this period, and when his cousin Elizabeth Campbell Brown learned of his frustration, she contacted influential friends in Washington to secure him a promotion. Ewell had fallen in love with his fair cousin, known by her friends as "Lizinka," at an early age, but she did not reciprocate his affections, and he coincidentally declared his vow of bachelorhood the same year she married another man. Yet, though devastated by his failure to win Lizinka's affections, he maintained a regular correspondence with her before the Civil War. Lizinka's efforts did not secure Ewell immediate rewards. Nonetheless, she wanted "to do something for Dick," and she suggested that he become a farm manager on one of her plantations. Lizinka explained her generosity to another relative: "The truth is I am excessively anxious about Richard, all the more for the sensitiveness which I fear unfits him for any position out of the army."[6]

After much agonizing, Ewell decided to stay in the army. He informed Lizinka of his decision via Thomas Gantt, who reported that "he [Ewell] would not hesitate to accept your [Lizinka's] proposal if you were a man, but he fears to take advantage of a poor weak woman in the matter of a bargain."[7] But this was a thinly veiled excuse. In truth, Ewell must have regarded Lizinka's proposal as a threat to his status as a Southern man: to depend on a woman's generosity would violate his primary responsibility as a provider and protector. The title of farm manager posed an even greater threat in terms of community acceptance, for some might have equated the job with the detested but accepted position of an overseer.

Lincoln's call for troops after the firing on Fort Sumter and Virginia's subsequent withdrawal from the Union ended Ewell's career in the United States Army. Like many of the upper South, he reluctantly accepted the breakup of the Union rather than draw his sword against his native state. Consequently, he tendered his resignation on May 7 and promptly returned to Old Dominion, where he was assigned to a cavalry regiment. By July, he received a promotion to brigadier general and commanded an infantry brigade.[8]

On his staff was Campbell Brown, Lizinka's son from a previous marriage. While Lizinka was visiting Campbell in Virginia, her relationship with Ewell quickly moved beyond friendship. Why she had a sudden change of heart is difficult to say. Her son rejoiced at the news of the romance but never thought the couple would reach the altar.[9] Nonetheless, the general proposed, and Lizinka, now a widow, accepted. Perhaps concern for Campbell Brown and a desire to keep close tabs on him might explain why she accepted the proposal, and no doubt the prospect of marriage would ensure that Ewell served as a protector and advocate for her son in the army—certainly, she never let her fiancé forget what a devastating blow it would be to her to lose Campbell to a Yankee bullet. Whatever her motives, the general seemed not to care. He eagerly looked to the future, telling Lizinka shortly after their engagement that her "expression 'in life or death we shall be united'" was "fraught with promise."[10]

After a solid performance as a brigade commander in the First Manassas campaign, Ewell emerged as one of the Confederacy's most promising officers. In the 1862 Shenandoah Valley campaign, he commanded a division under Stonewall Jackson. But despite repeated battlefield victories, Jackson exasperated Ewell with his secretive ways. While Stonewall battled the Federals at McDowell on May 8, he left Ewell with vague orders to remain at Swift Run Gap and guard against an approaching Union force. "I tell you, sir, he is as crazy as a March hare," Ewell exploded to a subordinate. "He has gone away, I don't know where, and left me here with some instructions to stay until he returns, but Banks' whole army is advancing on me and I haven't the most remote idea where to communicate with General Jackson. I tell you, sir, he is crazy and I will just march my division away from here."[11] However, Ewell never acted on his threat: He stayed at Swift Run Gap and even came to appreciate and admire his eccentric superior. Despite their personality differences, both officers jelled on the battlefield, united in purpose by their penchant for the offense.

After a credible performance during the Seven Days campaign, when Lee drove the Federal army away from Richmond, Ewell anticipated what would become a bitter debate in the Confederacy when he called for the South to arm slaves. "It is astonishing to me that our people do not pass laws to form regiments of blacks," he wrote on July 20. "The Yankees are fighting low foreigners against the best of our people whereas were we to fight our Negroes they would be a fair offset. We would not be as now fighting kings against men to use a comparison from chequers." He also heard reports of Yankee depredations against Southern civilians. "The Yankee are now in Culpeper, and, I learn, are systematically destroying all the growing crops and everything the people have to live on." Reports of Union cavalrymen riding "into the fields" and swinging "their sabres to cut down the growing corn" infuriated Ewell. He thought the enemy was "bent on starving out the women and children left by the war."[12]

A vengeful Ewell accompanied Jackson on his famous march around John Pope's Union army during the Second Manassas campaign. When the Federals located Stonewall's troops near Brawner's Farm on August 28, Ewell's men blunted the Union advance. As the general observed the enemy's movements while crouching under a tree, a bullet shattered his right knee. Ewell became extremely weak as his body hemorrhaged from the grievous wound. At a field hospital the respected surgeon Hunter McGuire amputated his leg, and it was not until November that he completed the journey to Richmond, where he convalesced. His impatience to rejoin the army led to imprudence. Against doctors' orders, he left his bed and took a hard fall, inducing another hemorrhage. By spring 1863, Ewell could not ride a horse or wear a wooden leg.[13]

After the war, Campbell Brown speculated that the general's crippling injury persuaded Lizinka to marry, and perhaps he was right, for she wrote an extremely revealing letter to her fiancé while he was resting in Richmond. The loss of his leg, she said, made her more "necessary" to him than ever before. Until that unfortunate incident, Lizinka told Ewell, she believed that he should "marry a younger woman, [but] now I will suit you better than any one else, if only because I will love you better." "The truth is," she added, "I have grown old very rapidly during the last six months [and] my eyesight is not good & my hair is turning grey, besides being thin & sallow."[14]

Although he had missed the fighting at Chancellorsville and Fredericksburg, when he returned to Lee's army in the spring of 1863, Ewell received a promotion to lieutenant general and command of Jackson's old Second Corps. A day later, on May 26, he and Lizinka took their vows at Saint Paul's Church in Richmond with the noted minister Charles F. E. Minnigerode presiding.

Shortly after the ceremony, Ewell rejoined the Army of Northern Virginia for its second northern raid. Before leaving for Pennsylvania, Lee "talked long and earnestly" with him about his "quick alternations from elation to despondency [and] his want of decision." After the war, Lee confided that he "had feared the old habit of E. when assigned him to the Corps, but had hoped he had gotten over it."[15] When the campaign started, Ewell acted with great swiftness, capturing a Union garrison at Winchester. But controversy surrounded the general at the ensuing Battle of Gettysburg. During the first day's fighting, when the routed Federals retreated through town, the commanding heights of Cemetery Hill seemed to invite a Confederate attack. Capturing this important ground would have compelled the Army of the Potomac to abandon the field completely.

Ewell quickly recognized the importance of Cemetery Hill and believed he could take the position with the assistance of A. P. Hill's Third Corps. Lee was also anxious for Ewell to attack, but he gave his subordinate vague instructions, allowing for any course of action as along as Ewell did not wreck his command. Without firm direction from above, Ewell lost his sense of urgency, and caution overwhelmed him when he realized that he would have to make the attack alone.

Why Lee did not order a combined assault between Ewell's and Hill's troops remains a mystery. The commanding general was on the field, near the Third Corps, where he could see the lightly defended heights. He, not Ewell, had the authority to launch a joint attack between the Second and Third Corps. Yet criticisms of Lee seem to be deflected onto Ewell, who would become one of many Confederate scapegoats for the defeat at Gettysburg.

After the war, Jubal Early, William Nelson Pendleton, Isaac Trimble, and other prominent Confederates blamed Ewell for failing to take Cemetery Hill and thereby squandering Lee's best chance for victory. Trimble bitterly wrote that Ewell had committed "a radical error, for had we continued the fight, we should have got in their rear & taken the Cemetery Hill and Culps Hill."[16] Other Lost Cause disciples conjured up Stonewall's ghost to argue that the outcome at Gettysburg and the fate of the entire war would have been different if Jackson had lived. The aggressive Stonewall, they contend, would have pressed the advantage, cleared the heights of Yankees, and delivered another impressive victory to the Army of Northern Virginia. This interpretation has captured the popular imagination, at the expense of Ewell's reputation.[17]

Immediate reactions after the battle suggest a strikingly different assessment of the Southern leadership. Alexander "Sandie" Pendleton, Ewell's chief of staff, thought Cemetery Hill would have fallen into Confederate hands if Hill's troops had supported the Second Corps. "There has been some mismanagement in this affair & while the fault may be with others," Pendleton concluded, "the blame must & should fall on Gen. Lee."[18] Jubal Early's official report written shortly after the battle contradicted his postwar ranting. In that report, he expressed his belief that additional support from A. P. Hill would have resulted in the capture of Cemetery Hill. He wrote: "Meeting with an officer of Major General Pender's staff, I sent word by him to General Hill that if he would send up a division, we could take the hill to which the enemy had retreated." Early and Ewell both wanted to take the high ground, but Lee never interceded to ensure that Hill properly supported the assault.[19]

The residue of defeat at Gettysburg created the impression that Ewell was not fit to command a corps. Most of his contemporaries (and even some historians) blamed his shortcomings as an officer and administrator on Lizinka. One soldier summed up the dominant opinion of the army: "From a military point of view the addition of the wife did not compensate for the loss of the leg. We were of the opinion that Ewell was not the same soldier he had been when he was a whole man—and a single one."[20] This officer touched on a popular idea that had gained acceptance among Lee's troops during the latter stages of the war. Once a soldier took his wedding vows, ran the common argument, he lost his aggressiveness in battle, his sense of duty to his men, and his purpose as a soldier. In reference to another Confederate general who married during the war, one Virginian officer observed "that no man who married during the war was as good a soldier after. It was a singular fact, because those men who came into the war as married men were as good soldiers as the single ones, but marriage during the war seemed to demoralize them."[21] Perhaps blaming womanly influences, not a general lack of manliness or courage in the ranks, provided an acceptable explanation of the army's decline for many Confederate soldiers.

Lizinka's constant presence at Ewell's headquarters and her influence over the general made her a favorite target of criticism from his staff. She further alienated herself by trying to secure promotion for her son at the expense of other officers. When a new bill was put before the Confederate Congress to enlarge the general staff of the Confederate army, a number of officers believed that Ewell was maneuvering to promote Campbell Brown. "Old Ewell," wrote Col. James Conner, "acted upon by feminine influences, is dead bent on pushing Campbell Brown, Mrs. Ewell's son, up to be a

Colonel, and to do it, he is trying to engineer his other staff officers out of the way." Many saw Ewell as a puppet-general—a figurehead controlled and manipulated by his wife. Conner wrote with disgust that "Old Baldy" was a "fond, foolish old man . . . worse in love than any eighteen-year older that you ever saw."[22] Although the staff bill received a pocket veto, the matter revealed the troubled state of affairs in the Second Corps.

Lizinka did not concern herself exclusively with issues of promotion and rank. She also tried to shape Ewell's conduct on the battlefield. Under no circumstances did she believe it necessary for her husband to expose himself to enemy fire, and keeping Ewell away from danger would also increase the chances that her son would remain out of harm's way. In a conversation with James B. Sheeran, a priest with the Louisiana Brigade, Lizinka asked if a general "is justified in carelessly exposing himself on the battlefield." Sheeran unequivocally said no. "A general in my opinion should keep himself as far as possible out of danger," he told her, "but in such a position as to see or hear of the movements in battle." He considered the general "the soul of the army [whose] fall always causes despondency and sometimes greater disaster to his command." A vindicated Lizinka turned to Ewell and boasted, "There now General, you see that the Father is just of my opinion."[23]

Although Lizinka never convinced Ewell to avoid enemy fire, she did succeed in keeping Campbell Brown a comfortable distance from the Yankees. A staff officer named Turner said Ewell once confided to him that "he had never exposed Campbell but once, and then was so miserable until he came back, that he did not know what to do." "If anything had happened to him," Ewell told the man, "I could never have looked at his Mother again." Turner repeated this story to a friend and then exclaimed, "Hang him [Ewell,] he never thinks of my Mother, I suppose, for he pops me around, no matter how hot the fire is." After Turner left, another staff officer remarked: "'Well, Turner is safe, but I am in a tight place. Campbell Brown hangs onto his mother's petticoats, and Turner is engaged to the little Brown girl [Lizinka's daughter], and she will prize him up, but I have to fight against the pair.'"[24]

Lizinka's influence in the daily operations of the Second Corps caused some of Ewell's staffers to wonder whom they served. Col. James Conner noted that Lizinka "manages everything from the general's affairs down to the courier's who carries his dispatches. All say they are under petticoat government."[25] Gen. Robert Rodes sardonically asked who commanded the Second Corps—the Widow Brown, Ewell, or Chief of Staff Sandie Pendleton; he hoped that it was the latter. The snide comments and the brusque manners of the staff had made it abundantly clear that the men resented Lizinka's presence during the winter of 1863–1864.

General Lee ordered all women to leave camp on April 12, 1864, but it appears that Lizinka defied the commanding general's edict and lingered at Ewell's headquarters for ten extra days before departing for Richmond. One soldier reported that just before she left, she turned to the staff and told them that "she knew every one here was glad to get rid of her and no one had politeness to say 'no.' " Without Lizinka's presence, the tension at Second Corps headquarters must have eased considerably, but its commander appeared morose. "Mrs. Ewell has gone away," Jedediah Hotchkiss wrote, "& the poor old General is almost disconsolate—gets up early in the morning & walks about nearly all day."[26]

As the army prepared for Grant's spring offensive, Lee entertained serious doubts about Ewell as a lieutenant general. His uneven performance at Gettysburg and persistent health problems raised troubling questions about his ability to lead a corps. The commanding general's worst fears materialized during the opening rounds of the Overland campaign. Initially, on May 5 at the Wilderness, Ewell fought exceptionally well in what was probably his finest moment in the Army of Northern Virginia. Even though most of his approximately fourteen thousand men lacked time to build breastworks and fought without proper artillery support, they successfully overcame at least two-to-one odds in repulsing portions of the Union Fifth and Sixth Corps. Many of Ewell's contemporaries recognized his skillfulness on May 5, among them Edward Porter Alexander, who wrote that "dear, glorious, old, one-legged Ewell, with his bald head, & his big bright eyes, & his long nose . . . sat back & not only whipped everything that attacked him but he even sallied out on some rash ones & captured two guns & quite a lot of prisoners."[27]

During the final day of action, however, Ewell lost his sense of decisiveness when Grant exposed his right flank. His subordinate, John B. Gordon, pleaded for permission to attack. Jubal Early, Ewell's senior divisional commander, disagreed and warned Ewell that it was too dangerous. Ewell vacillated, wasting precious daylight as he tried to decide which course to follow. In his highly romanticized memoirs, Gordon considered Ewell's behavior at that moment reminiscent of his actions at Gettysburg. "No intelligent military critic," Gordon observed, ". . . will fail to sympathize with my lament, which was even more bitter than at Gettysburg, over the irreparable loss of Jackson."[28]

Historians have followed Gordon's lead in condemning Ewell without looking at the circumstances that made a full flank attack unrealistic. The Second Corps commander did not have the troops for a concentrated assault. Every available man had been committed to the front and was pinned down by the enemy. It was also prudent for Ewell to listen to his senior divisional commander, Early, rather than Gordon, who was only a brigadier. Furthermore, although Lee's hopes for a concentrated assault might have been realized in 1862, when the army had plenty of reserves, attempting such an offensive stroke was not realistic in May 1864. Army headquarters nonetheless took note of Ewell's inaction, reinforcing the growing perception that he lacked the aggressive instincts necessary for command.

The physical demands of active campaigning once again preyed on Ewell's frail health and irritated his raw emotional state. After the Federals broke Confederate lines on May 12 at Spotsylvania, an agitated Ewell lost his composure as he tried to rally some fleeing soldiers. One witness described him as a "tower of passion" as he hurled a "terrible volley of oaths," calling some of the stragglers "cowards." "Yes, goddamn you, run," he shouted, according to the witness. "The Yankees will catch you. That's right, go as fast as you can." When Ewell started to hit some of the fleeing soldiers on their backs with his sword, Lee ordered him to restrain himself. "How can you expect to control these men when you have lost control of yourself?" Lee reportedly asked. "If you cannot repress your excitement, you had better retire." Seven days later, on May 19, Ewell suffered an emotional breakdown when he inspected Grant's flank. In a postwar conversation with William Allan, Lee recounted that Ewell "lost all presence of mind, and that he found Ewell prostrate on the ground, and declaring he could not get Rodes' division out."[29]

Shortly after this incident, Ewell left on sick leave, but he sought reinstatement just before Jubal Early departed for the Shenandoah Valley on the campaign that would take him and the Second Corps to the very outskirts of Washington. Lee tried to put off Ewell because of the latter's illness, but Ewell insisted that he was physically capable of resuming command. Reluctantly, Lee informed him that he had been permanently relieved and that his replacement, Early, was better suited to lead a corps. It was a wrenching decision, Lee later told Allan, but one that was necessary for the good of the cause. When Ewell received a secondary assignment to the Richmond defenses near the end of the war, he handled his duties in a professional manner, but he would have preferred a more important command. He then accompanied Lee's army on its retreat only to be captured at Sayler's Creek, just three days before Appomattox. Federal officials withheld paroles to Confederate generals, forcing captured officers such as Ewell to languish in prison while enlisted men were sent home.

Lizinka wanted the immediate release of her husband and thought she could cash in on her prewar connections with Andrew Johnson, even though Johnson despised the planter class and remained a staunch Unionist. Instead of directly petitioning the president, she wrote a peculiar letter to his wife, calling her "Dear Mother" and referring to Andrew Johnson as "the Governor." However, Mrs. Johnson was incapable of assisting Lizinka, and her plea infuriated the president, who promptly had her arrested and detained in Saint Louis. Johnson's forceful response stunned Lizinka.[30]

For portions of June and July, Lizinka lived with a prominent Rhode Island family so she could be near her husband: Prison would not insulate Ewell from his wife's stern advice. After he complained about his eyesight, for instance, Lizinka bluntly told him: "Do get over your delusion about a stigma—it is a queer idea. Read the 46th Psalm."[31] Not until late July was Ewell released from Fort Warren, and after a short stay in Virginia, the reunited couple returned to Tennessee. Although Ewell quickly adapted to civilian life and prospered as a farmer, Lizinka detested living on her plantation. She felt isolated and pleaded with her husband to move to Richmond, Virginia. He refused and immersed himself in farming. When Ewell frequently left Lizinka for business trips to Mississippi, she condemned him for abandoning her, writing that "I think it is due to the woman you considered respectable enough to be your wife not to be left as I have been this winter with the additional mortification when asked, when will your husband be home? to be compelled to answer, I have no idea. Looking back, I can't see how I have deserved it. I have declined leaving you even to go to my children & I thank you for teaching me the folly of so doing."[32] Ewell consistently ignored her demands and traveled for months at a time. This pattern continued until a typhoid epidemic took both of their lives in January 1872.[33]

Far less has been written about Richard Ewell than any of Lee's other primary subordinates, and those historians who *have* examined Ewell have not been generous in their evaluations. Too many have assumed that his poor performance at Gettysburg established a similar pattern of inept behavior for the remainder of the war. Such an interpretation focuses too heavily on personality traits and the supposed disruptive influences of Lizinka Brown. That fact that Ewell followed the legendary Jackson as the Second Corps commander has only compounded the problem, for Stonewall achieved his remarkable victories when the Army of Northern Virginia possessed an offensive capacity to strike the enemy with hard, decisive blows. This impressive benchmark was impossible to match when Ewell led the Second Corps because the muscle behind Lee's offensive punch had been shredded at Chancellorsville and Gettysburg. Suffering more than forty thousand casualties in those two engagements as well as earlier losses made the slashing movements Jackson employed relics of the past. Few have examined Ewell's generalship within the specific context of commanding a Confederate corps during the last two years of the war. With such a perspective, we can better understand the range of choices that faced Ewell without delving into the pointless scenarios of armchair generals.

Notes

1. For the definitive biography of Richard S. Ewell, see Donald C. Pfanz, *Richard S. Ewell: A Soldier's Life* (Chapel Hill: University of North Carolina Press, 1997).

2. Richard Taylor, *Destruction and Reconstruction: Personal Experiences of the Late War* (1879; reprint ed., New York: Longmans, Green, 1955), 36–37; Herman Hattaway and Archer Jones, *How the North Won: A Military History of the Civil War* (Urbana: University of Illinois Press, 1983), 405.

3. Percy Gatling Hamlin, *Richard Stoddert Ewell: "Old Bald Head" (General R. S. Ewell)—The Portrait of a Soldier and the Making of a Soldier: Letters of General R. S. Ewell* (1935, 1940; reprint ed., Gaithersburg, MD: Combined by Ron R. Van Sickle Military Books, 1988), 10.

4. Ibid., 11.

5. Ibid., 39.

6. Lizinka Brown to David Hubbard, December 23, 1855, David Hubbard Papers, Tennessee State Library, Nashville, Tennessee (hereafter cited as TSL).

7. Thomas Gant to Lizinka Brown, November 2, 1855, Campbell Brown–Richard S. Ewell Papers, TSL. Before Ewell made his final decision in December, the reasons he gave to Gant the previous month kept him from accepting Lizinka's offer.

8. Hamlin, *Richard Stoddert Ewell,* 60.

9. Ewell letter-book, Box 2, Folder 2, Campbell Brown–Richard S. Ewell Papers, TSL.

10. Hamlin, *Richard Stoddert Ewell,* 78–79.

11. Ibid., 84.

12. Ibid., 113.

13. Ibid., 129–33.

14. Lizinka Brown to Richard S. Ewell, September 9, 1862, Campbell Brown–Richard S. Ewell Papers, TSL.

15. William Allan, "Memoranda of Conversations with General Robert E. Lee," in *Lee: The Soldier*, ed. Gary W. Gallagher (Lincoln: University of Nebraska Press, 1996), 11.

16. William Starr Myers, ed., "The Civil War Diary of General Isaac Ridgeway Trimble," *Maryland Historical Magazine* 17 (March 1922): 11.

17. On the Confederate debates surrounding Gettysburg and the Lost Cause interpretation of Richard S. Ewell in Pennsylvania, see J. William Jones et al., eds. *Southern Historical Society Papers*, 52 vols. (1876–1959; reprint ed. with 2-vol. index, Millwood, NY: Kraus, 1977–1980), esp. vols. 4–6; also, Thomas L. Connelly and Barbara L. Bellows, *God and General Longstreet: The Lost Cause and the Southern Mind* (Baton Rouge: Louisiana

State University Press, 1982), 30–31. Ewell has particularly suffered at the hands of modern historians. For recent scholarship on Jackson that indicts Ewell for failing to seize Cemetery Hill, see Bevin Alexander, *Lost Victories: The Military Genius of Stonewall Jackson* (New York: Henry Holt, 1992), 330; Paul D. Casdorph, *Lee and Jackson: Confederate Chieftains* (New York: Paragon House, 1992), 396; and John Bowers, *Stonewall Jackson: Portrait of a Soldier* (New York: William Morrow, 1989), 356. For other critical assessments of Ewell, see Glenn Tucker, *High Tide at Gettysburg: The Campaign Pennsylvania* (Indianapolis: Bobbs-Merrill, 1958), 189; Douglas Southall Freeman, *Lee's Lieutenants: A Study in Command,* 3 vols. (New York: Scribner's, 1942–1944), 3:93; Clifford Dowdey, *Death of a Nation: The Story of Lee and His Men at Gettysburg* (New York: Knopf, 1958), 142; and Herman Hattaway, *Shades of Blue and Gray: An Introductory Military History of the Civil War* (Columbia: University of Missouri Press, 1997), 143.

18. Alexander S. Pendleton, letter to [?], July 1863, Ellinor Porcher Gadsden Papers, University Library of Washington and Lee University, Lexington, Virginia.

19. See Early's Gettysburg report in the U.S. War Department, *The War of the Rebellion: Official Records of the Union and Confederate Armies,* 128 vols. (Washington, DC: U.S. Government Printing Office, 1881–1901), vol. 27, pt. 2, p. 830.

20. James Conner, *The Letters of General James Conner, C.S.A.* (Columbia, SC: The State Co., 1933), 114–15.

21. Eppa Hunton, *Autobiography of Eppa Hunton* (Richmond, VA: William Byrd Press, 1935), 127.

22. Conner, *The Letters of General James Conner,* 114–15.

23. James B. Sheeran, *Confederate Chaplain: A War Journal of Rev. James B. Sheeran, c.ss.r 14th Louisiana, CSA,* ed. Joseph T. Durkin, S. J. (Milwaukee: Bruce Publishing Co., 1960), 75.

24. Conner, *The Letters of General James Conner,* 115.

25. Ibid.

26. Jedediah Hotchkiss to his wife, April 26, 1864, Jedediah Hotchkiss Papers, Reel 4, Library of Congress, Washington, DC (hereafter cited as LC); Jedediah Hotchkiss to his wife, April 24, 1864, Jedediah Hotchkiss Papers, Reel 4, LC.

27. Edward Porter Alexander, *Fighting for the Confederacy,* ed. Gary W. Gallagher (Chapel Hill: University of North Carolina Press, 1989), 353.

28. John B. Gordon, *Reminiscences of the Civil War* (1903; reprint ed., Dayton, Ohio: Morningside Press, 1985), 260–61. For a critical assessment of Ewell's performance at the Wilderness, see Freeman, *Lee's Lieutenants,* 3:442; Clifford Dowdey, *Lee's Last Campaign: The Story of Lee and His Men against Grant, 1864* (1960; reprint ed., New York: Barnes and Noble, 1994), 170; Edward Steere, *The Wilderness Campaign* (New York: Bonanza, 1960), 448; Gary W. Gallagher, "The Army of Northern Virginia in May 1864: A Crisis of High Command," *Civil War History* 36 (June 1990): 115; Gordon C. Rhea, *The Battle of the Wilderness: May 5–6, 1864* (Baton Rouge: Louisiana State University Press, 1994), 444–45.

29. Quoted from Gordon C. Rhea, *The Battles for Spotsylvania Court House and the Road to Yellow Tavern, May 7–12, 1864* (Baton Rouge: Louisiana State University Press, 1997), 255–56; Allan, "Memoranda of Conversations with General Robert E. Lee," 11.

30. Elizabeth Campbell Brown Ewell to Andrew Johnson, July 9, 1865, Polk-Brown-Ewell Papers, Southern Historical Collection, Chapel Hill, North Carolina (hereafter cited as SHC).

31. Lizinka Campbell Brown Ewell to Richard Stoddert Ewell, July 9, 1865, Polk-Brown-Ewell Papers, SHC.

32. Elizabeth Campbell Brown Ewell to Richard S. Ewell, n.d., Campbell Brown–Richard S. Ewell Papers, TSL. This letter was probably written after 1868.

33. *Nashville Republican Banner,* January 1, 1872, 4.

4

Raphael Semmes
Rebel Seadog

Spencer C. Tucker

It is all too easy to forget that the Civil War was not fought solely on the North American continent, much less in the hundred-mile stretch between Washington and Richmond. In fact, the actions and reverberations of the conflict literally spanned the globe. One of those who carried it to far distant seas was Confederate naval officer Raphael Semmes. His life reveals much about the nature of the Civil War at sea and those who fought it.

In this chapter distinguished naval historian Spencer C. Tucker, professor of history at the Virginia Military Institute, Lexington, Virginia, and author of many books including a recent biography of Andrew H. Foote, describes Semmes's remarkable career and offers insights into the Confederate captain's bitter attitude toward the flag he had once called his own.

Raphael Semmes, captain of the *Alabama*, was the best-known Confederate naval commander. Our knowledge of him comes chiefly from his memoirs and from books written by two of his officers. Born on September 27, 1809, in Charles County, Maryland, of French Catholic ancestry, Semmes lost his parents early in his childhood and was raised in Georgetown, DC, by an uncle and aunt. In 1825, President John Quincy Adams appointed him a naval midshipman. Although he was second in his class in the Naval School at the Gosport (Norfolk) Navy Yard, there were too many officers in the United States Navy when he graduated, and it was February 1837 before Semmes made lieutenant. During long leaves of absence ashore, he took up the study of law, a profession he followed when he was not at sea. In 1834, he was admitted to the Maryland bar. Three years later he married Anne B. Spencer. From 1837 until the Mexican War, Semmes spent most of his time on survey work along the southern coast and the Gulf of Mexico. In 1841 the navy ordered him to survey Mississippi sound, and at that time, he established his legal residence in Alabama.

During the Mexican War, Semmes took command of the *Somers* on blockade duties. On December 8, 1846, the brig went down while off the eastern coast of Mexico in a sudden squall; half of her crew members were lost, but a court-martial acquitted Semmes of blame and even commended him on his seamanship.

In March 1847, Semmes took part in the capture of Vera Cruz. He also participated in the expedition against Tuxpan and was detailed on special duty to accompany Gen. Winfield Scott's forces to Mexico City, serving as an aide to the division commander, Maj. Gen. William Worth, who cited him for bravery.

After the war, Semmes again found himself in a navy with too many officers and spent much of his time ashore awaiting orders. In November 1847, he returned to his home on the Perdido River in Alabama, where he had established his family in 1845 and where he lived until moving closer to Mobile in 1849. In 1852, Semmes published *Service Afloat and Ashore during the Mexican War,* detailing his wartime experiences. Ironically, in view of later events, Semmes argued that if Mexico had used privateers against U.S. shipping, they should have been treated as pirates. In 1855, he was promoted to commander and was posted to Washington as a member of the lighthouse board a year later.

Following his state's secession and the creation of the Confederate States of America, Semmes resigned his U.S. Navy commission on February 15, 1861, and traveled to Montgomery, Alabama, to present himself for service to the Confederacy. Shortly thereafter, President Jefferson Davis sent him into the North to purchase military and naval supplies and manufacturing equipment. In his absence, he was commissioned a commander in the Confederate States Navy. Semmes returned to Montgomery, and on April 17, after the shelling of Fort Sumter, he met with Secretary of the Navy Stephen R. Mallory, another proponent of commerce raiding.

Commerce raiding was not a new phenomenon in American naval history, and it was a natural course for a nation facing a more powerful naval foe with an extensive and vulnerable merchant marine. Southern leaders hoped that raiding might hurt the North financially and weaken its resolve; even a few raiders would force some Union naval assets from blockade duties.

Mallory gave Semmes command of the *Habana,* a 437-ton steamer packet that had been employed on the New Orleans–Havana route. Renamed the *Sumter* and commissioned on June 3, she was the first Confederate navy commerce raider.[1] Semmes said the *Sumter* was "as unlike a ship of war as possible."[2] She was armed with an 8-inch shell gun on pivot amidships and four 32-pounders in broadside.

On June 30, 1861, after nearly two weeks of waiting, Semmes got the *Sumter* to sea past two blockading Union warships. Mallory's orders to him were to "do the enemy's commerce the greatest injury in the shortest time."[3]

On July 3 the *Sumter* took her first prize, a valuable U.S. merchant bark. Semmes wrote of this event, "Our first prize made a beautiful bonfire and we did not enjoy the spectacle the less because she was from the black Republican State of Maine."[4]

Because Great Britain, France, Spain, the Netherlands, and Brazil all declared their neutrality in the Civil War, there were few places where the Confederates could sell captured vessels. As a result, most U.S. merchantmen taken as prizes were burned. Neutrality laws also limited the time raiders could spend in port and prohibited a captain from improving a vessel's fighting characteristics, but Semmes used his legal knowledge to circumvent these laws; he also became adept at deception.

Over the next six months the *Sumter* cruised the Caribbean, capturing nine other vessels. Semmes then sailed her to Brazil and back to the West Indies but took only two prizes. Believing he would have better success in European waters, he sailed the *Sumter* across the Atlantic, taking six Union vessels en route.

On January 3 the *Sumter,* now in poor condition, put into Cadiz. Spanish authorities allowed Semmes to make only minor repairs before ordering him to depart. He took two other prizes before arriving at Gibraltar. British authorities there were more accommodating, but several U.S. Navy warships, including the screw sloop *Kearsarge*, soon set up a blockade. This forced Semmes to lay up the *Sumter* and pay off most of her crew before departing for Britain, whence he planned to return home.[5]

Although the *Sumter* had been both too small and too slow for an effective commerce raider, Semmes had taken eighteen prizes in her. Mallory was well pleased, and on August 21, 1862, the Confederate Congress promoted Semmes to captain; on September 9, it voted him special thanks. He had already left Britain and was in the Bahamas, hoping to catch a blockade runner to the South, when he received an order from Mallory to return to England and take command of a ship nearing completion at Liverpool. This ship had been contracted for on August 1 by Confederate captain James D. Bulloch. First identified as Hull No. 290, she was launched on May 15, 1862, as the *Enrica*.

U.S. diplomats in Britain were certain she was intended for the Confederacy, and the British government was also aware of what was transpiring. Bulloch was therefore warned to get the ship to sea to avoid her being impounded. Fortunately for the Confederates the cabinet order was held up, and the *Enrica* departed British waters on July 30.

Bulloch ordered her British captain to sail her around Ireland to avoid the USS *Tuscarora*, which had been sent to intercept her. Her destination was Terceira Island in the Azores.[6] At the same time,

Bulloch sent another ship, the *Agrippina,* to Terceira, carrying the commerce raider's ordnance, ammunition, stores, and coal. On August 13, Bulloch, Semmes (who had arrived in Liverpool after the *Enrica* sailed), and other officers left Liverpool aboard the *Bahama.* Semmes brought along his large law library, which would be useful in adjudicating condemnation cases.

The *Enrica* arrived at Terceira on August 9. Portuguese officials were told she was the *Barcelona,* bound from London to Havana for the Spanish government. The *Agrippina* arrived at the island on August 18, joined by the *Bahama* two days later.[7]

Semmes supervised the taking on of coal, stores, and ordnance, and on August 24, he commissioned the new ship the *Alabama.* In a rousing speech, he persuaded eighty crewmen from the other ships to sign on with him, promising them double the standard wages in gold and prize money for any ships they destroyed.[8]

A sleek, three-masted, bark-rigged sloop of oak with a copper-sheathed hull, the *Alabama* had a screw propeller that could be detached so that she could run faster (ten knots) under sail alone; she could make thirteen knots under the combined force of steam and sail. Semmes characterized her as "a very perfect ship of her class."[9]

The *Alabama* had a fully equipped machine shop to enable her crewmen to make all ordinary repairs themselves, and she could carry coal sufficient for eighteen days of continuous steaming. Semmes preferred to rely on sail whenever possible. In fact, all but about a half dozen of the *Alabama*'s subsequent captures were made under sail alone.[10]

The *Alabama* mounted eight guns: six 32-pounders in broadside and two pivot-guns (a 7-inch, 110-pounder rifled Blakeley and a smooth-bore, 8-inch, 68-pounder) amidships. She had a 120-man crew and 24 officers.[11] If she could provision from captured prizes, the *Alabama* could remain at sea a long time.

The *Alabama* took her first prizes, all whalers, in the vicinity of the Azores. In approaching a targeted ship, Semmes would fly a false flag, presenting the *Alabama* as a British or Dutch vessel or even a U.S. Navy warship. Only when the targeted vessel had replied with the U.S. flag did Semmes order the Confederate ensign hoisted.

In just two weeks in the Azores, the *Alabama* took and burned ten prizes, eight of them whalers. Semmes would first remove any supplies or merchandise that might be useful for his own ship, as well as the doomed vessel's chronometer and flag—the last two items destined for his rapidly growing collection. Most of his captures were burned, although Semmes occasionally used one for target practice.

If land was close, Semmes usually put the crew and passengers of the captured vessel into their ships' boats, which they then rowed to shore. If no land was nearby, they might be kept on board the *Alabama* or on their own vessel for a time before being released. On occasion, Semmes bonded a ship, a practice whereby a captain signed a paper guaranteeing to pay a set sum equal to the ship's worth to the Confederate government at the end of the war.

Semmes was an excellent captain who paid attention to detail and was a stickler for order and cleanliness; indeed, none of his crewmen ever died of disease. A small man, he was an introvert who did not socialize with his officers, but his leadership, though quiet and calm, was unquestioned. A staunch Catholic, Semmes was opinionated, wordy, and given to hyperbole.

Proud and entirely self-satisfied, he never saw any faults in his own cause and only evil and unfairness on the part of his adversaries. His memoirs reveal a great hatred of the North and contempt for the U.S. Navy. His imperial style, martial bearing, chin whiskers, and long waxed mustaches that ended in fine points led his sailors to refer to him as "Old Beeswax" and "Marshal Pomp."

The vast majority of the *Alabama*'s crew members were British. In November 1862, Semmes seemed well pleased with them, noting in his journal: "I have never seen a better disposed or more orderly crew. They have come very kindly into the traces."[12] In time, however, his opinion changed: On August 1, 1863, he wrote that "I have a precious set of rascals on board, faithless in the matter of abiding by their contracts, liars, thieves and drunkards."[13]

Crew conduct was especially a problem during the infrequent occasions when the ship was in port. Although Semmes tried to maintain tight discipline and rarely allowed the men ashore, he never succeeded in welding them into a smooth-working team. In fact, only about half of the crew remained with the ship during her nearly two years of existence, but because volunteers were readily available, Semmes was never short of men. If his crew was somewhat indifferent, however, Semmes's officers were quite capable. The first three lieutenants had been with him in the *Sumter*. First Lt. John McIntosh Kell and 4th Lt. Arthur F. Sinclair later wrote books about their experiences at sea.

In two weeks, Semmes decimated the Union whaling fleet in the Azores, but on September 18, as his crew was torching a whaler, a gale came up. Semmes remembered the day in these words:

> This burning ship was a beautiful spectacle, the scenes being wild and picturesque beyond description. The thunder began to roll, and crash, and the lightning to leap from cloud to cloud in a thousand eccentric lines. The sea was in a tumult of rage, the winds howled,

and floods of rain descended. Amid the turmoil of the elements, the *Dunbar*, all in flames, and with disordered gear and unfurled canvas, lay rolling and tossing upon the sea. Now an ignited sail would fly from a yard, and scud off before the gale; and now the yard itself released from the control of its braces, would swing about wildly, as in the madness of despair, and then drop into the sea. Finally the masts went by the board and then the hull rocked to and fro for a while, until it was filled with water, and the fire nearly quenched, when it settled to the bottom of the great deep, a victim to the passions of man and the fury of the elements.[14]

The *Alabama* survived the storm unscathed, and Semmes sailed west to the Newfoundland banks, where Union vessels laden with midwestern grain would pass on their way to Europe. In October, he took eleven vessels, destroying eight and granting bond to the remainder. From one, he kept an African American named David White. Semmes recalled:

This was a likely negro lad of about seventeen years of age—a slave until he was twenty-one, under the laws of Delaware. This little State, all of whose sympathies were with us, had been ridden over, rough-shod, by the Vandals north of her, as Maryland afterward was, and was arrayed on the side of the enemy. I was obliged, therefore, to treat her as such. The slave was on his way to Europe, in company with his master. He came necessarily under the laws of war, and I brought him on board the *Alabama,* where we were in want of good servants, and sent him to wait on the ward-room mess.[15]

In his memoirs, Semmes noted the "howl" in the North over White's "capture" but mentioned how happy "Dave" was in his new surroundings and during leave ashore. He claimed to have entered him in the ship's books as a crew member with pay. Semmes asserted that Northerners "know as little about the negro and his nature as they do about the people of the South."[16]

A hurricane interrupted the *Alabama*'s activities, and the crew forgot about commerce raiding as they fought to save their vessel. The storm reached its height on October 16 and snapped the ship's main yard, but she survived. By this time more than a dozen Union warships were searching for the *Alabama,* but they were always a little too late or their captains were looking for her in the wrong locations. Although he was a capable commander, Semmes was also lucky.

He then sailed the *Alabama* into the Caribbean. On November 18, she joined the *Agrippina,* already at Fort de France. The crew soon smuggled liquor on board, which led to drunkenness and talk of mutiny. Semmes ordered his officers armed and the crew beaten to quarters. He then picked out the drunkards and had them placed in irons, ordering the quartermasters to douse the worst offenders with buckets of seawater as they gasped for breath until they were sober. Semmes noted with satisfaction that it was "my first, and only mutiny on board the Alabama."[17]

Apprehensive over the possible appearance of a U.S. Navy warship, Semmes did not attempt to coal the *Alabama* at Fort de France. The next morning, he ordered the *Agrippina* to Blanquilla Island off Venezuela. This was fortunate because the tender was hardly clear of the harbor when the U.S. Navy screw frigate *San Jacinto* arrived. Her captain soon identified the *Alabama* and blockaded the harbor.

Although the Union frigate had double the armament and crew of the *Alabama,* she was old and slow (making only seven knots under steam), and that night, Semmes took advantage of a rain squall to escape with lights out and guns manned. He then sailed to Blanquilla to rendezvous with the *Agrippina* for recoaling. There, Semmes learned that Union forces had taken Galveston, Texas, and that an expeditionary force was expected to invade Texas in January. He also knew the Galveston harbor was shallow and that Union transports would have to anchor offshore. Thus, he intended to take the *Alabama* to Galveston and destroy a number of transports before escaping.

On the way to Texas, he hoped to intercept steamers from Panama. In those days, travelers to California went by steamer from New York to Aspinwall (now Colón) and then by rail across the Isthmus of Panama, where they caught another steamer to San Francisco. Semmes hoped to snare at least one such ship traveling northward with gold.

On November 29 the *Alabama* sailed for the Mona Passage between San Domingo and Puerto Rico, the usual route for mail steamers on their way north. Among the ships Semmes took was the *Ariel.* A third larger than the *Alabama,* she was its most important prize. Unfortunately for Semmes, however, she was outward bound, carrying more than 700 people, including 500 passengers and 140 U.S. Marines. Semmes disarmed the latter and paroled them.

Unable to fall in with another merchantman on which he could place the *Ariel*'s passengers, Semmes was forced to let the ship go under a bond of $216,000. He was sorely disappointed that he could not burn her, especially since she was owned by Cornelius Vanderbilt, who had given a fast steamer to the U.S. government to hunt down Confederate commerce raiders.[18] Semmes then sailed the *Alabama* into the Gulf of Mexico. On December 23, he rendezvoused with the *Agrippina* off the coast of Yucatán, where his crew spent a week taking on supplies and coal before being given liberty on some uninhabited coral islands.

Semmes planned to arrive at Galveston during daylight, note the disposition of Union ships, and then return for a night attack. This plan seemed likely to succeed because the *Alabama* was faster than the blockading U.S. Navy warships. But when the *Alabama* arrived off Galveston in the late afternoon of January 11, 1863, Semmes found that the Confederates had retaken Galveston ten days before and that the Union expedition had been diverted to New Orleans. Instead of a fleet of Federal transports, he found five Union warships lobbing shells into the port city.

Semmes took his ship in too close, and Union seamen sighted the *Alabama*. Their suspicions were aroused when she stopped some twelve miles offshore. The Union squadron commander, Commodore Henry H. Bell, dispatched the *Hatteras,* under Lt. Cmdr. Homer C. Blake, to investigate the suspicious ship. A former Delaware River excursion side-wheel steamer mounting only four 32-pounders and a 20-pounder rifle, the *Hatteras* was a poor match for the *Alabama*, although this did not stop Semmes from claiming that the ensuing battle was an equal one.[19]

Semmes had not decided what to do next and was thus relieved to see the *Hatteras* put out to sea. The *Alabama* moved slowly along the coast, drawing the *Hatteras* away from the other Union warships. When it was dark and the two ships were about twenty miles from the Federal squadron, the *Alabama* lay to and turned toward the *Hatteras* under steam. The two ships were within hailing distance when Blake demanded his opponent's identity. Semmes identified his ship as "Her Britannic Majesty's steamer *Petrel*" (some accounts say "*Ariel*"). Blake then demanded the right to inspect the ship's registry as verification. After a boat had been lowered and was under way from the *Hatteras,* Semmes called out, "This is the Confederate States steamer *Alabama*. Fire."[20]

Blake tried to ram Semmes's ship, but the *Hatteras* was too slow, and the *Alabama* easily avoided contact. In just thirteen minutes, with two crewmen dead, five others wounded, his ship sinking, and the *Alabama* in position to rake her, Blake surrendered. The *Alabama,* which had only two men wounded, took the remainder of the *Hatteras*'s crew on board and departed without lights. On January 20, she arrived at Jamaica, where Semmes paroled his prisoners. He kept the *Alabama* in the West Indies for the next month.

On January 25, after recoaling, the *Alabama* departed Jamaica to sail east to Brazil. Soon after her departure, she took a prize, which Semmes ordered destroyed. He described the scene:

A looker-on upon that conflagration would have seen a wonderful picture, for besides the burning ship, there were the two islands mentioned [Saint Domingo and Jamaica] sleeping in the dreamy moonlight on a calm bosom of a tropical sea, and the rakish-looking "British pirate" steaming in for the land, with every spar and line of cordage brought out in bold relief by the bright flame—nay, with the very "pirates" themselves visible, handling the boxes and bales of merchandise which they had "robbed" from this innocent Yankee, whose countrymen at home were engaged in the Christian occupation of burning our houses and desolating our fields.[21]

On April 10 the *Alabama* arrived at the island of Fernando de Noronha off Brazil. In three months of sailing off Latin America, Semmes took fifteen prizes, never spotting a U.S. Navy warship. Semmes took the *Alabama* to sea on April 22 and headed for Bahia, capturing several prizes before arriving there on May 11. Two days later the CSS *Georgia* arrived. The CSS *Florida* was then only 100 miles to the north. The sole Union warship in the South Atlantic, the screw sloop *Mohican,* missed the Confederate cruisers in several locations by just a few days.[22]

On May 21, 1863, the *Alabama* sailed from Bahia. She then cruised off the Brazilian coast between Bahia and Rio de Janeiro and took eight more prizes, one of which was the 500-ton bark *Conrad*. A fine clipper, the *Conrad* could be easily handled with a small crew. Semmes armed her with two 12-pounder cannons and commissioned her the *Tuscaloosa,* noting, "It was meet that a child of the *Alabama* should be named after one of the towns of the State."[23] Two officers and a dozen men from the *Alabama* made up her crew.[24] Semmes ordered the *Tuscaloosa* to cruise independently and rendezvous with him at Cape Town. She subsequently captured two merchantmen, but British authorities at Cape Town ultimately seized her as an uncondemned prize.[25]

Semmes next took the *Alabama* to the Cape of Good Hope to intercept vessels homeward bound from the East Indies. He first put in at Saldanha Bay, about seventy-five miles northwest of Cape Town, for maintenance. This done, he sailed for Cape Town. On August 15, Semmes again took the *Alabama* to sea. By then, weariness had set in, and he recorded in his journal, "How tiresome is the routine of cruising becoming."[26] On returning to Cape Town, he learned of the fall of Vicksburg and Port Hudson.

In two months of patrolling off South Africa, the *Alabama* had taken only one prize. But more important, Semmes learned that the more powerful U.S. Navy steamer *Vanderbilt* was searching for him. Time was running out. The year 1863 was, in fact, the high point for Confederate commerce destroyers; the *Alabama* took only three prizes in the first six months of 1864.

Semmes then took his ship into the Pacific. On September 24, she left Cape Town to sail through the Indian Ocean and into the

China Sea. On October 16, the anniversary of the hurricane a year before, the *Alabama* encountered a bad storm. Semmes then put the crew to work repairing damage and painting the ship.[27] He had high expectations, hoping he could make serious inroads into U.S. trade with the Orient. In the first half of November the *Alabama* took four prizes, but problems with the crew were increasing. The diary entries written by the chief officer of a prize, made while he was a prisoner on the *Alabama,* reflected the situation: "Crew much dissatisfied, no prize money, no liberty, and see no prospect of getting any. Discipline very slack; steamer dirty, rigging slovenly. Semmes sometimes punishes but is afraid to push too hard; men excited; officers do not report to captain; crew do things for which they would be shot on board American man-of-war."[28]

It was also apparent to Semmes that the *Alabama* herself was wearing out. Her hull's copper plating was loosening, and her boilers were so corroded that it was dangerous to use full steam.[29] Uncertainty and strain were showing on all, including Semmes. Lieutenant Sinclair noted that Semmes "must have a rugged constitution and iron nerves to pull through as he does. At all hours of the day and night he may be seen bent over his chart in the cabin, or on deck conning the surroundings."[30]

On December 21 the *Alabama* arrived at Singapore. Rumors of the ship's arrival had preceded her, and Semmes counted twenty-two U.S. merchant ships safely laid up in the harbor. He also heard of others secure at Bangkok, Canton, Shanghai, and Manila. At almost every port she touched, some men deserted; at Singapore, twelve men left the ship, although another six signed on. Semmes soon learned that the U.S. Navy screw sloop *Wyoming* was patrolling Sunda Strait between Sumatra and Java. Knowing that the *Alabama* was a more powerful warship, he resolved to attack the *Wyoming*. But although at one point the two ships were only twenty-five miles apart, they never actually met. The *Alabama* then sailed through the Straits of Malacca and took two more U.S. merchant ships the day after Christmas, bringing the year's total to thirty-seven. By now, morale on board was quite low, and Semmes decided to seek a modern shipyard in Britain or France to carry out a complete overhaul of his vessel.

On December 31 the *Alabama* reentered the Indian Ocean. In the Bay of Bengal, she made a brief call on the southwestern Indian coast, where Semmes landed prisoners. She then sailed west to the Comoro Islands near the coast of Africa to reprovision. With Islam the religion of the area and with no legal sale of alcohol allowed, Semmes gave his men shore leave. Then, on February 12, the *Alabama* left the Comoros, retracing her course back through the Indian Ocean to Cape Town, where she arrived on March 20. On the return trip, Semmes took only one vessel.

By now the *Alabama* had been in commission for almost twenty months. Her bottom was foul, and her machinery was in poor repair. Semmes noted, "Many of the beams of the ship are splitting and giving way, owing to the greenness of the timber of which she was built."[31] On March 25 the *Alabama* left Cape Town for Europe. During her passage, she took her last two prizes. Semmes burned both.

As his ship sailed north, Semmes wrote in his journal on May 21: "Our bottom is in such a state that everything passes us. We are like a crippled hunter limping home from a long chase."[32] In his memoirs, he was more poetic about the *Alabama* and stressed the cost of the voyage on himself:

> She was like the wearied fox-hound, limping back after a long chase, foot-sore, and longing for quiet and repose. Her commander, like herself, was well-nigh worn down. Vigils by night and by day, the storm and the drenching rain, the frequent and rapid change of climate, now freezing, now melting or boiling, and the constant excitement of the chase and capture, had laid, in the three years of war he had been afloat, a load of a dozen years on his shoulders. The shadows of a sorrowful future, too, began to rest upon his spirit.[33]

On June 11, 1864, the *Alabama* dropped anchor at Cherbourg. Since her commissioning, she had sailed seventy-five thousand miles, taken sixty-six prizes, and sunk a Union warship. In the *Sumter* and the *Alabama,* Semmes had taken a total of eighty-four Union merchantmen. He estimated he had burned $4,613,914 worth of shipping and cargoes and bonded others valued at $562,250. Another estimate places the total at nearly $6,000,000. Moreover, twenty-five Union warships had searched for the *Alabama*, costing the Federal government over $7 million. Her exploits had also been a considerable boost to Confederate morale.[34]

French officials rejected Semmes's request to put the *Alabama* into dry dock for repair. They pointed out, as Semmes already knew, that the Cherbourg facilities were reserved for ships of the French navy. They suggested he move his ship to Le Havre or another port with private dockyard facilities. Semmes did secure a relaxation in the one-day rule regarding the presence of a belligerent warship in a French port. He also sent prisoners from his last two captures ashore and granted his men leave.

Word of the *Alabama*'s arrival spread quickly. On June 12 the U.S. minister in Paris telegraphed the news to Flushing, Holland, where the Union's third-rate screw steam sloop *Kearsarge,* commanded by Capt. John A. Winslow, was at anchor, monitoring the *Georgia* and *Rappahannock* at Calais.

Winslow knew Semmes well, as they had served together. A Southerner by birth, Winslow had been educated in New England

and married a Boston woman. He also became an ardent abolitionist who believed in the moral duty of the North to eradicate slavery. Winslow had spent a year searching for the *Alabama,* and he was determined that she would not again elude him. He soon had the *Kearsarge* under way, and she arrived at Cherbourg on June 14.

Despite the fact that his ship was in poor condition and slowed by her foul bottom, Semmes did not hesitate to do battle. Perhaps it was a matter of pride; after all, the war was about over, and there had been little glory in sinking merchantmen. In any case, he had little choice. Delay would only bring more Union warships.

Semmes sent a sarcastic message to Confederate agent Auguste Bonfils at Cherbourg: "I desire you to say to the U.S. consul that my intention is to fight the *Kearsarge* as soon as I can make the necessary arrangements. I hope these will not detain me more than tomorrow evening or after the morrow morning at the furthest. I beg she will not depart before I am ready to go out."[35] Meanwhile Semmes and his crew did all they could to prepare the *Alabama.* She took on a full load of coal, which would help protect her machinery from shot. Nonessential spars and rigging were removed, the deck was holystoned, and weapons were cleaned. Semmes also put the crew through gunnery drill. He took the precaution of sending ashore the ship's valuables: his collection of chronometers from each of his captures, the *Alabama*'s gold (forty-seven hundred gold sovereigns), her payroll, and the ten ransom bonds on ships he had released. As a point of pride, however, he kept aboard his collection of prize flags.[36]

Semmes informed French authorities that he would be fighting the next day, and then he attended mass. The following morning at 9:00 when the boilers were lit, Semmes called the crewmen aft and addressed them for the last time:

> Officers and Seamen of the *Alabama:* You have at length another opportunity of meeting the enemy—the first that has been presented to you since you sank the *Hatteras.* In the meantime, you have been all over the world, and it is not too much to say that you have destroyed, and driven for protection under neutral flags, one half of the enemy's commerce, which, at the beginning of the war, covered every sea. This is an achievement of which you may well be proud; and a grateful country will not be unmindful of it. The name of your ship has become a household word wherever civilization extends. Shall that name be tarnished by defeat? The thing is impossible! Remember that you are on the English Channel, the theatre of so much of the naval glory of our race, and that the eyes of all Europe are at this moment upon you. The flag that floats over you is that of a young Republic, who bids defiance to her enemies, whenever, and wherever found. Show the world that you know how to uphold it! Go to your quarters.[37]

Wearing his dress uniform, Semmes positioned himself on the quarterdeck.

Sunday, June 19, 1864, was a perfect day, with a calm sea and a light wind from the west. The battle that ensued between the USS *Kearsarge* and the CSS *Alabama* in the English Channel off Cherbourg was one the most spectacular of all the Civil War naval engagements. Some fifteen thousand people observed it from the cliffs on the coast and windows of houses ashore, although most saw the battle only as smoky smudges on the horizon.

Despite Semmes's later claims that the *Kearsarge* had the advantage in size, weight of ordnance, and number of guns and crewmen, the two ships were actually closely matched. He admitted as much in a journal entry of June 15: "My crew seems to be in the right spirit, a quiet spirit of determination, pervading both officers and men. The combat will no doubt be contested and obstinate, but the two ships are so equally matched that I do not feel at liberty to decline it. God defend the right and have mercy upon the souls of those who fall as many of us must."[38]

The deciding factor in the hour-long battle that began at about 11:00 A.M. in international waters some six or seven miles offshore was the pivot-mounted, 11-inch Dahlgren guns aboard the *Kearsarge*. But the crew of the Union warship was fortunate that one shell from the large Blakeley gun on the *Alabama* failed to explode. It lodged in the *Kearsarge*'s wooden sternpost, and had it gone off it would have destroyed her steering and made her unmanageable. Semmes later wrote that if the fuse had worked, "I should have been called upon to save Captain Winslow's crew from drowning."[39]

The *Kearsarge* also had the advantage of having chain strung over the vital middle parts of the ship to protect her engines, boilers, and magazines from enemy fire; this technique had been proven in fighting along the Mississippi River, and the chain had been in place on the *Kearsarge* for some time. An outward sheathing of 1-inch wood painted the same color as the rest of the hull concealed the chaining from Confederate observation, but the French had informed Semmes about it. Semmes might have used chain in the *Alabama*'s lockers for the same purpose. But later, he claimed he had been unaware of the *Kearsarge*'s chain mail, which he said was an unfair advantage in that it made the vessel a "concealed ironclad." He seems to have convinced himself that this factor was the only reason the *Alabama* lost the battle. But as one writer has noted, "This is a curious misconception of the character of warfare to take possession of the mind of a professional naval officer of life-long training, whose own vessel was born in deception and who for nearly two years had been disguising her with false colors to decoy unarmed merchantmen."[40]

Lieutenant Sinclair later wrote that Semmes knew about the chain and was critical of him for not equipping the *Alabama* in the same fashion: "Winslow, for protecting his ship with chain-armor, should, in the humble judgment of the writer, submitted with diffidence, be accounted as simply using proper prudence in the direct line of duty. He had not given, accepted, or declined a challenge. But it was his duty to fight if he could, and win. Semmes knew all about it, and could have adopted the same scheme. It was not his election to do so."[41]

Throughout the battle, Winslow was able to dictate range because his vessel was both faster and more maneuverable than that of his opponent. Shells from the 11-inch Dahlgrens tore into the *Alabama* and had a terrible effect on the ship and her crew. The raider's hull was repeatedly hit, and large holes were ripped in her side.

With his ship sinking, Semmes sent a dinghy to the *Kearsarge* to notify Winslow that he was ready to surrender. Semmes and Sinclair later wrote that the *Kearsarge* continued to fire on his ship after her colors were struck and a white flag displayed; Winslow said that he had ordered fire halted when the *Alabama*'s colors came down and a white flag went up at her stern but that, shortly afterward, his opponent had opened fire again, from the two guns on the port side. He said he then moved his ship into position to rake his antagonist but, seeing the white flag still flying, had again held fire.

With the *Alabama* sinking, Semmes ordered that "All hands save yourselves" be piped. All but two of her boats had been destroyed in the battle, and one of these had been damaged, so most men simply leaped in the sea. Semmes gave his papers to a sailor who was a good swimmer, hurled his sword into the water, and then jumped in himself.[42]

The *Alabama* sank stern first with forty-one casualties: Nine men died and twenty were wounded in the engagement, and twelve others drowned.[43] Only three men were wounded aboard the *Kearsarge*, one of whom later died of his injuries.[44] Semmes unfairly blamed Winslow and wrote: "Ten of my men were permitted to drown."[45] An English yacht, the *Deerhound,* rescued forty-two men from the *Alabama,* including Semmes, and took them to Southampton. The British government rejected demands that they be turned over to U.S. authorities.

Semmes paid off his remaining crew and sent allotments to relatives of the dead. He then traveled to Belgium and Switzerland, returning to London at the end of September. On October 3, he embarked on a steamer to Saint Thomas. From there, he traveled to Havana, where he arrived at the end of October and took passage on a small ship to Bagdad at the mouth of the Rio Grande on the Mexican side of the Texas border.[46]

Semmes made his way to Brownsville and then to Richmond. Promoted to rear admiral in February 1865, he took command of the James River Squadron of three ironclad rams and seven wooden steamers. This command lasted barely three months. The squadron was largely immune from attack as long as it was protected by powerful shore batteries, but when Confederate forces abandoned Richmond, Semmes had no choice but to destroy his vessels. This he did on the night of April 2, 1865: The ships were set on fire, scuttled, or blown up. The men of the squadron then formed into a naval brigade under Semmes as a brigadier general and retreated to Greensboro, North Carolina, where the unit joined Gen. Joseph E. Johnston's army and later surrendered.

Paroled on May 1, 1865, Semmes returned to Mobile, where he was arrested by order of Secretary of the Navy Gideon Welles on December 15, despite the protection his parole should have afforded. He was transported to Washington and held there for three months. Evidently, Welles planned to try him before a military commission on charges that he had violated military codes by escaping from the *Alabama* after her colors had been struck. But after the Supreme Court denied jurisdiction of the commissions, Semmes was released, and he again returned home.

Semmes was a probate judge of Mobile County but was forced out of that office after a brief term. He then accepted the chair of moral philosophy and English literature at Louisiana State Seminary (now Louisiana State University) at Baton Rouge. When political pressure again forced him out, he became editor of the *Memphis Daily Bulletin* but was also hounded from that post. After a profitable lecture tour he resumed the practice of law. In 1869, he published *Memoirs of Service Afloat, during the War between the States*. Semmes died on August 30, 1877, leaving his wife and six children. He is buried in Mobile.[47]

Notes

1. For information on the *Sumter,* see Paul H. Silverstone, *Warships of the Civil War Navies* (Annapolis, MD: Naval Institute Press, 1989), 214.

2. Raphael Semmes, *Memoirs of Service Afloat, during the War between the States* (Baltimore: Kelly, Piet and Co., 1869), 96.

3. *Appleton's Cyclopaedia of American Biography,* ed. Grant Wilson and John Fiske, 7 vols. (New York: D. Appleton and Co., 1888), 4:341. Also, Adm. David D. Porter, *Naval History of the Civil War* (1884; reprint ed., Secaucus, NJ: Castle Books, 1984), 605–6.

4. Semmes, Journal, in *Official Records of the Union and Confederate Navies in the War of the Rebellion* (Washington, DC: U.S. Government Printing Office, 1894) (hereafter cited as *ORN*), series 1, 1: 695.

5. On her cruise, see Porter, *Naval History of the Civil War*, 606–20.

6. Philip Van Doren Stern, *The Confederate Navy: A Pictorial History* (Garden City, NY: Doubleday and Co., 1962), 117; George W. Dalzell, *The Flight from the Flag: The Continuing Effect of the Civil War upon the American Carrying Trade* (Chapel Hill: University of North Carolina Press, 1940), 131–36.

7. Charles M. Robinson III, *Shark of the Confederacy: The Story of the CSS* Alabama (Annapolis, MD: Naval Institute Press, 1995), 28.

8. Dalzell, *The Flight from the Flag*, 136–47; Robinson, *Shark of the Confederacy*, 33.

9. Semmes, *Memoirs of Service Afloat*, 402.

10. Ibid., 419–20.

11. Ibid.

12. Semmes, Journal, November 16, 1862, in *ORN*, 1:805.

13. Dalzell, *The Flight from the Flag*, 149.

14. Semmes, *Memoirs of Service Afloat*, 444.

15. Ibid., 464.

16. Ibid., 465–66.

17. Ibid., 511–13.

18. Dalzell, *The Flight from the Flag*, 142–43; Frank M. Bennett, *The Monitor and the Navy under Steam* (New York: Houghton Mifflin, 1900), 189; Robinson, *Shark of the Confederacy*, 65–66; Semmes, *Memoirs of Service Afloat*, 535.

19. Semmes, *Memoirs of Service Afloat*, 449.

20. Robinson, *Shark of the Confederacy*, 74.

21. Semmes, *Memoirs of Service Afloat*, 566. Calling the *Alabama* the "British pirate" was a sarcastic reference to the way the Union press referred to the *Alabama*.

22. Robinson, *Shark of the Confederacy*, 97–98.

23. Semmes, *Memoirs of Service Afloat*, 627.

24. Sinclair, *Two Years*, 124–25.

25. Silverstone, *Warships of the Civil War Navies*, 218.

26. Semmes, Journal, September 13, 1863, in *ORN*, series 1, 2:765.

27. Robinson, *Shark of the Confederacy*, 108–9, 111, and 113.

28. Dalzell, *The Flight from the Flag*, 154

29. Robinson, *Shark of the Confederacy*, 115.

30. Sinclair, *Two Years*, 164.

31. Semmes, Journal, April 3, 1864, in *ORN*, series 1, 3:669.

32. Semmes, Journal, May 21, 1864, in *ORN*, series 1, 3:674.

33. Semmes, *Memoirs of Service Afloat*, 749–50.

34. U.S. Navy Department, *Civil War Naval Chronology*, pt. 6, 192; Robinson, *Shark of the Confederacy*, 194; "Vessela Overhauled by the C.S.S. Alabama," *ORN*, series 1, 3:677–81.

35. Semmes to Bonfils, June 14, 1864, in *ORN*, series 1, 3:648.

36. Semmes to Barron, June 14, 1864, in *ORN*, series 1, 3:651.

37. Semmes, *Memoirs of Service Afloat*, 756.

38. Semmes, Journal, June 15, 1864, in *ORN*, series 1, 3:677.

39. Semmes, *Memoirs of Service Afloat,* 762; Frank M. Bennett, in *The* Monitor *and the Navy under Steam,* takes exception to the claim that this one shell, had it exploded, would have decided the battle.

40. Semmes, *Memoirs of Service Afloat,* 759–62; *ORN,* series 1, 3:758; Dalzell, *The Flight from the Flag,* 163.

41. Sinclair, *Two Years,* 263.

42. Ibid., 258–60; Semmes, *Memoirs of Service Afloat,* 757.

43. Sinclair, *Two Years,* 281.

44. Dalzell, *The Flight from the Flag,* 160; Bennett, *The* Monitor *and the Navy under Steam,* 187.

45. Semmes, *Memoirs of Service Afloat,* 759.

46. Ibid., 789–92.

47. *Dictionary of American Biography,* ed. Dumas Malone, 21 vols. (New York: Charles Scribner's Sons, 1935), 16:977.

5

Charles Henry Foster
A Unionist in Confederate North Carolina

Donald E. Collins

In the decades after the end of the Civil War and Reconstruction, political pundits spoke of the "Solid South," a region said to be thoroughly monolithic in its political opinions. That assessment was probably never true in an absolute sense, even in regard to white Southerners, and it certainly was not true during the Civil War itself. Each Confederate state had among its people those who, for reasons ranging from expedience to heartfelt conviction, remained loyal to the Union, and every Confederate state except South Carolina fielded a regiment or more of white Union troops. North Carolina provided two such regiments, one of them raised by the enigmatic Charles Henry Foster, an unprincipled mountebank who switched back and forth between antislavery and proslavery "convictions," as the author of this chapter points out, "solely for the purpose of self-promotion into the ranks of political and/or military leadership." Foster was not typical of Southern Unionists, but he *was* typical of those individuals, from the North and the South, whose primary purpose was self-aggrandizement.

In recounting Foster's story here, Donald E. Collins, associate professor of history at East Carolina University, Greenville, North Carolina, author of *Native American Aliens* (1985), and an expert on the Civil War in North Carolina, also tells us something about the divisions within the Southern body politic and how they contributed to Confederate defeat.

Charles Henry Foster was an enigma. Like a chameleon, he was able to adapt to the community around him and become whatever he believed others wanted him to be. Although a New England Yankee of abolitionist tendencies, he assumed the role of a champion of Southern rights in his adopted state of North Carolina. And when war came, Foster just as easily reversed his publicly proclaimed beliefs in slavery and states' rights to champion the Lincoln administration and the cause of the Union. Yet Foster the patriot was also Foster the shameless con man, for whom even the most fantastic and improbable schemes were not off-limits in his pursuit of high political office or military rank. To leading North Carolina Unionists and Confederates alike, he was "Humbug Foster"—a scoundrel, liar, and fraud.[1] Despite his motives, however, he significantly advanced the cause of the Federal government in the Confederate state of North Carolina.

Foster was born in Orono, Maine, on February 18, 1830, the first-born child of local merchant Cony Foster and his wife Caroline, a daughter of Benjamin Brown, one of the wealthiest men in the state. As a youth, he showed an intelligence and ability beyond his years. Detailed diaries kept by Charles and his brother Benjamin show that he was well read and an exceptional writer. Like his parents, he opposed slavery and generally supported the Democratic Party. As a young teenager, he developed an early and deep passion for journalism and politics—a passion that only death would end. At the age of seventeen, he used the press to attack slavery as "a curse" that violated "the first principles of humanity" and was therefore "utterly, totally and fully wrong."[2] Only days before his twentieth birthday, Benjamin recorded in his diary that "Charles is completely smashed with politics, and he thinks, writes and publishes *sans cesse,* if not *sans varier.*"[3]

In 1850, Charles and Benjamin entered Bowdoin College, where they became acquainted with future leaders of the state and country, including Joshua L. Chamberlain, future governor of Maine and a hero of Gettysburg; Harriet Beecher Stowe, author and wife of professor Calvin Stowe; and future U.S. Supreme Court Chief Justice Melville W. Fuller. In 1852, Charles publicly demonstrated his antislavery beliefs when he took copies of Stowe's recently published book, *Uncle Tom's Cabin,* to Portland to sell for the author. The two brothers were elected to Phi Beta Kappa honorary fraternity and graduated with honors in 1855.[4]

Prior to entering college, Charles studied law under the direction of Israel Washburn, who would soon become the Civil War governor of Maine. Following graduation, he completed his law studies and was admitted to the Maine bar. Washburn is reputed to have offered him a partnership in his firm, which Charles declined.[5] Instead, he spent 1856 as a teacher and principal at Cony School for Boys in Augusta, Maine.

In 1857, Foster the abolitionist dramatically changed his career and political philosophy, opting for a life in the South as editor of the *Southern Statesman,* a Democratic Southern rights newspaper, and later as assistant editor of a larger paper, the *Norfolk Day Book.* On January 1, 1859, he moved to Murfreesboro, North Carolina, where he purchased the *Citizen,* a weekly Democratic newspaper, and became its editor. On May 1, 1860, he married Susan Carter, daughter of Perry Carter, a locally prominent merchant and large slaveholder, and took up residence in the Carter home, Rose Bower.

Foster now became a staunch and emotional defender of the South and its institutions. He fiercely attacked "Black Republicanism," the John Brown raid on Harpers Ferry, and abolitionists. At the same time, he just as staunchly defended secession, states' rights, slavery, and the expansion of slavery into the territories.[6]

In March 1860, Foster attended the Democratic National Convention in Baltimore, Maryland, as an alternate delegate for his district. On the fifth day in session, he joined other North Carolina delegates in bolting the convention, which was dominated by supporters of Stephen A. Douglas, to hold a separate convention and nominate the states' rights candidate, John C. Breckinridge of Kentucky, for president.[7] During the campaign, Foster used his newspaper to support the Breckinridge-Lane ticket.

On December 1, 1860, following the election of Abraham Lincoln, Foster again used the *Citizen* to argue for state sovereignty and secession. He argued that allegiance to one's state was supreme and that secession was constitutional because once a state was kept in the Union by force, it had lost its sovereignty and was reduced to the status of a "subjugated province."[8] Soon after making this argument, however, he sold the *Citizen,* probably in anticipation of moving to Washington, DC, where he had accepted a minor position in the U.S. Post Office.

In late February, only a week after the birth of his first child, Foster left his family behind in Murfreesboro and headed for the national capital. As events occurred in North Carolina that would lead to that state's secession on May 20, 1861, Charles followed a course that would lead to his ejection from the state as an outright Unionist. On April 12, Southern forces fired on Fort Sumter in Charleston harbor, South Carolina. Three days later, North Carolina refused to provide troops to suppress the rebellion. About the same time, Foster enlisted in the Clay Guard, a volunteer battalion being raised in Washington for the temporary defense of the city against a rumored attack from Virginia. He was damned for this anti-Southern act when the news became known in Murfreesboro.[9]

Foster, perhaps unaware of the hostility that awaited him in North Carolina, returned to Murfreesboro to visit his family. There, he found his wife's family, as well as his brother Lyman (who had followed him from Maine to North Carolina), fully in support of the new Confederate States of America. Foster also discovered that the residents of Murfreesboro were greatly agitated against him. Some believed him to be a Union spy, and others spoke of lynching him. He found himself a virtual prisoner in the home of his father-in-law and was ordered not to leave town until his case was referred to Gov. John W. Ellis.[10]

Although there can be little doubt that Foster had already thrown his support to the Union, he saw no way out of a dangerous situation but to convince the governor of his continued and firm loyalty to the South. "I am," he wrote, "bound by my oath never to take up arms against the South."[11] Fearing the worst, however, he fled North Carolina under the cover of darkness, heading for Southampton County, Virginia, where he safely boarded a train for Washington, DC.

For the next few years, Foster would follow a path of conspiracy and deceit designed solely for the purpose of self-promotion into the ranks of political and/or military leadership. To track his several schemes, it is necessary to understand his relationship with E. W. Carpenter, a man he apparently met soon after taking his position in the post office. Prior to the war, Carpenter had read law under Winfield Smith, attorney general of the state of Wisconsin, who described him as an impudent, ignorant man whose most marked traits were energy, a gift for flattery, and an almost irresistible inclination to lie. Carpenter, he added, knew enough law to keep out of the penitentiary and to practice the barroom acts useful for obtaining public positions and a low notoriety.[12] Nonetheless, Carpenter became Foster's man Friday and an essential element in their mutual schemes to deceive the government for Foster's benefit.[13]

On June 24, 1861, Foster informed President Lincoln of his intention to campaign for the *United States* House of Representatives to represent the *Confederate* state of North Carolina. According to Foster's logic, Congress should include representatives from the Southern states; after all, he and the president both agreed that these states were still in the Union. Foster intended to be his adopted state's congressman, and he was serving notice on Lincoln and his cabinet of his candidacy. "Your silence," he boldly informed the president, would be "considered as implying assent to these propositions."[14]

Foster followed up his announcement with a campaign for office based solely on newspaper propaganda that he and Carpenter wrote themselves. According to the plan, they would report on the fictitious campaign ostensibly from within North Carolina while actually maintaining a low profile in Pennsylvania and Maryland.[15] Fraudulent dispatches written by the two men were then printed in the *New York Tribune* and picked up by other Northern papers to give the impression that an actual campaign was being conducted.

Dispatches allegedly written from Salisbury, Morganton, Raleigh, Weldon, and other North Carolina towns informed Northern readers of the fictitious campaign's progress. On September 2, 1861, Foster told the public, "I was elected to Congress from this State by a large vote" and "shall claim my seat in December next."[16]

With Foster's conversion to Unionism now public knowledge, his wife, Susan, broke relations with him in a letter published in an August 1861 issue of the *Petersburg (Virginia) Daily Press*. "As a true woman of the South," she wrote, "I am desirous that my indignation and contempt be shown for the course [he has taken]." Every tie "which has heretofore bound me to Charles H. Foster" was, she declared, "virtually dissolved forever."[17]

Foster's reported election awakened a bitter enemy in the person of Benjamin F. Hedrick. The former chemistry professor had gained a national reputation as a Southern abolitionist and supporter of the Union when he was dismissed from the University of North Carolina for expressing support for John C. Frémont, the antislavery Republican candidate for president in 1856. Foster appears to have initiated the feud when, on December 7, 1859, he placed in the columns of the *Citizen* a virulent attack on Hedrick for stealing Southern money to finance abolitionist attacks on the South. Intemperately describing the former professor as a "Benedict Arnold" to the South, Foster warned North Carolinians that Hedrick's treachery would bring rape, murder, and slave insurrection to his native state.[18]

Now an official in the U.S. Patent Office in Washington, DC, Hedrick was centrally located to campaign against Foster, whom he regularly described as a humbug, cheat, liar, and fraud. He began a three-year campaign against Foster, firing off a stream of letters to the president, cabinet members, congressional committees, politicians, newspapers, and various other Unionist North Carolinians within and outside the state.[19] Although Foster would gain the support of North Carolina's poor whites (the so-called poor white trash), leading native Unionists lined up against him, among them Edward Stanly, soon to be appointed military governor of the state, and Hinton Rowan Helper, author of the *Impending Crisis of the South*.

Without waiting for the verdict of Congress on the validity of his election, Foster entered into yet another scheme, this one aimed at winning a ranking position in the Union army. The campaign was initiated in the *New York Tribune* of September 2, 1861. Carpenter, in his guise as a special correspondent reporting the alleged Federal congressional campaign in North Carolina, informed readers that "Col. Foster" had enrolled a full brigade of loyal men in the eastern part of the state. "Why not," the correspondent suggested, "appoint Col. Foster a brigadier-General and arm and equip his men at once?" Within weeks, the "Congressman-elect" personally offered Lincoln the services of his brigade. The scheme failed when the president referred Foster's offer to Secretary of War Simon Cameron; with a note of sarcasm, he suggested that if arms *were* put in the hands of a regiment of Unionist North Carolinians, they probably would not remain in their hands for long.[20]

Foster's failure to gain official recognition from Congress or the president through his various political and military schemes did not discourage his efforts. On August 28 and 29, 1861, Union forces under Gen. Benjamin Butler invaded North Carolina and gained control of Hatteras Island, off the northeastern coast. Federal forces quickly found a sizable amount of Union sentiment among the residents of the island as well as in the adjacent Confederate-held coastal plains. Foster seized on these pockets of Unionism, seeing in them still another opportunity for gaining political office. The leader among the Unionists on Hatteras Island was Methodist minister Marble Nash Taylor. By October, Foster had moved from Washington to Hatteras, where he would remain off and on for the following seven months, residing near Reverend Taylor. There, he and the clergyman jointly planned for a government that even many local natives would have difficulty taking seriously.[21]

In late October, Foster and Taylor visited New York City to win support for their proposed government and to plead for clothing, food, and other aid for the loyal citizens of Hatteras. While Taylor accomplished this goal in a meeting at Cooper Institute, Foster worked to gain support for their planned government from North Carolinians in exile. On November 11, he reported that he and Taylor had conferred with every North Carolinian they found in New York. These individuals, he claimed, "concur[red] heartily" in the plan for creating a provisional government. Indeed, sixty thousand people would recognize that government, he said, as soon as the "intimidation of rebel pressure were removed."[22]

Once again on Hatteras, the two men called for a convention to meet on November 18, 1861, and take the necessary steps to create the proposed government. Forty-five counties were said to be represented either by delegates or proxies collected in New York; the actual number of delegates present totaled a scant six or eight. Taylor was declared provisional governor, and the ordinance of secession was declared to be null and void. Without delay, "Governor" Taylor declared that an election for a representative to Congress from the Second Congressional District would be held on November 28, 1861.

The election was confined to Hatteras Island, the only area of the state then under Union control, and Foster was the unanimous choice of the 268 voters. Two days later, the "Hon. C. H. Foster, member of Congress," left Hatteras in the company of his associate E. W. Carpenter to claim his seat in the House of Representatives. But on December 18, 1861, the House's Committee of Elections rejected Foster's bid to become a member of that body.[23]

With the failure of Congress to seat Foster, a meeting was held on Hatteras Island at which it was decided to hold a second election on January 16, 1862, to fill the district's still-vacant seat. However, bad weather and the arrival of Gen. Ambrose Burnside's invasion fleet at Hatteras inlet prompted the voters themselves to delay the election until January 30. When it finally took place, Foster gained thirty additional votes from Chicamacomico Precinct, bringing his total to 298.

While Foster's claim to a seat in the House of Representatives made its slow way toward a hearing by the Committee of Elections, Union forces under General Burnside moved to take control of the upper coastal region of North Carolina from Roanoke Island southward to New Bern and Beaufort. Roanoke fell to Union arms on February 8, and in March, Federal forces occupied New Bern, Beaufort, Plymouth, Washington, and Fort Macon. For the most part, these areas would remain in Union hands until the end of the war. The presence of the Northern army on the land and Federal gunboats in the sounds and rivers of eastern North Carolina provoked numerous expressions of Union sentiment, and Foster, who considered himself a member of Congress until proven otherwise, was quick to exploit that sentiment.

In March or early April 1862, he left Hatteras and moved his base of operations to New Bern. Once there, he advertised his intention to hold a political rally on April 23. When General Burnside heard of his plans, he sent a tersely worded letter denying him the right to speak. "You occupy no official political position in the State," he wrote, and in light of the president's appointment of a provisional governor (Edward Stanly) who represented the "views and feelings of a majority of the people of North Carolina, I cannot consent . . . to embarrass either him or the Government . . . by allowing any one else to initiate any civil policy." Because "none of the citizens have represented to me that they desire a meeting of this kind [it] cannot be allowed to assemble."[24]

Foster's last hope for entering Congress was pinned on the growing Union movement that was becoming increasingly evident within the native population of the coastal counties. Beginning in May 1862, eastern North Carolinians began to enlist in the First North Carolina Union Volunteer Infantry Regiment, a new Union army unit created specifically for white residents of the state. It was here and in the related Free Labor movement that was also beginning to appear among the poor whites in the region that Foster would find support for still another try at Congress, as well as the officer rank in the Union army that he had failed to obtain earlier.

The initial attraction of both these movements for North Carolinians appears to have been economic self-interest rather than nationalism. Federal recruiters found that "Union talk" failed to attract enlistments. Poor whites, many of whom wanted to remove both free and enslaved blacks from the state in order to secure employment for members of their own race, often became avid abolitionists.[25] Although Foster apparently regarded slavery as an issue better left for later times, his appeals for the Union and his oratorical skills would win numerous adherents to the First North Carolina regiment and the Free Labor movement.

Plans for creating the First North Carolina regiment were conceived in April 1862 by Unionists in the village of "Little" Washington, on the Pamlico River. The idea of forming the unit received a positive reception from Gen. John G. Foster and General Burnside, and recruiting posters began to appear on May 1. These posters promised the prospective enlistee that he would serve as a home guard within his county of enlistment and he would be under the protection of the U.S. government.[26] With Carpenter's continuing aid, Foster saw the native North Carolina regiment as another opportunity for furthering his own career and quickly assumed a role as regimental recruiter, although he had no formal relationship with the unit.

Carpenter, writing as a special correspondent to the *New York Tribune,* resorted to outright fiction in order to enhance Foster's reputation in this regard. In a dispatch datelined New Bern, May 3, 1862, the self-described congressman was reported to be laying the foundation for a second regiment of native North Carolinians in Hyde, Tyrrell, and Washington Counties. This phantom unit was said to be armed and equipped, with a portion already "in the field, on [its] way to the scene of action."[27] Regimental records, however, fail to show a single enlistment in the three counties during the period cited by the *Tribune* "correspondent."

The following month, Foster took time off from recruiting the First North Carolina regiment and his own mythical unit to return to the Federal capital and plead his case for a seat in Congress, based on his earlier election under the short-lived Hatteras government. The House Committee of Elections met on June 5 and 6 to consider his case. A new impediment, however, had been introduced to dilute Foster's argument. On May 19, Lincoln had appointed Edward Stanly as military governor of North Carolina. Thus, Foster could no longer claim the existence and support of a de facto or de jure Hatteras government.[28] His case now rested solely on expressions of public opinion rather than any previous election, as it had been carried out under the unrecognized Taylor "provisional government." On June 16, 1862, a negative decision was handed down. Noting that "this is the fourth time that [he] has claimed to have been elected a representative to the thirty-seventh Congress" from the First and Second Congressional Districts of North Carolina, the decision stated that "it is difficult to understand how anyone can, in seriousness and in good faith, claim this to be an election of a representative [to Congress]."[29]

Foster, who had suffered so many previous rebuffs, was still not discouraged. He continued to speak at Union meetings, where he actively campaigned for recruits for the North Carolina regiment and, at the same time, picked up support for yet another try at Congress. Free Labor associations in the various counties, in some cases led by and largely made up of intensely abolitionist members of the First North Carolina, would form the core of his support.[30] By September, Foster was openly accepted by the commander of the First North Carolina as a civilian recruiter for the regiment.[31]

On August 21, 1862, the Washington correspondent of the *New York Times* reported that President Lincoln had authorized North Carolina's military governor, Edward Stanly, to order an election for the First and Second Congressional Districts of North Carolina. Stanly, however, delayed a decision on the matter because, according to the New Bern correspondent for the *New York Times,* "undesirable persons would be elevated to office."[32] One such undesirable person was Charles Henry Foster.

To block Foster, Stanly brought in Jennings Pigott, a North Carolinian who was then residing in Washington, DC, to run against him in case an election was held. Native Unionist opponents of Foster believed that Pigott would win easily over their detested enemy. On December 10, Stanly announced that an election would be held on January 1, 1863, for a seat from the Second Congressional District. The only serious candidates were Foster, Pigott, and Stephen D. Willis of Beaufort (city).

Pigott and Willis officially announced their candidacy on December 20, 1862, and Foster's failure to remove his name from the ballot left all three men in the race. On election day, the turnout was low primarily because most of the congressional district lay either in Confederate-controlled counties or in areas strongly contested by Southern guerrillas. Pigott won with 549 of the 864 votes cast.

Pigott's victory was immediately challenged by Foster's supporters. They expressed outrage and prepared a series of documents to contest his election. On January 2, 1863, Pvt. Abraham Congleton of the First North Carolina claimed that he had challenged at the polls over forty people "known personally as secessionists and to be open enemies to the government." The entire roster of Company F and thirty-six members of Company G of the First North Carolina signed petitions swearing that they had voted for Foster and refused to recognize the validity of the election.[33]

Foster gathered these and other documents purporting to show the illegitimacy of the election and forwarded them to the Committee of Elections in Washington, DC. When it met in mid-February 1863, Foster appeared as a witness and was angered when his lengthy presentation was cut short by committee members. In the committee's view, the low turnout and the inability of so large a number to attend the polls because of the danger of Confederate guerrillas was sufficient reason to declare that a valid election had not taken place; the arguments of both sides were therefore irrelevant and need not be considered.[34]

Foster's defeat in the House of Representatives was softened when, on February 5, 1863, he was finally tendered an officer's commission in the Federal army and authorization to raise a second regiment of white North Carolina Union troops. While in the capital for the hearings on the congressional race, he received notice from Adj. Gen. Lorenzo Thomas that the secretary of war authorized him to raise a regiment of volunteer infantry in North Carolina. He left Washington in March with "the written promise of the President" that he would be appointed captain, with authority to recruit such a unit, on receiving the approval of Maj. Gen. John G. Foster, commander of Union troops in North Carolina.[35]

On March 18, 1863, Charles Foster reported to General Foster at the headquarters of the Eighteenth Army Corps in New Bern, where his application as captain and recruiting officer for North Carolina was accepted. Shortly after presenting his papers to General Foster, however, and while the general's approval was in the process of final acceptance in Washington, DC, Charles inexplicably began to make public threats against General Foster and former Governor Edward Stanly, who had resigned after a disagreement with the administration over Union policies in the state. His actions are difficult to comprehend given General Foster's generous approval of a recommendation that Charles's commission date from September 1862, in recognition of his work in recruiting for the First North Carolina Union Volunteer regiment.[36]

Perhaps in a display of unnecessary bravado, Charles arrogantly threatened to "ruin" General Foster if he failed to get his application as the state's recruiting officer approved and secure for him the higher rank of colonel in the Second North Carolina regiment. He had, he falsely bragged, played a major role in removing Governor Stanly, and he could do the same to the general. Capt. N. P. Pond of the Third New York Cavalry and naval lieutenant T. J. Woodward, to whom Foster addressed his comments, reported him to military authorities.[37]

As he had not yet been mustered into the service, authorities decided to try Charles Foster as a civilian before a military commission that would meet in New Bern on April 22, 1863. He was charged with using language prejudicial to good order and military discipline. Brig. Gen. I. N. Palmer headed the court. Foster acted as his own attorney but failed to persuade the court of his innocence. On April 25, 1863, he was found guilty and ordered to leave North Carolina and promise never to return.[38]

Despite this forced exile from his adopted state, Charles managed to overcome the commission's sentence. In danger of losing all he had worked for, he appealed to General Foster, the man he had maligned, for a private interview to present an explanation for his actions before the general acted upon the findings of the commission.[39] On May 2, General Foster, now supporting Charles Foster, wrote to Maj. Gen. John A. Dix, in Fortress Monroe, Virginia, with a request that Charles be permitted to work under him "in carrying out the wishes of the authority given by the President." He further asked that Charles be given aid in raising a regiment in Chowan County and adjacent northeastern North Carolina counties.[40]

Following his visit to General Foster, Charles traveled to Washington, DC, where he apparently lobbied successfully with administration officials. On May 8, Secretary of War Edwin M. Stanton wrote to inform him that the "President . . . has appointed you Captain in the 2d Regiment North Carolina Volunteers," with orders to report for duty to Maj. Gen. J. G. Foster.[41] On May 22, Captain Foster left the nation's capital for Norfolk, Virginia, where he received orders from the general to report to Maj. Gen. John D. Peck at Suffolk. His designated task would be to "recruit from that portion of the population of [North Carolina] lying between Albemarle Sound and the borders of Virginia." Any recruits obtained were to remain in Suffolk "until such time as the force under my command will admit the reoccupation of Elizabeth City [North Carolina]."[42]

Foster's exile in Virginia was short-lived, and by June 7, 1863, he was writing from New Bern for permission to accompany a military expedition into the northeastern counties in order to retrieve his family (with whom he had reconciled); they were still residing in the Confederate-held interior. On July 27, he entered Murfreesboro aboard a Federal gunboat, only to find that his wife and daughter had already departed for Union territory, where the family would later be reunited.[43]

On October 3, 1863, Foster received the authorization he had long awaited to begin recruiting operations. Special Orders No. 45, issued by General Peck, commander of the Army and District of North Carolina, was notable because it was signed by Benjamin Foster, Charles's brother, who was now serving as assistant adjutant general on Peck's staff, a position that undoubtedly worked to Charles Foster's benefit during his tenure with the Second North Carolina regiment.[44]

Foster placed his highest and almost exclusive priority on recruitment, which would not be easy. General Foster had noted, four months earlier, that recruits were no longer to be had in the occupied region below Albemarle Sound. Eastern North Carolinians who were true Unionists and those who had joined in order to eliminate slavery in the state had enlisted in the First North Carolina regiment more than a year earlier. This left Charles Foster in the unenviable position of relying almost exclusively on poor whites with families to feed and shelter and Confederate deserters fleeing combat on the battlefields of Virginia as the primary sources for building the regiment. The motivation to fight for the Union was largely absent from these men.

Unable to use patriotism as a motivating force, Foster had three inducements to encourage such men to enlist in his regiment: bonuses of three hundred dollars, the equivalent of a year's salary, for merely signing enlistment papers; promises of food and shelter for families of poverty-stricken poor whites; and safety under the protection of Union forces for Confederate deserters and draft resisters who had no desire to be sent to the front lines in Virginia and elsewhere. In January 1864, Foster even attempted to recruit light-skinned free blacks who professed reluctance at enlisting in black regiments. This latter practice ceased following a request for approval to General Butler, who apparently believed that such recruitment would interfere with the formation of Brig. Gen. Edward A. Wilde's African Brigade, which was then being recruited in North Carolina. Even these inducements, however, would be insufficient to attract men in the numbers necessary to form a complete regiment.[45]

On February 1, 1864, Foster's regiment received a crushing blow from which it would never fully recover. Fifty-three men of Company F were captured during a surprise attack on New Bern by Confederate forces under Gen. George Pickett. The men were stationed at Beech Grove, a Union outpost eight miles east of New Bern. Largely made up of former Confederates, its function was to intercept and enlist deserters fleeing from the Southern stronghold of Kinston, about fifteen miles east. Surprised by Pickett's troops and unable to escape, the men were taken as prisoners to Kinston. Nearly all of the captured men would die within two months, most in Confederate prisons in Richmond, Virginia, and Andersonville, Georgia. Twenty-two, however, were court-martialed as deserters from the Confederate army, found guilty, and sentenced to be hanged. Mass public executions took place in Kinston between February 5 and 22, 1864.[46]

Although Foster protested the executions and attempts were made to bring Pickett to justice, the immediate effect was panic and demoralization among the men of the two white North Carolina regiments. Sgt. George W. Jones, whose brother had been hanged in Kinston, complained that "I am looked upon as a traitor and coward by the majority of the North as well as the South, and neither feel willing to protect me." Therefore, "I no longer feel willing to serve [as] I feel like a prisoner whom his sentence is death awaiting the day of execution."[47]

Conditions continued to deteriorate in Foster's regiment following the hangings. Desertions increased, discipline declined, and, on at least two occasions, mutinies were put down.[48] While he was trying to turn conditions around, Foster's dream of military glory burst.

His downfall was brought about by General Butler, who only recently had appointed Foster to the rank of lieutenant colonel on the recommendation of his predecessor. On March 12, Butler informed Secretary of War Stanton that he had received an unspecified paper in connection with Foster that caused him to conduct further inquiries. Foster's "movements in 'Sixty-one, the method he took to get back into the service [following his ordered removal by the military commission], his seeming want of efficiency, and his fickleness of purpose, render it not desirable that he should be retained in the service."[49] Special Orders No. 124, issued by the War Department on March 22, 1864, however, simply alluded to "improper conduct relative to his appointment and . . . unfitness for the position of an officer, as reported by the Commanding Officer, Department of Virginia and North Carolina, and other General Officers."[50]

At the time of his dismissal from the service, Foster had built a regiment of 413 men. Of these, most members of Company F had been captured at Beech Grove, and within a month of his discharge, another two companies would be captured at the Battle of Plymouth, leaving only two of the regiment's five companies available for duty. On April 4, 1864, Lt. Col. Walter S. Poor assumed command. He found a regiment whose morale was destroyed, whose discipline was almost nonexistent, and whose administrative affairs were in disarray.[51] The regiment that Foster had conceived and built was in an irreversible decline. By August 1864, poor morale and fear of capture led Poor to request permission for the Second North Carolina to lose its identity by merging with a Northern regiment. This move, it was believed, would make North Carolina Union soldiers indistinguishable from their Northern brethren and protect them from execution if captured.[52] The request was denied, but merger with the First North Carolina was approved, and on February 27, 1865, the Second North Carolina disappeared as a regiment.

Foster never recovered from the humiliation of his dishonorable discharge and would never mention it in later writings about his life. Following his dismissal, he remained for a month or more in Beaufort, where he attempted to obtain a reduction, if not complete reversal, of his sentence; at the very least, he hoped to save face by being allowed to resign from the service. Failing in this effort, Foster returned to his parent's home in Orono, Maine, to carry on the struggle to clear his name.

In July, he made an unsuccessful effort to return again to the South as an agent for Massachusetts and recruit soldiers for that state in the occupied areas of the Confederacy. Approval for the position apparently depended on securing a reversal of his dishonorable discharge from the service. With this in mind, Foster wrote to Secretary of the Treasury William P. Fessenden, a politician from Maine and, like himself, a Bowdoin alumnus. Foster pleaded for understanding of his actions in North Carolina, describing himself as a "refugee, with my family dependent on me, without a home save my father's roof." He begged Fessenden to intercede with President Lincoln for "clemency in causing the cruel order dismissing [him] dishonorably from the service to be rescinded." Apparently tiring of Foster's entreaties, Fessenden filed away his request with the written comment, "This man Foster has had his case twice examined and twice adversely decided. The last application, I thought, had exhausted the case."[53]

With his appeals denied, Foster drifted from job to job, never completely successful at any until near the end of his life. In early 1865, he attempted to earn a living as a freelance lecturer in Boston, a career that he interrupted to go to North Carolina when his wife decided to return to her parents' home in Confederate-occupied Murfreesboro. Foster remained alone in the coastal region, eking out a meager living as a lawyer. When Richmond fell in April 1865, he reunited with his family and opened a mercantile establishment with the help of his father-in-law. Over the next few years, he tried his hand again at law and then established a short-lived news bureau in Raleigh, the state capital. His role in Reconstruction North Carolina was minimal. In 1867, he ran unsuccessfully to serve as the delegate from his county to the state constitutional convention called for by the states' military commander, Gen. Edward S. Canby.

In 1878 the Fosters left North Carolina, reportedly because of concern for Susan's health, and settled in Philadelphia. There, Charles was employed as a traveling salesman, going from door to door and business to business selling subscriptions and advertisements for the Norfolk *Virginian* and other Southern newspapers. In June 1878, he was approved to practice law before the Philadelphia bar and opened an office with George W. Reid. His real love, however, was journalism, and he would work late into the night writing articles for a number of newspapers and other periodicals. He became a regular visitor to the offices of Philadelphia's papers, offering to sell his articles for publication.

In November 1879, Foster realized his childhood ambition of becoming a successful newspaperman when he was hired by the *Philadelphia Record,* and over the next three years, he rose to become its lead editorial writer. The success that had eluded him for so long was now his. Only three years later, however, on March 8, 1882, he developed signs of pleurisy, which turned into pneumonia. He died peacefully at home the following Tuesday, March 14, surrounded by his family.

Charles Henry Foster had all the makings for success. Possessed of a brilliant mind, he was a gifted writer who was acquainted with many of the literary, political, and military leaders of his day. Yet he squandered a promising career in journalism, his first love, for dreams of political and military glory. The success of the First North Carolina Union Volunteer Regiment owes much of its success to his recruiting ability. For all his brilliance, however, he was not an able leader of men, and the failure of the regiment was due largely to his own shortcomings. His lack of administrative ability, combined with his lapses in ethics, caught up with him at the height of his glory and brought him down to smashing defeat. Nonetheless, he made his mark on history, and the cause of Unionism in North Carolina during the Civil War benefited by his presence in the state.

Notes

1. Benjamin S. Hedrick Collection, Perkins Library, Duke University, Durham, North Carolina (hereafter cited as Hedrick Collection). Numerous letters from several persons in this collection describe Charles Henry Foster in strongly negative terms.

2. Benjamin Brown Foster, *Down East Diary,* ed. Charles H. Foster (Orono, ME, 1975), 35–36.

3. Ibid., 262.

4. Ibid., 308–11, 337, 341–42, 345, 347, 361.

5. Cleaveland Packard, Nehemiah Packard, and Alpheus Spring Packard, *History of Bowdoin College* (Boston, 1882), 696; newspaper clipping, Charles Henry Foster Alumni Biographical File, Special Collections, Bowdoin College Library, Brunswick, Maine.

6. *Murfreesboro (North Carolina) Citizen,* November 23 and 31, 1859; February 9, 1860; August 30, 1860.

7. Norman C. Delaney, "Charles Henry Foster and the Unionists of Eastern North Carolina," *North Carolina Historical Review* 37 (1960):350; Thomas C. Parramore, "In the Days of Charles Henry Foster," *Daily Roanoke Chowan News* (Ashoskie, NC), 1960, 146–155; *Murfreesboro (North Carolina) Citizen,* June 28, 1860.

8. *Murfreesboro (North Carolina) Citizen,* December 1, 1860.

9. Parramore, "In the Days," 148.

10. Ibid., 149.

11. *Raleigh (North Carolina) Register,* May 21, 1862.

12. J. A. Noonen to Benjamin S. Hedrick, September 14, 1863, Hedrick Collection.

13. Benjamin Marshall to Benjamin S. Hedrick, January 9, 1862, Hedrick Collection.

14. Charles Henry Foster to Abraham Lincoln, June 24, 1861, Abraham Lincoln Papers, series 1, Library of Congress, on microfilm (hereafter cited as Lincoln Papers).

15. *Congressional Globe,* 37th Cong., February 23, 1863, 1211.

16. *New York Tribune,* August 10, 1861, September 2, 1861, September 12, 1861.

17. Parramore, "In the Days," 154.

18. *Murfreesboro (North Carolina) Citizen,* December 7, 1859.

19. Much of the Benjamin S. Hedrick Collection at Duke University Library is devoted to correspondence with civilian, military, and government officials in regard to Foster.

20. Richard Nelson Current, *Lincoln's Loyalists: Union Soldiers from the Confederacy* (Boston, 1992), 61.

21. *Boston Journal,* March 17, 1862.

22. Delaney, "Charles Foster," 356–57; U.S. War Department, *The War of the Rebellion: Official Records of the Union and Confederate Armies,* 128 vols. (Washington, DC: U.S. Government Printing Office, 1881–1901), series 1, vol. 1, p. 631.

23. House Miscellaneous Document, No. 21, Thirty-seventh Congress, Second Session; House Miscellaneous Document, No. 2, Thirty-seventh Congress, Second Session.

24. *Raleigh (North Carolina) Register,* May 21, 1862.

25. Norman D. Brown, "A Union Election in Civil War North Carolina," *North Carolina Historical Review* 43 (1966): 391–92; *New York Tribune,* December 25, 1862.

26. "To the People of Eastern North Carolina" (recruiting poster), Henry Toole Clark Papers, Private Collection No. 235, North Carolina Department of Cultural Resources, Division of Archives and History, Archives and Records Section, Raleigh, North Carolina.

27. *New York Tribune,* May 8, 1862.

28. Delaney, "Charles Henry Foster," 361.

29. House Report, No. 118, Thirty-seventh Congress, Second Session.

30. Brown, "A Union Election," 391.

31. [Written endorsement by] J. M. McChesney, Commanding, First North Carolina Union Volunteer Infantry, May 9, 1863, Charles Henry Foster Papers, M-3498, Southern Historical Collection, University of North Carolina Library, Chapel Hill, North Carolina (hereafter cited as Foster Papers).

32. Brown, "A Union Election," 386; *New York Times,* November 14, 1862.

33. House Miscellaneous Document, No. 14, Thirty-seventh Congress, Third Session.

34. House Report, No. 41, Thirty-seventh Congress, Third Session.

35. Lorenzo Thomas, Washington, DC, to Charles Henry Foster, February 5, 1863, Second North Carolina Union Volunteer Infantry, *Regimental Books,* RG-94, Records of the Office of Adjutant General, U.S. National Archives, Washington, DC (hereafter cited as *Regimental Books*); Charles Henry Foster, to Samuel C. Pomeroy, April 11, 1863, Lincoln Papers.

36. Court Martial of Charles Henry Foster, Eighteenth Army Corps, Department of North Carolina, Proceedings of a Military Commission Held at New Berne, N.C., April 21, 1863, RG 153, U.S. National Archives, Washington, DC.

37. Ibid.

38. Ibid.; John G. Foster to Benjamin S. Hedrick, August 31, 1863, Hedrick Collection; Delaney, "Charles Henry Foster," 362.

39. Charles Henry Foster to John G. Foster, April 21, 1863, Charles H. Foster File, Miscellaneous Card Abstracts of Records, Roll 25, Compiled Service Records of Volunteer Union Soldiers Who Served in Organizations from the State of North Carolina, National Archives Microfilm Publications, Microcopy no. 401, U.S. National Archives, Washington, DC, 1962 (hereafter cited as Foster File).

40. John G. Foster to John A. Dix, May 2, 1863, Foster Papers.

41. Edward Stanton to Charles Henry Foster, May 8, 1863, Foster Papers.

42. Charles Henry Foster to John G. Foster, May 22, 1863, Foster File; John G. Foster to John D. Peck, June 6, 1863, Foster Papers.

43. Charles Henry Foster to John G. Foster, June 7, 1863, Foster File; Parramore, "In the Days," 154–55.

44. Special Orders No. 45, Headquarters, Army and District of North Carolina, New Bern, Foster File; I. Graham Tull to Benjamin S. Hedrick, February 22, 1864, Hedrick Collection.

45. Second North Carolina Union Infantry, *Regimental Books*. The information comes from an examination of many documents scattered throughout regimental records.

46. Donald E. Collins, "War Crimes or Justice? General George Pickett and the Mass Execution of Deserters in Civil War Kinston, North Carolina," chap. 3 in *The Art of Command in the Civil War*, ed. Steven Woodworth (Lincoln: University of Nebraska Press, 1998), 60–66.

47. George W. Jones File, [Roster of the] Second North Carolina Union Infantry, Compiled Service Records of Volunteer Union Soldiers Who Served in Organizations from the State of North Carolina, National Archives Microfilm Publications, Microcopy no. 401, U.S. National Archives, Washington, DC, 1962.

48. Charles Henry Foster to Benjamin B. Foster, March 12, 1864, *Regimental Books*; Walter S. Poor to Benjamin F. Butler, April 11, 1864, *Regimental Books*.

49. Delaney, "Charles Henry Foster," 365; Benjamin F. Butler, *Private and Official Correspondence of General Benjamin F. Butler During the Period of the Civil War*, 5 vols. (Norwood, MA, 1917), 3:520.

50. Special Orders No. 124, March 22, 1864, Foster File.

51. Walter S. Poor to Benjamin F. Butler, April 11, 1864, April 12, 1864, *Regimental Books*.

52. Lieutenant Colonel, Commanding, 2nd North Carolina Volunteers, to J. A. Judson, August 21, 1864, *Regimental Books*.

53. Charles Henry Foster to William P. Fessenden, July 21, 1864, Foster File.

6

Francis Nicholls
"A Brave Soldier Whose Life Was One Long Battle"

Richard Selcer

The crucible of war tends to develop and reveal the true character of men and women, sometimes for better and sometimes for worse. Although both sides in the Civil War might regret the presence of unscrupulous characters such as Charles Henry Foster, both could also point with pride to men and women of outstanding character—individuals who rose to the challenges of adversity, endured amazing hardships, and displayed profound nobility through circumstances as varied as the fortunes of war. One such exemplary character was Francis Nicholls of Louisiana, and his story, recounted here by prolific Civil War author Richard Selcer, vividly illustrates both the sacrifice and the perseverance of the generation of Americans that fought the Civil War. Selcer teaches history at Northlake College in Dallas, Texas, and is the author of *"Faithfully and Forever Your Soldier," General George E. Pickett, C.S.A.* (1995).

On July 24, 1876, Louisiana state senator F. W. Goode stood up before a deadlocked Democratic Party convention in New Orleans to proclaim in a voice that rang from the rafters, "Gentlemen, I nominate all that's left of General Nicholls for Governor!"[1] The crowd responded in wild support of the one-armed, one-legged Confederate veteran, and on the fourth ballot in that steamy hall, the delegates overwhelmingly nominated Francis Nicholls, a man who had assiduously shunned the spotlight of fame all his life. It was a historic moment in both Louisiana and national politics.

The same man who went on to win the governor's office in a bitter, hard-fought election later that year was the most reluctant of politicians; in fact, he had not even campaigned for the general's commission that was given to him years before in the Confederate army. But if he was not eager to be hailed by his fellows, neither did he refuse to accept responsibility when duty called. In everything he did all throughout his life, Francis Nicholls's quiet, unassuming nature and his rock-solid integrity won him the admiration of all he met. He was like Cincinnatus, the Roman citizen-soldier who reluctantly left private life to lead his people on the battlefield only to return to civilian ranks as soon as the job was done. He wanted neither glory nor high office nor the wealth that came with them. Fame seemed to pursue him rather than the reverse, allowing him to cram several lifetimes' worth of living into seventy-eight years.

He came into the world on August 20, 1834, the eighth child of Louisa Hannah and Thomas Clark Nicholls of Donaldsonville, Louisiana. The family could trace their ancestry back to the mists of English history, and concepts such as honor and heritage were instilled in him from the beginning. Like many Southern aristocrats of his day, he was christened with four names; three were not enough to properly represent the distinguished family tree. Francis Redding Tillou Nicholls was the latest addition to a community-minded family that considered the law and soldiering to be equally honorable callings. At the age of fifteen, he left home to find his place in the world. Two years later, he found that place at the United States Military Academy, arriving at West Point just two months shy of his seventeenth birthday. At the time, he was the first boy from his parish ever to pursue higher education and the only cadet at the academy hailing from Louisiana. The next four years saw him grow up rapidly in mind and body, thriving under the strict regimen of West Point. He endured the usual indignities of cadet life, stood countless inspections, and wore full-dress uniforms in all sorts of weather. When he graduated, he was six feet tall but rail thin, still little more than a boy.

Nicholls graduated twelfth out of thirty-four in the class of 1855, a ranking guaranteed to put him into either the cavalry or the artillery but not good enough for the prestigious engineers. He accepted his (brevet) second lieutenant's commission in the artillery, facing the happy prospect of three career options: He could take up an offer of a professorship at Columbia College, New York; he could follow in his father's footsteps by studying law; or he could fulfill his two-year obligation to the government and begin a military career by serving out his time in the army. He chose the army and never looked back. Like other fourth-year men, he was eager to see action, and in the summer of 1853, that meant participating in the Seminole conflict in Florida, the aftermath of two bitter wars fought to subdue the recalcitrant Indians. The last war had officially ended in 1847, but flare-ups and border skirmishes continued to demand the presence of large numbers of U.S. Army troops in the state well into the 1850s.

Although the Florida climate might have been reminiscent of Louisiana, the living conditions he soon encountered were nothing like young Nicholls had ever experienced. A tour of duty in the malarial swamps bordering the Everglades while doing battle with an elusive enemy convinced him that army life was not his calling after all. When he asked for reassignment, he was transferred to Fort Yuma, California, where he was forced to endure desertlike conditions that improved neither his health nor his morale. His biggest physical ailment, which plagued him all his life, was a sensitive stomach that reacted to any sudden change in diet or stress with an attack of gastritis. He finally resigned his commission in 1856, suffering from poor health and worried about supporting his family back home on a soldier's meager pay. He returned to Louisiana and in 1857, after passing the bar, opened a law practice in Assumption Parish with two partners. But he saw lawyering as only a step on the way to his true goal, which was to sit on the opposite side of the bench as a judge.

On April 26, 1860, he married Caroline Guion, daughter of a prominent family of jurists with deep Louisiana roots. Barely five feet tall and possessing grace and spunk in equal parts, she was described as "a small, fairy-like creature, plucky as a terrier," the perfect wife for Nicholls.[2] Both the bride and the groom represented the finest of Louisiana's landed gentry. Thus, the marriage united two distinguished families and forged a husband-wife partnership that was to last for the next fifty-two years. Caroline was the last piece in the puzzle of his personal life that he needed to complete before his career could shift into high gear. Unfortunately for his well-mapped career plans, the Civil War intervened in 1861.

In the secession crisis before the war, Nicholls positioned himself as a moderate: he was neither a fire-breathing defender of states' rights nor a die-hard Unionist, and he was certainly no abolitionist. Mostly he kept his political opinions to himself. His natural reticence and always-pleasant manner hid a quiet strength that attracted numerous admirers and caused them to listen carefully when he spoke. Although he refused to commit himself publicly to the new order after Louisiana seceded from the Union, he agonized over his choices before eventually coming down on the side of the Confederacy. Realistically, he seemed to have no option but to join his friends and neighbors in their chosen course, and in short order he joined the Phoenix Guards, a parish militia company attached to Maj. Roberdeau Wheat's soon-to-be-famous Louisiana Tiger Battalion.

When the men reported to Camp Moore, north of New Orleans, to receive their training, there was as much politicking as drilling, for by tradition officers up through the regimental level were popularly elected. Although Nicholls's politics may have been lukewarm in the eyes of Southern fire-eaters, his local standing was good enough to convince the men of the company to promptly elect him captain, with his brother Lawrence voted in as first lieutenant.

Training at Camp Moore was unlike his earlier West Point experience. Most of the men in his unit were amateurs, playing at war. Discipline was made more difficult by the easy availability of liquor. Every rank (or so it seemed) indulged liberally, "even to Captains & Lieutenants," wrote one disgusted recruit in a letter home. But though the rules were in place to keep the stuff out of enlisted men's hands, there was no shortage of friendly captains willing to boost their popularity by distributing liquor in the ranks. Captain Nicholls was not one who pandered to the baser instincts of his men, though the pressure to be a "regular guy" was great.[3]

The regiment to which the Phoenix Guards were attached numbered among its colorful recruits "free booters and robbers," cutthroats, and pickpockets, as well as a fair share of lawyers' and planters' sons.[4] There was also a strong leavening of foreigners in all ranks, but from the first, Nicholls got along well enough with all the disparate elements of the command to be nominated for one of the top two positions in the Eighth Louisiana regiment—colonel or lieutenant colonel. During the run-up to the election, there was some confusion about which position he really desired, and his chief rival for the second-in-command spot did not campaign as hard as he might have otherwise. On election day, Nicholls's name appeared on the ballot for lieutenant colonel, and he handily won the contest. Whether his win was the result of shrewd politicking on his part, dumb luck, or even "cowardly deceitfulness," as his rival charged, was never established. The end result was that fortune had smiled on Nicholls in a political campaign for the first time.

Determined to be where the hottest action was, he wrote to President Jefferson Davis, offering his services to the Confederacy. He received no reply, but soon enough orders came through that sent the regiment to Virginia just in time for the first big battle of the war, called Bull Run in the North or Manassas in the South, on July 1, 1861.

In the fall, Richard Taylor, son of former President Zachary Taylor and a self-made military officer, took over the Louisiana Brigade, including Nicholls's Eighth Infantry regiment. The Louisianans were attached to Stonewall Jackson's Army of the Valley when it moved into the Shenandoah Valley in early 1862, and they played a vital role in the subsequent history-making campaign for control of that valley. "To General Taylor and his brigade belongs the honor of deciding two battles . . . Winchester (May 25) and Port Republic (June 9)," Maj. Gen. Richard Ewell stated when he assessed their contribution.[5]

At Winchester, the Tigers were ordered by Jackson to take a Union battery on a hill anchoring the enemy's right. The men climbed the hill under a furious barrage of artillery and musket fire, with the Eighth regiment on the left flank. One Union colonel wrote admiringly, "They were received with a destructive fire of musketry, yet they moved on, but little shaken."[6] At one point, they were charged by a squadron of Federal cavalry, but Nicholls expertly turned his troops to face the new threat. On his command the men delivered a well-aimed volley, unseating dozens of horsemen and scattering the rest. The final rush of the Louisianans has been described as "one of the most spectacular of the Civil War, a picture-book assault."[7]

Unfortunately, Nicholls was not present at the climax of the battle. He had been wounded while halfway up the hill, his elbow shattered by a minié ball. He was carried from the field, bleeding profusely, and before the day was out, his arm had to be amputated at a Confederate field hospital in Winchester. The excruciating surgery was performed without modern anesthetics, antibiotics, or transfusions, none of which were available in that day. Men survived such primitive procedures because of strong constitutions and the grace of God, not because of medical expertise, and many more died than survived major surgery.

Meanwhile, the Federal army was retreating down the valley toward the safety of the Potomac, but the victory was not complete. Two more Yankee armies were closing in, so Jackson ordered his troops back to Strasburg, Virginia, six days after the battle. The most grievously wounded, including Lieutenant Colonel Nicholls, had to be left behind in Winchester, their fate entrusted to the mercies of the Northerners. Shortly before the Confederates pulled out, Gen. Richard Taylor visited Nicholls in his recovery room at a private home in the area. They were both advised by the surgeons that the wounded man's condition was too critical to permit him to travel. As Taylor sadly commented, "Much to my regret and more to his own, he was left."[8] Nicholls resigned himself to captivity as he lay on his cot listening to the fading sounds of the Southerners marching out of town. When the Federals occupied the town, he was placed under guard, which allowed him to continue his recuperation but otherwise curtailed his freedom. He would have suffered far worse had he been sent north to a Yankee prison camp.

That was not the end of the matter, however. In the weeks that followed, reports reached the Confederates that Nicholls had been not merely captured but also placed under arrest as a spy because he was dressed in civilian clothes at the time of his capture. The Louisianans were outraged and talked about taking revenge on the next Union officer who fell into their hands, but the story ultimately proved to be a wild rumor. Nonetheless, it caused enough concern that no less an eminence than Union major general George McClellan himself, commander of the Army of the Potomac, personally investigated the charges and pronounced them groundless.[9] Nicholls was saved from a lengthy trial or worse, but he remained a prisoner of war.

Fortunately, his imprisonment did not last long because at this point, the two warring governments were still exchanging prisoners (which did much to alleviate suffering but actually prolonged the war). On September 21, 1862, Nicholls was exchanged at Aikens Landing, Virginia, and furloughed home for some much needed rest and recuperation. Four months in a Yankee prison awaiting exchange had left him weaker in both body and mind. Yet the loss of his arm was just one of a series of blows that fate dealt him at this time. On his way home via Lynchburg, Virginia, he received news that his brother had been killed in action on June 28 while leading the Eighth regiment at the Battle of Gaines Mill, Virginia. Lawrence had been as much of a father figure to his younger brother as a sibling, and the news hit Francis hard. In little more than a month, he had lost, successively, his favorite brother and one arm. The only bright spot in the recent months was his promotion to full colonel, which had come through while he was still a prisoner. No sooner had he received the commission than he accepted command of the Fifteenth Louisiana regiment. But the Army of Northern Virginia was campaigning far away in Maryland at this time, so he took a leave of absence until it returned.

Antietam was a hard campaign for his old brigade, the Tigers. The troops were decimated at Antietam in September, forcing a complete reorganization. On October 14, Nicholls was promoted to brigadier general and given command of the new Second Louisiana brigade, although he did not join his unit until January 1863.[10] When he arrived to take up his duties at Fredericksburg, Virginia, he found his brigade a mere skeleton, most of the men listed on the rolls being sick or wounded or, in some cases, absent without leave. Eventually, most of the ill and injured returned to the ranks, and new conscripts filled many of the empty places. But nothing could meet the need for arms, food, and especially shoes.

Nicholls was still with Stonewall Jackson, though now as a part of the Second Corps, and everybody knew that wherever Jackson was, the fighting would be heaviest. Jackson's aggressive tactics were especially hard on general officers, who were expected to lead from the front.

Nicholls was with Jackson at Chancellorsville in May 1862, taking part in the surprise attack on Fighting Joe Hooker's left flank and positioned as usual at the head of his troops. On the evening of May 2, after the famous flank attack had run out of steam, a Union battery zeroed in on the disorganized Confederates on Plank Road as they celebrated their victory, raking them mercilessly with shot and shell. While the men were throwing themselves on the ground to avoid the hailstorm of lead, Nicholls spurred his horse forward, trying to bring some order to his panicked troops. Suddenly, a solid shot whizzing through the trees ripped through his horse's abdomen, taking off Nicholls's left foot as it exited. With a herculean effort, he managed to throw himself free from the dying animal as it keeled over on the same side as his shattered leg, but he could do no more. He lay on the road in danger of bleeding to death while everybody around him hugged the ground, trying to avoid a similar fate. Only when the barrage finally lifted after half an hour did ambulance crewmen come upon him in the darkened woods. Dimly seeing his empty sleeve and blood-soaked limb, they moved on, leaving him for dead. Some 312 of his men lay dead or wounded around him, and he himself was close to joining the former group. Groping in the darkness for his mutilated leg, he was astonished to find that the wound had stopped bleeding by itself. But he was still not in the clear; he would undoubtedly have died before the night was over, but some of his men, searching the bushes for their fellows, found him and carted him to the rear in a stretcher improvised out of a blanket. While awaiting succor, he had calmly chatted with his worried staff, cracking wise both to reassure them and to keep up his own spirits. If he survived the war after this latest wound, he observed mordantly, he would be "too one-sided for a judge." His calmness, punctuated by humor, probably kept him from bleeding to death before he could get to a field hospital, where he endured his second major amputation in less than a year. This time, he lost his lower leg.[11]

Ironically, the beloved commander Stonewall Jackson had suffered a similar wound on what was otherwise a glorious day for Confederate arms. Jackson's wounding also came at the end of the day and in the same woods not far from where Nicholls was hit. He received immediate medical attention befitting his rank, but soon after his left arm was amputated, he contracted pneumonia and died nine days later.

The same fate that took Jackson also spared Nicholls. His survival was almost as remarkable as his unbelievably bad luck. In the two battles in which he participated, he had suffered two terrible wounds, either one of which would have laid most men low permanently if they survived. Remarkably, the Louisianan came back both times thanks to his amazing recuperative powers. However, after Chancellorsville, his men began to whisper that he was jinxed, which, based on his brief combat record, was not an unreasonable conclusion.

At the headquarters of the Army of Northern Virginia, General Lee was less concerned with jinxes than with how to replace a valuable brigadier. He commented that if he made a poor choice in assigning a man to take over the Second Louisiana brigade, "its service, I fear, will be lost to the army." Reluctantly, he decided to leave the position open indefinitely, putting a colonel in temporary command until Nicholls recovered or some other officer emerged from the pack.[12]

Nicholls's latest battlefield wound brought him another promotion; after he recovered sufficiently to resume service, he was recommended for major general's rank. As soon as he heard this news, however, he declined the promotion because he saw it as more of a consolation for his terrible wounds than an earned reward. He could have returned to the field (as did another unlucky Confederate general, John Bell Hood, who also lost an arm and a leg in separate battles), but he chose instead to acknowledge his physical unfitness for further field service. Yet he was not ready to be put on the shelf either, so he accepted command of the military district of Lynchburg, Virginia, where he was in charge of transportation, reserve troops, and prisoners of war. An important railroad junction in the antebellum period, Lynchburg became the South's largest "outpost hospital center" during the war. At least twenty thousand patients, both Union and Confederate, passed through the center during four years of fighting.[13] But there were never enough surgeons, never enough medicines, never enough of anything except dead and dying men, and as a result, Nicholls's administrative skills and ability to improvise were put to the test as never before. Still, in his new position, he continued to display the same cool composure that had characterized his earlier service. During the last year of the war, he successfully defended Lynchburg against Yankee general David Hunter's Valley army, and he served on the court-martial board trying Gen. Lafayette McLaws and Gen. Felix Robertson in February 1864 after they were charged by Gen. James Longstreet with dereliction of duty in the ill-fated Knoxville campaign. In this assignment, he put his prewar legal training to good use, but he had to travel an arduous two hundred miles to participate.

In the summer of 1864, he was ordered to the Trans-Mississippi Department to organize the conscript bureau, with headquarters in Marshall, Texas. He quickly ran afoul of Gen. Edward Kirby Smith, who considered the department his personal feifdom. When the war ended, Nicholls was still in Marshall, striving mightily to keep the carcass of the trans-Mississippi Confederacy alive a little longer. He wrapped up his official duties and painfully made his way home to Donaldsonville. Though limping gingerly on a new wooden leg, he still walked erectly and proudly, just as he always had.

During the years of Reconstruction, Nicholls remained loyal to the now discredited Democratic Party. He also maintained his basic honesty and integrity through the Federal occupation and the corrupt, homegrown administrations that followed. Personal disaster struck again in 1867 when one of the periodic yellow fever epidemics that plagued the Mississippi delta carried away his sister Martha. Less than a year later, his sister Josephine also succumbed to the same disease. Her loss was particularly poignant because he had always considered her to be his "second mother." Fate seemed to be burying his family, one by one.

Meanwhile, the official policy of disenfranchising former Confederate officers kept him from running for public office or even voting in the early years of Reconstruction. Yet his character, moral strength, and serenity in the face of adversity appealed strongly to his fellow citizens, who looked to him for leadership. He was able to think under pressure and, when necessary, to hide his emotions. Of course, his obvious personal sacrifice to the Southern cause did not hurt his popularity. He offered a model of behavior for a defeated people, much as General Lee did in Virginia. Although he was not an unreconstructed rebel by any means, he nonetheless refused to accept the role of second-class citizen, inferior to the Yankee conquerors. He desired a quick return to home rule for Louisiana and the rest of the South—but not in order to oppress the freedmen or plunder the state treasury, as so many public figures did.

By 1876 this country lawyer from Bayou LaFourche had transformed himself into an up-and-comer in state politics and a white knight for the Democratic Party. Fellow party members, including New Orleans machine Democrats and Delta Bourbon Democrats, appreciated his unsullied public image: He had no political record to justify and no enemies to guard against. Also, though he was a former rebel, Francis Nicholls was a white man whom black Louisianans could respect and even support politically. By the time the state Democratic convention rolled around on July 24, 1876, he was a force to be reckoned with in the high-stakes wheeling and dealing. When it was over, his party had tapped him as their candidate for governor, and he found himself running his first political race that fall. He beat the Republican candidate fairly in November, but a bitter dispute over the propriety of the balloting kept him from taking office, and both candidates claimed rightful possession of the state house. Nicholls shrewdly outmaneuvered his opponent, S. B. Packard, and when the Republican administration in Washington refused to intervene, he took over with the complete approval of the overwhelming majority of voters. On January 8, 1877, he took the oath of office in a ceremony some had thought would never happen without bloodshed. Nicholls's inauguration brought the biggest turnout on the streets of New Orleans since the announcement of the Louisiana Purchase.

As governor of Louisiana, he promoted racial peace and honest government. One observer said, "There was a reverent quality about [him]; he was truly one of us yet apart. He seemed so noble and always in command of his senses and emotions."[14] He favored national reconciliation of all political factions and an end to strife and turmoil, not just in Louisiana but also throughout the nation. He urged the citizens of his own state to be "law-abiding, just, and moderate."[15] With the state legislators, a notoriously fractious bunch, he walked a tightrope, winning their confidence and support for his programs, which included paying off all public debts accrued during Reconstruction (a "sacred obligation," he said), defusing the issue of revenge against carpetbaggers and freedmen, and revamping the decrepit financial system of the state. With one eye on economic expansion and the other on a traditional political power base, he expanded the state's railroad network and resuscitated the Louisiana militia. Thanks to having established his Southern bona fides during the "Late Unpleasantness," he was free to bring black citizens into public affairs without fear of a backlash from white voters, and this he did. He appointed African Americans to "small offices" and placed them on boards where they could work side by side with suspicious white men. His motives were not entirely pure, as he hoped through his actions to break the entrenched political power of the Republican Party, but he also consciously pursued "a conciliatory course to the colored race" that was truly visionary. Years later, looking back on his racial policies, he said, "I was particularly anxious by kindness and strict justice and impartiality to the colored people and consideration to them to do away with the belief which the Republican leaders had imbued them with, [namely] that Democratic rule was inconsistent with their rights and prosperity." The "momentary dissatisfaction" that some of his fellow citizens felt about this course of action was ultimately allayed by the positive results it produced.[16] His record on race relations was more progressive than that of any other Southern governor of the late nineteenth century.

Nicholls also pushed through a complete reorganization of state agencies, and for his pièce de résistance, he had the capital moved from New Orleans to Baton Rouge—away from the malignant influence of the French Quarter and entrenched interests. He accomplished all this in three years, rather than the customary four, because the state approved a revised constitution in 1879 that required new elections. Nicholls chose not to run for a second term.

His one great regret as a first-term governor was that he was unable to destroy the Louisiana State Lottery Company. Chartered by the Republican-dominated legislature in 1868, the company was a thoroughly corrupt operation from top to bottom. In 1878, Nicholls succeeded in getting the legislature to repeal the company's twenty-five-year charter, but the federal courts struck down the measure as a violation of contract. Subsequently, the charter was incorporated in the 1879 constitution, seemingly placing it beyond the political ebb and flow. The company enjoyed a monopoly over the lottery business in Louisiana and attracted a large nationwide following, and it also received tax-exempt status—all in return for a modest annual payment of $40,000 to the state. Former Confederate generals Jubal Early and Pierre G. T. Beauregard were employed by the lottery in a public relations capacity to help deflect criticism, but in reality, the company's wealth and political connections made it practically unassailable. This did not, however, deter Nicholls from waging war against it.[17]

Even before his term was up, Nicholls was approached by party leaders about running for the U.S. Senate in 1878. The party was behind him 100 percent, they promised, and there seemed little doubt that the voters would rally around him in such a race. But he was not infatuated with public office and felt that he had promised citizens when first elected that he would serve his full term as governor. Although no court would ever have considered that promise a binding contract, he considered it a moral obligation that he had to fulfill.

When the new constitution was approved, putting him out of a job, he stepped down willingly. He firmly resisted all pleas to run for reelection, though, in truth, everyone knew the new constitution was at least partly an end run by the gambling syndicate and machine politicians to get a new, lottery-friendly regime into office. Though frustrated by his inability to bring down the lottery, Nicholls was hardly crushed by the premature demise of his political career. Three years in office was long enough. In his view, he had performed his civic duty; now, like Cincinnatus, he would return to private life. He had never seen himself as a career politician.

He left office in 1881 with an excellent record. Scrupulously honest, he was admired by Louisianans of all political stripes and colors, notwithstanding the opposition of the lottery interests. He retired from office with his reputation intact and his popularity at an all-time high, two accomplishments practically unheard of in public service.

He returned to his law practice in Napoleonville. But seven years later, he again answered the call of the electorate by running for governor a second time. Like all of his decisions, this move was carefully weighed before he threw his hat into the ring. In part, unfinished business from his first term drove him to reenter politics, for the Louisiana lottery remained the richest and most powerful institution of its kind in the United States, collecting an estimated

$500 million per year from players in every state and holding the Louisiana political machinery in thrall. In any event, he was reelected, and during his second term, he continued to improve the state's infrastructure and to fight for the rights of its black citizens, but he dedicated himself to the great crusade of destroying the lottery. No one thought he could succeed; indeed, most felt he was committing political suicide by taking on this challenge. But he was undeterred. He stumped the state in a tireless campaign, assaulting the lottery with the same vigor that he had assaulted Union lines a quarter century earlier. He fought the bottomless coffers of the Louisiana State Lottery Company with stirring words, irrefutable logic, and every ounce of personal prestige he possessed. This time, his battle against "demon gambling" paid off: In July 1892, after he had left office, a constitutional amendment to put the lottery beyond political reach was defeated forty to one. This represented the most one-sided defeat of any issue in Louisiana history to that date.[18]

Nicholls walked out the door of the governor's mansion for the last time in May 1892, but he was not out of public office for long. In 1893, he was appointed chief justice of the state supreme court by his successor as governor. Just after he took his seat, the famous black civil rights case, *Plessy* v. *Ferguson* came before the bench. The court upheld the well-entrenched Jim Crow laws, but Justice Nicholls was so new to the court that he played no role in the decision.[19]

He served nineteen years on the Louisiana supreme court, the first twelve as chief justice. As he grew older and his energy flagged, he preferred to turn the reins of power over to others. In the end, he engineered his own ouster by working behind the scenes with the state legislature to place term limits on the position of chief justice.

Although his health was failing in his final years, he was never one to retire to a rocking chair. He soon accepted an appointment to become president of the board of visitors of the United States Military Academy, demonstrating not only his vigor but also the fact that his public esteem was not limited to the Bayou State. He also continued to be a familiar figure on the streets of Baton Rouge. Young and old alike doffed their hats in respect when the old warrior passed.

He died at home on January 4, 1912, while the population of the entire state maintained a death vigil. His wife and children were at his side at the end, as were many friends and admirers who had come to pay their final respects. He was seventy-eight years old, and he had led a rich and productive life, most of it answering the call of duty in one way or another. Throughout his years, he had heeded his mother's admonition to him as a young man going off to the Mexican War: "'Tis your country that calls you; heed her summons, obey."[20] Later, when first the South and then his state called, he answered just as promptly, though it disrupted his life and cost him dearly. One of his closest friends, Joseph Breaux, who had succeeded him on the state supreme court and served alongside him during the years that followed, aptly described his friend when he paid tribute to "this brave soldier whose life was one long battle."[21]

Notes

1. C. Howard Nichols, "Some Notes on the Military Career of Francis T. Nicholls," *Louisiana History* 3, no. 4 (1956): 306.

2. Ibid.

3. Terry L. Jones, *Lee's Tigers: The Louisiana Infantry in the Army of Northern Virginia* (Baton Rouge: Louisiana State University Press, 1987), 11–12.

4. Captain J. W. Buhoup to St. John R. Liddell, April 26, 1861, Box 14, Folder 91, Moses and St. John R. Liddell Family Papers, Special Collections, Louisiana State University, Baton Rouge. Also see Jones, *Lee's Tigers*, 5.

5. T. Michael Parrish, "Richard Taylor," in *The Confederate General*, ed. William C. Davis, 6 vols. (Harrisburg, PA: National Historical Society, 1991), 6:29.

6. U.S. War Department, *The War of the Rebellion: Official Records of the Union and Confederate Armies*, 128 vols. (Washington, DC: U.S. Government Printing Office, 1881–1901) (hereafter cited as *OR*), series 1, vol. 12, pt. 1, p. 617.

7. Jones, *Lee's Tigers*, 79.

8. Richard Taylor, *Destruction and Reconstruction: Personal Experiences of the Late War*, ed. Richard B. Harwell (1879; reprint ed., New York: Longmans, Green and Co., 1955), 67.

9. Evans J. Casso, *Francis T. Nicholls: A Biographical Tribute* (Thibodaux, LA: Nicholls College Foundation, 1987), 82–83. Also see Jones, *Lee's Tigers*, 82.

10. John Dimitry, "Brigadier-General Francis T. Nicholls," in *Confederate Military History* (Extended Edition), ed. Clement A. Evans, 17 vols. (1899; reprint ed., Wilmington, NC: Broadfoot Publishing Co., 1988), 13:313–14.

11. Barnes F. Lathrop, ed., "An Autobiography of Francis T. Nicholls, 1834–1881," *Louisiana Historical Quarterly* 17 (1934):252. Also see Nichols, "Some Notes," 308–9.

12. Robert E. Lee to Jefferson Davis, May 20, 1863, *OR*, vol. 25, pt. 2, p. 810.

13. Cameron Smith, "To Rest in the Shade of Trees," *Southern Partisan Magazine* 26 (Fourth Quarter 1996): 36.

14. Elisa Richard LeBlanc Babin, quoted in Casso, *Francis T. Nicholls*, 136.

15. Ibid., 127.

16. Lathrop, "An Autobiography of Francis T. Nicholls," 257.

17. B. C. Alwes, "The History of the Louisiana State Lottery Company," *Louisiana Historical Quarterly* 17 (October 1944): 964–1118. See also R. H. Wiggins, *Louisiana Historical Quarterly* (July 1948); Judith Fenner Gentry, "Louisiana State Lottery Company," in *The Encyclopedia of Southern History,* ed. David C. Roller and Robert W. Twyman (Baton Rouge: Louisiana State University Press, 1979), 752.

18. Casso, *Francis T. Nicholls,* 161.

19. A. M. Bickel, *The Supreme Court and the Idea of Progress* (New Haven, CT: Yale University Press, 1970). Also see E. F. Waite, *Minnesota Law Review* (March 1946).

20. Casso, *Francis T. Nicholls,* 175.

21. Joseph A. Breaux, "Francis T. Nicholls, An Address," Nicholls Family Papers, Special Collections, Tulane University Library, New Orleans, Louisiana.

7

Anna Dickinson
Abolitionist Orator

J. Matthew Gallman

A woman's role in mid-nineteenth-century American society was fairly well defined. Her realm was generally domestic, and she was definitely not expected to be oriented toward public advocacy. In this regard, the culture of Civil War America was by no means unique or even unusual, either in the world of its time or in the flow of history. Anna Dickinson, however, did not fit this mold, as she made for herself an impressive career as an orator on issues of popular controversy. In fact, the very novelty of her actions added to her success, since the same mid-nineteenth-century American culture also assumed that women, by nature domestic creatures, were more pure and less grasping than men. Thus, the conventions that she flouted gave increased weight to the messages she carried—messages presumably powerful enough to have moved a young woman out of her natural sphere.

J. Matthew Gallman, who recounts Dickinson's story, is Henry R. Luce Professor of the Civil War Era at Gettysburg College, Gettysburg, Pennsylvania, and is author of *Mastering Wartime: A Social History of Philadelphia during the Civil War* (1990) and *The North Fights the Civil War: The Home Front* (1994).

In December 1863, Anna E. Dickinson, a young Quaker Philadelphian still shy of her twenty-second birthday, received the following short note:

> Miss Dickinson,
>   Heartily appreciating the value of your services in the campaigns in New Hampshire, Connecticut, Pennsylvania & New York, & the qualities that have combined to give you the deservedly high reputation you enjoy; & desiring as well to testify that appreciation as to secure ourselves the pleasures of hearing you, we write in cordially inviting you to deliver one or more addresses this winter at the Capitol, at some time suited to your own convenience.

The invitation was signed by more than one hundred Republican senators and congressmen. Less than a month later, Dickinson found herself in the House of Representatives standing atop a makeshift platform in front of the Speaker of the House's desk, flanked by the Speaker and the vice president. As she spoke, President Abraham Lincoln and Mary Todd Lincoln took seats in the audience.[1]

It is difficult to picture this strange moment in the midst of the American Civil War. It is harder still to make sense of it. The tone of the invitation and the presence of Dickinson before such a gathering defy so many of our notions of mid-nineteenth-century gender norms that one scarcely knows where to begin in coming to terms with the occasion. Moreover, the virtual absence of Dickinson from our collective knowledge of the war calls into question our understanding of those historical norms. This chapter will sketch Dickinson's wartime activities and suggest a few ways in which we might use her experiences to reach a better understanding of the war years and of the position of women in public life during the mid-1800s.

American women's historians have gone to great lengths to uncover the importance of gender in shaping access to public life in the first half of the nineteenth century. The early waves of scholarship noted crucial gender distinctions—both in expectations and in behavior—between private and public spheres. In the nation's first decades, the scholars argued, women were principally limited to the private sphere of home and family, but within that separate sphere, they enjoyed an expanded sense of autonomy and authority. By the second quarter of the nineteenth century, women had successfully parlayed this culturally acknowledged distinctiveness into an enhanced public voice in limited arenas, including religion, benevolence, and social reform. Even in the early interpretive stages, the scholarly participants in the discussion of separate spheres noted its limitations. The distinctions between male and female spheres were most clearly drawn and demonstrated not in actual behavior but in prescriptive literature.

Later scholarship forced a rethinking of the terms shaping this analysis. The earliest work had emphasized the experiences of middle-class, Northern, white women. Later studies introduced the importance of class, region, race, and marital status in determining gender roles. After all, the idealized roles of middle-class New England women might well have had only a limited impact on the experiences of working-class women in New York City and a negligible role in dictating gender experiences in a South Carolina slave cabin. Meanwhile, the very notion of the public arena was reconsidered, and in the process, traditional ideas about the true dimensions of "public" behavior were challenged. Women, it turned out, routinely appeared in public space in various guises, which called into question earlier understandings of what constituted public or even political participation.

Still, despite a host of challenges to the primacy of separate spheres as an organizing concept, some crucial points survive. Even if social norms differed according to class, race, and place, there were clear legal and political lines dividing the genders. One of the most radical and certainly the most famous of the critiques of those gender roles was produced at Seneca Falls, New York, in 1848. In the "Declaration of Sentiments," Elizabeth Cady Stanton and her colleagues assailed a world of rules and customs that limited women's economic, legal, and political roles. Even this radical gathering itself demonstrated the power of such divisions: James Mott, the husband of women's rights advocate and abolitionist Lucretia Mott, chaired the proceedings, and the only plank that failed to win unanimous approval was a call for woman's suffrage.

Two of the most intransigent notions in antebellum America were that women should not speak before mixed public gatherings and that women should not enter the arena of partisan politics. True, by 1860 quite a few women had taken to podiums and pulpits to speak of the social issues of the day, most prominently abolitionism and women's rights. But when they spoke to mixed audiences, the topics were generally quite circumscribed and the audience usually composed of the politically converted. Certainly partisan politics remained a man's purview. And women's suffrage was still more than a half century away.

Anna Dickinson's Antebellum Experiences

Anna Dickinson, the child of an old Philadelphia Quaker family, made her first tentative steps into the public arena in 1855 at age thirteen when she published an antislavery article in William Lloyd Garrison's abolitionist newspaper, *The Liberator*. Dickinson came to this abolitionist passion naturally: Her father, who had been a prominent member of the antislavery Liberty Party, reportedly delivered an abolitionist speech shortly before he died. Dickinson was just two when she lost her father, and she and her four siblings were raised by their mother, who ran a school and took in boarders. Anna contributed to the family finances from an early age, working in a publishing house and as a schoolteacher while still in her teens.[2]

In April 1860, seventeen-year-old Dickinson attended an open forum at Philadelphia's Clarkson Hall, where locals gathered to discuss the reform issues of the day. On hearing one speaker's dismissive comments about the position of women in public life, she leaped from her seat in the audience and unleashed an impassioned attack on the man and his conservative ideas. Clearly this early experience in public oratory struck a nerve. The following week, Dickinson returned to the same forum and delivered a more extensive discourse on "The Rights and Wrongs of Women." Soon, she was giving more formal speeches at gatherings across eastern Pennsylvania. That fall, with the crucial presidential election of 1860 only a few weeks away, the young Quaker was invited to speak at the twenty-third anniversary meeting of the Pennsylvania Anti-Slavery Society at Kennett Square.[3]

The Kennett Square speech turned out to be an important milestone for Dickinson. Addressing the slave issue before some of the nation's leading abolitionists, Anna had the opportunity to attract a much wider audience for both her ideas and her oratorical skills. These skills were put to the test when she advanced the controversial argument that slavery was, indeed, as the *Dred Scott* decision had contended, protected by the Constitution, thus forcing abolitionists onto more radical terrain in defending their cause. Several members of the audience interrupted her speech with lawyerly objections, insisting that the Supreme Court—and Dickinson—had erred in finding constitutional support for slavery. The series of exchanges made excellent theater and became the centerpiece for a lengthy account in the *Philadelphia Press*. Anna was already well known in many local quarters, but this article helped establish her as an important radical, orator, and public novelty.

The *Press* also set patterns of reporting Dickinson's speeches that would become familiar in the years to come. On the one hand, the reporter certainly took her ideas seriously, carefully summarizing her main themes. On the other hand, the article's allusions to Dickinson's age and gender clearly helped shape the popular response to her public appearance. In describing Anna's reply to her challengers, for example, the reporter noted that "the lady rallied with a pluck and resolution extraordinary for a girl of her years." As the attacks persisted, according to the article, another speaker on the stage interceded, pointing out that "Miss Dickinson was but 17 years of age, and necessarily timid, while the doctor [her adversary] was used to public speaking." Once the challengers had been silenced, the story continued, "Miss Dickinson then proceeded to address mothers, young men, and young girls upon the enormities of slavery. . . . The beauty and talent of the young woman exercised a talismanic effect upon even the rudest." Anna's performance deserved attention on its merits, but the *Press* reporter and the audience clearly noted—and appreciated—the importance of hearing the words of a striking young woman.[4]

As the nation stood poised on the verge of civil war, Anna Dickinson was ideally situated to step from her still rather insular, working-class Quaker world into the public eye. Her family and educational background had left her with a deep commitment to radical causes, particularly abolitionism and women's rights, and with the intellectual tools to form and defend her positions. Moreover, Anna clearly had both a gift for oratory and a passion for the public stage. Perhaps even she was surprised by her actions on that first night at Clarkson Hall, but the decision to return the following week bespoke her love of the rhetorical contest as well as the enthusiastic support of her friends and family. Chief among these supportive friends were Elwood Longshore and his wife, Dr. Hannah Longshore, a Philadelphia couple who soon took on the role of informal guardians and advisers.[5]

Before long, Anna's circle of friends and correspondents would include many of the nation's leading abolitionists, women's rights advocates, and partisan Republicans. In February 1861, one of her strongest supporters, Lucretia Mott, introduced Anna to a large audience at Philadelphia's Concert Hall. In this, her first full-length address to a paying audience, Anna once again spoke on "The Rights and Wrongs of Women." Picking up on themes that she had first raised at Clarkson Hall, she devoted most of her two hours to calling for expanded access to the professions for women.

Like the printed responses to her Kennett Square speech, the newspaper reports of Dickinson's Concert Hall lecture revealed a range of contemporary attitudes about her role in the public arena. One common analytic theme praised her performance while belittling her ideas. "It was the words of mediocrity spoken through the lips of genius," reported one paper. The *Philadelphia Evening Bulletin* published a generally favorable summary of her arguments but concluded that "we were sorry to hear the lady damaging her cause by claiming intellectual equality with men. She seems ignorant of the fact that though woman can be as great as man, the equality is not in kind but in degree—the equality of noblest intuition with noblest intellect." If the *Bulletin* made some effort to celebrate gender difference while dismissing the notion of true gender equality, a New Jersey paper was more openly critical: "The young lady in question cannot do better than exchange the harassing duties of public life for those serener and domestic walks so befitting her sex."[6]

War and the Rise of a Public Personality

Perhaps a final force behind Anna's entrance into the public arena was her desire for a profession: Her family needed her income, and she would soon discover that she preferred the lecture hall to the schoolhouse. When the Civil War broke out in April 1861, she left her teaching position and took a job at the United States Mint. In beginning work in a federal office, Dickinson moved into one of the few areas of expanded employment opportunities for women during the war. But in her case the opportunity would not last long. For the first several months of the war, Anna pored over the newspaper reports of the conflict while continuing to accept occasional speaking engagements. With the war moving slowly and often going badly for the Union, she shared in the sense of frustration that plagued much of the North. And whereas many of her radical associates—both abolitionists and women's rights advocates—spurned the rough-and-tumble of partisan politics and military affairs, Anna was clearly drawn to the world of political infighting.

Shortly after the disastrous Battle of Ball's Bluff, the Pennsylvania Anti-Slavery Society invited Dickinson to return to Kennett Square for their annual meeting. There, to an audience of fellow abolitionists (including her hero, William Lloyd Garrison), she delivered a detailed critique of the progress of the war. She saved her most vigorous attacks for the Democratic commander of the Union army. "Future history will show," she declared, "that this battle was lost not through ignorance and incompetence, but through the treason of the commanding general, George B. McClellan." Such colorful (and outrageous) charges reached receptive ears in Kennett Square, but they soon cost Dickinson her job with the mint, thus forcing her to seek other means of support.[7]

During the first months of 1862, Anna visited friends in Rhode Island, where she delivered the occasional speech on "The National Crisis" or women's rights. In March, after returning to Philadelphia for several more lectures, she wrote to Garrison to ask the abolitionist's help in obtaining paid engagements in New England. Garrison managed to arrange an invitation for her to speak at Boston's Music Hall, as well as a series of smaller engagements across the state. During these months, Dickinson really made the transition from an occasional orator to an accomplished, professional stump speaker. She delivered well-attended lectures in Providence on her way to Boston, where she settled into several weeks of paid speaking.[8] Although public oratory was now her source of income—and a source of support for her family back in Philadelphia—Dickinson maintained a passion for her causes and a youthful enthusiasm for life on the road. When she arrived in Boston, she was almost immediately asked to step in to replace an ailing Wendell Phillips, one of the nation's leading abolitionists. The twenty-year-old Quaker could barely contain her enthusiasm in a letter to her sister. "Think of *that* mum—this small snip—acting as Wendell Phillipses substitute," she exclaimed.

> Well I had a great cram—4 or 5 thousand people, Wendell Phillips himself & all the literary fragments about Boston floated up there to listen—& they all said it was a magnificent success—Mr. Phillips called next day to say he had *never* been so gratified,—

and so deeply moved—"actually my dear Anna brought tears into my eyes—they had almost forgotten the sensation."—I see him almost every day—as well as a great many other splendid people— & indeed they have almost devoured me.—one would suppose that no such had ever been seen in these quarters, Mr. Garrison says he has been over run with thanks for finding me—however I will stop blowing my own trumpet—being somewhat out of breath & will send you a paper or two.

But even in the midst of these heady experiences, Dickinson did not lose track of her larger financial goals. In the same letter, she added:

I do not expect to be very rich,—in pocket wealth this time.—shall have *some.*—but I am making my way & name now. —when I come again next winter Mrs. Dall says—"You can, to a great extent— . . . demand your own price." & that is doing wonderfully I say.— think so?[9]

The following week, Garrison introduced Anna—fresh from her Boston successes—to New York's Antislavery Society at the Cooper Institute. The *New York Herald*'s response to her speech was characteristic of the nation's mainstream press. The generally supportive article found Dickinson to be "a young lady of prepossessing appearance, who, in a clear, musical voice, made a plea for the downtrodden of her sex." "But," the article went on, "it is needless to add that Miss Dickinson's brain did not produce anything more striking or original upon the vexed question than Garrison, Phillips or Cheever." The *National Anti-Slavery Standard,* in contrast, took Dickinson's words much more seriously, recognizing the speech as principally a political attack on the South and a call for turning the conflict into a war for abolition. Following the Cooper Institute lecture, Anna returned to Massachusetts to complete her series of lectures before returning home to Philadelphia for the summer.[10]

By this point, she had an established reputation among abolitionists and women's rights advocates, but she was still unable to fill her calendar with paid speaking engagements. So, like many patriotic Northern women, she began volunteering at the local military hospitals. During the war years a relatively small cohort of Northern women, under the supervision of Dorothea Dix, entered the previously male-dominated world of professional nursing. Thousands of other women and men, like Dickinson, were drawn to the hospitals, where they offered the wounded men company and comfort. But in Anna's case, conversations with the soldiers became fodder for future lectures. That fall, she delivered a new lecture on "Hospital Life" in Concord, New Hampshire, followed shortly by a Lyceum lecture in Boston on the same topic. Rather than merely describing the

physical hardships of the wounded men she had met, Dickinson—
ever the political partisan—used their plight to attack the institution of slavery and critique the progress of the war effort.[11]

The Lyceum lecture earned Dickinson a large (one hundred
dollar) honorarium, but no similar invitations were forthcoming.
Instead, she occupied herself with several fund-raising speeches in
New Hampshire while privately despairing of ever earning a living
as an orator. And as she awaited further speaking opportunities, her
financially beleaguered family peppered Anna with calls for assistance. In December 1862 her sister Susan wrote: "I hope, however,
both for thy sake and ours that thee will be pretty well paid for what
thee gets to do, both for thy sake and ours. What a weight would be
taken off if we were only fairly out of debt." The following month,
with much of the nation's attention focused on the new Emancipation Proclamation, Susan reported from Philadelphia that "there is
no prospect of anything in the lecturing line here," adding that

> I have been thinking lately whether it would not be well for thee to
> give practical readings after the fashion of Miss Kimberly, Murdock
> etc. Thee has voice enough, and has had it trained enough to suc-
> ceed, and it is likely to pay a great deal better than lecturing at
> present. . . . I commend it to thy serious attention. Also while things
> are stagnant in the lecturing line and we are so in need of devising
> ways and means to make money would thee not do well after thee
> comes home to have a private class or classes in reading for
> awhile?[12]

Even if Dickinson's family shared her political opinions, their more
immediate concern was financial survival.

The Emergence of a Political Partisan

Although Dickinson ended 1862 with deep concerns about both
her prospects as an orator and her family's economic fortunes, the
seeds of a successful future had already been sown. The secretary of
New Hampshire's Republican State Committee had been in the
audience during her Concord speech and concluded that the charis-
matic young woman might be a perfect addition to the party's
upcoming political campaigns. With the controversial Emancipation
Proclamation now on the books, the war dragging on, and enlistments dwindling, the Republican Party—still in its infancy—had
ample reason to worry. The crucial 1863 state elections promised to
be an important test, setting the stage for Lincoln's reelection bid
the following year. Therefore, based on the party secretary's enthusiastic recommendation, the New Hampshire Republicans invited
Dickinson to assist in the campaign.

Suddenly, Anna was launched into a flurry of activity, delivering twenty lectures across the state in the month of March alone. When the Republicans carried most of the state in the hotly contested election, she received her share of the credit, earning particular praise from the governor-elect. As the Republican *Granite State Free Press* declared, "We are confident that had Miss Dickinson spoken in every town in the State, the result would have been more gratifying." Her triumph was only enhanced by the news that a local candidate who had declared "don't send that damn woman down here to defeat my election" was among the party's few casualties.[13]

Having received widespread credit for the victories in New Hampshire, Dickinson found her services in great demand in political circles. She went directly from New Hampshire to Maine for another round of campaign speeches, followed immediately by several weeks of engagements for the Republican Party in Connecticut. Although she arrived late in the Connecticut campaign, she soon had a place of prominence in the party's strategy. After spending most of the campaign speaking to enthusiastic crowds in the state's smaller cities and towns, she was given the ultimate honor of delivering the party's closing address on election eve in Hartford. Printed notices for her final campaign appearance placed her name prominently above those of other Republican luminaries—all male—from across the state and the nation. The packed Allyn Hall crowd heard her deliver a rousing two-hour speech that was reported with enthusiasm by the local and state press.[14]

When the Republicans won important victories in both Maine and Connecticut, Dickinson once again received praise for her performances and some public credit for the party's electoral success. In just a few months, she had established herself as not only a political radical but also a passionate party spokesperson. Without setting aside her deep commitment to abolition and women's rights, she had proved to be an adept orator, even directing clever—and enthusiastically reported—barbs at the occasional Democratic heckler. Most of her radical abolitionist colleagues stayed above such partisan squabbles, often eyeing Lincoln and his moderate Republican compatriots with cautious skepticism, if not outright distaste. Dickinson might well have adopted a similar attitude had it not been for Lincoln's Emancipation Proclamation.[15] Still, the lure of speaking fees (and perhaps the temptation of new audiences to conquer) certainly helped lead her into the Republican fold.

Following on the heels of her political successes, Dickinson suddenly found herself in great demand. She returned to Boston for another address, and then, in April 1863, Anna journeyed south to New York, where she delivered a strong prowar speech to a packed audience of five thousand at Cooper Union. Flanked by legendary abolitionists Henry Ward Beecher and Horace Greeley, she once again applied her abolitionist convictions to the military cause, attacking the slaveholding South while returning to a favorite theme of earlier years: the allegedly treasonous behavior of Gen. George McClellan. The Cooper Union speech was a success, gaining Dickinson extensive coverage in the influential New York press and setting the stage for her victorious return to Philadelphia at the Academy of Music. The lecture also earned Dickinson an enormous (one thousand dollar) speaker's fee and opened the door for similarly profitable engagements in the future.[16]

A National Celebrity

In hindsight, we can recognize the summer of 1863 as a crucial phase for the Union army's eventual military victory. In the first few days of July the army in the east successfully stopped Robert E. Lee's invasion at the Battle of Gettysburg, and the Confederate stronghold of Vicksburg fell one day later after a lengthy siege, giving the Union control of the upper Mississippi River. But despite these victories, there was still reason for concern in the Northern states: Lee had once again managed to escape with his army intact; military morale was down and recruitment disappointing; and internal conflicts over conscription and emancipation continued to plague the North, erupting in terrible antidraft rioting in New York City.

One solution to the growing manpower problem was to enlist black recruits to fill the ranks. In July, Dickinson joined leading black abolitionist Frederick Douglass at a Philadelphia meeting to encourage black enlistment. In so doing, she—and Douglass—called on black men to join the Union military cause despite the fact that the government persisted in paying them less than their white counterparts. A few weeks later Anna, attended a public review of the Sixth U.S. Colored troops at Philadelphia's Camp William Penn, where she ended up giving a brief, impromptu speech to the assembled soldiers and guests. In this fashion, she threw her weight behind the use of black troops in what she now saw as a war for emancipation.[17]

That fall, Dickinson returned to the campaign trail, spending six weeks stumping for Pennsylvania Republicans before making a brief political appearance in Buffalo, New York. In these large and politically vital states, Dickinson was only one star in a crowded Republican galaxy rather than the focal point of the party's campaign strategy. Nonetheless, the Pennsylvania Republicans recognized the power of her words and reputation, particularly among working-class voters, and offered her one thousand dollars a day for twelve days of speeches in the state's notoriously violent and strongly Democratic coal counties. Party officials calculated that Dickinson's working-class roots and gender might earn her a less hostile reception than other Republican orators received. Perhaps they were right, but the young Quaker was certainly not welcomed with open arms. During her Shamokin appearance, her legend grew when an angry Irish miner fired a pistol at her, shearing off a lock of her hair.[18]

As it turned out, the Pennsylvania Republicans reneged on the promised twelve thousand dollars, drawing Dickinson's wrath and perhaps encouraging her to shift her focus from political speaking to more remunerative engagements. Rather than remaining in New York to campaign for state Republicans there, she arranged to return to New England for a series of paid lectures. But Anna ended up postponing these engagements in order to travel to Chicago, where she was a featured speaker at the Northwestern Sanitary Fair to raise money for the regional branch of the United States Sanitary Commission. Her lectures were wildly successful, both as fund-raisers and as public oratory. But the Chicago speeches also thrust Dickinson into a new round of controversy when it came to light that she had earned a healthy six hundred dollars for her two fund-raising appearances. Her adversaries charged her with hypocritically profiting from the war emergency, whereas her defenders—and hosts—insisted that the young Quaker had earned far more for the cause than she had charged. Dickinson's own defense was quite telling. The fees, she pointed out, only compensated her for the income that she gave up during her journey to the Midwest. In short, although her heart was with the war effort and the goals of the Sanitary Commission, Dickinson could not afford to lose sight of her economic needs, particularly when her services were in such demand.[19]

Even before she ventured to Chicago, Anna's fame had attracted the attention of Republican members of the U.S. House of Representatives. Spurred on by the efforts of Judge William D. Kelley, a congressman from Philadelphia and a longtime Dickinson supporter and adviser, Republican representatives had agreed to invite Anna to Washington for a lecture. The politically savvy Dickinson held out for an invitation to speak in the Hall of Representatives itself, and on December 16, 1863, she eventually received that invitation, signed by more than one hundred representatives and senators. When she arrived at the hall on January 16, 1864, she faced an audience filled with political dignitaries. According to the *History of Woman Suffrage* (edited by Elizabeth Cady Stanton, Susan B. Anthony, and Matilda Joslyn Gage), Dickinson "was honored as no man ever had been before."[20] The speech itself was of familiar vintage. She attacked traitorous Northern Democrats while supporting emancipation and calling for better treatment of the black troops. The true drama began when Dickinson turned her attention to the Lincoln administration. Just as she began a detailed attack on Lincoln's lenient new proposals for reconstructing the Union, the president and his wife entered the hall. Anna continued her assault on the moderate Republican's conciliatory approach to the Confederacy but then surprised the audience by doing an about-face and supporting Lincoln's candidacy for reelection.

Dickinson's Washington speech won praise in most quarters. To many, it was a triumphant performance in an arena where women had never before ventured. Some Democrats criticized her for turning the occasion into a partisan performance with her explicit support for Lincoln's reelection. And Dickinson's radical friends were disappointed with her endorsement of the president, suggesting that she had been swept up in the excitement of the moment and the surprise at seeing the Lincolns in the audience. Shortly after the lecture, Anna admitted to Whitelaw Reid, a close friend and fellow abolitionist, that she had erred in supporting the moderate Lincoln.

That spring, she was once again a national favorite, accepting offers to speak across the Northeast and dutifully sending her earnings home to her mother and sister. These political lectures renewed her attacks on Lincoln's plan for Reconstruction while omitting her earlier endorsement of the president's reelection bid. In April she secured a private meeting with Lincoln in order to express her disapproval of his mild overtures toward the Confederacy. No formal record of that meeting survives, but in her subsequent speeches, Dickinson routinely used the episode as fodder for attacks on Lincoln and his policies.

By summer, Anna faced a complex personal and political decision. The embattled president had managed to secure his party's renomination and faced the Democratic candidate, General McClellan, in the crucial election of 1864. Although Dickinson had become almost outrageous in her attacks on the president, it would have been hard to imagine any leading figure she would have favored less than her old adversary McClellan. Whereas many leading abolitionists—including her friends and confidants Whitelaw Reid and Susan B. Anthony—declined to endorse either of these political "evils," Dickinson refused to remain on the sidelines. Instead, she once again reversed herself and declared her support for the Republican candidate, even while acknowledging that she would have preferred another standard-bearer. In the months preceding the election, Dickinson once again hit the campaign trail, emphasizing colorful attacks on the Confederacy and on the Democrats' candidate.[21]

Once Lincoln won reelection, Anna returned to her familiar rhetorical themes, demanding racial justice for freedmen and attacking the administration for its proposed leniency toward the rebels. But with Lincoln's assassination, coming quickly on the heels of Lee's surrender at Appomattox, Dickinson lost her principal rhetorical target. Despite her reputation as a Lincoln antagonist, however, Anna received numerous offers to eulogize the fallen president, and on May 10, 1865, the twenty-two-year-old celebrity returned to New York's Cooper Union to speak to a large audience, remembering Lincoln fondly and linking his name with the cause of freedom.[22]

Anna Dickinson's surprising public career did not end with Appomattox. In the decade after the war, she became one of the nation's most celebrated lyceum speakers, earning an annual income that was matched by only a handful of male orators. All the while, she maintained her radical proclivities: defending the rights of freedmen, critiquing monopoly capitalism, assailing political corruption in Washington, and periodically returning to the stump to support Republican candidates.

Personal and political conflicts and shifting public tastes eventually drove her from the podium into other equally public endeavors. She supplemented her reduced lecture earnings by trying her hand as a novelist, actress, and playwright but never matched her success as an orator. Eventually, years of declining fame, poor health, and a variety of political and legal battles took their toll on Dickinson. Her story took a melancholy turn in 1891 when her sister Susan arranged for Anna to be committed to Pennsylvania's State Hospital for the Insane. Ever the fighter, Anna took her case to the press and the courts, eventually winning her freedom in a celebrated jury trial.[23]

Conclusion

What should the historian make of Anna Dickinson's role in the Civil War? In the simplest—and most traditional—terms, she can be recalled as a participant in some of the critical debates that shaped the war years. It is certainly true that, although she played an important part in several state elections, she probably did not personally dictate the course of any particular vote or event. Moreover, it is likely fair to say that Dickinson's ideas, although firmly held and vigorously defended, were not entirely original. But it is the rare historical figure who single-handedly redirects the course of events through personal actions or entirely original ideas. In the most traditional sense, Anna Dickinson should be remembered—

perhaps more than she has been—as an important (and not merely an interesting) figure.

Nonetheless, if we try to understand the historic moment in its own context and on its own terms, we are led to a broader set of conclusions. During the war years, Dickinson was fabulously popular. Crowds flocked to her public appearances. Lecture organizers paid her huge honoraria. State Republican organizations vied for her services. Newspaper reporters hung on her every word and gesture. Today's reader might hear a reference to a mid-nineteenth-century "Miss Dickinson" and immediately imagine the poet of Concord, Massachusetts; a Northerner in 1863 would almost certainly picture the spirited young Philadelphia Quaker. In an age in which the public lecture was a crucial source of entertainment and information, the significance of such popularity should not be discounted. Even if her ideas were borrowed from Garrison or Phillips, how many other people's opinions were, in fact, swayed by the power of her rhetoric?

We may learn still more about both Dickinson and the Civil War era by concentrating on the sources of her popularity rather than the weight of her impact. Exactly what nerve did she touch in the popular imagination? Contemporary accounts offer ample, if sometimes contradictory, explanations. Some observers, particularly those most sympathetic to her message, described a speaker of mesmerizing skills. She clearly possessed a remarkable charisma that could reach the far corners of a lecture hall and also captivate individual associates and admirers. Friend and foe alike routinely commented on Anna's appearance, dress, and gestures, suggesting that the crowds had come to watch this striking young woman perform and not merely to hear her ideas. In fact, Dickinson's critics implied that it was merely her novelty, not her intellect, that attracted such attention, taking pains to point out that her message largely rehashed the words of older male abolitionists. All would acknowledge that an Anna Dickinson lecture was an event to be reckoned with and that the same words delivered by another speaker might have attracted far less interest. But it is hard to imagine her rising to such prominence as both a radical lecturer and a political stump speaker unless audiences were, indeed, interested in what she had to say. Of course, this, too, was open to a cynical reading: Dickinson's unrestrained style and habit of leveling outrageous charges helped draw large audiences who were anxious to hear what the young Quaker would say next.[24]

Whatever the mix of forces contributing to her particular appeal, Anna's wartime popularity was testimony both to the heightened national concern for all things military and political and to the more general midcentury enthusiasm for lectures and similar public events and spectacles. In the North in particular, the events of the crisis were woven seamlessly into the fabric of everyday life. The same individual who attended a lecture by Anna Dickinson or William Lloyd Garrison one evening might go to hear a mesmerist or to see Gen. Tom Thumb the next. As a celebrated public figure, Anna was also moving in a highly gendered world. Women were still quite rare on the lecture circuit and almost unheard of in partisan political discourse.

This last observation returns us to where we began. What can a distinctive figure such as Anna Dickinson teach us about gender roles during the Civil War? Despite her unique character and history, her career does illustrate some crucial aspects of women's wartime experiences. Like many women (and men), Anna became wrapped up in the events of the day, developing a fascination with and expertise in both political and military matters. Although most Northern women did not have the opportunity to offer such public critiques of governmental policy and military strategy, Dickinson was certainly not alone among her peers in framing opinions about the events of the day. And like many women in both the North and the South, Anna felt compelled to aid the war effort, even though she was not permitted to take up arms for the cause. To be sure, her contributions took an unusually public form, but Dickinson's wartime activities had much in common with those of more anonymous Northern women: She volunteered in military hospitals, helped raise funds for the Sanitary Commission, and contributed to the efforts to raise and support black regiments.

Moreover, like many other women, Anna acted out of both patriotic convictions and economic necessity. True, the war did not rob the Dickinsons of a male breadwinner, for Mrs. Dickinson was a widow long before the fighting began. But Anna's wartime lecturing is still a good example of how women with limited occupational opportunities made ends meet before and during the conflict.

In truth, Anna Dickinson was not typical of Northern women or of any other group. Still, her departure from gender norms provides a useful window through which to observe contemporary attitudes about the role of women in public space. Somehow, we must reconcile the notion that women were not supposed to appear in the political arena with the obvious fact that Anna Dickinson was a regular performer on the public stage. It is clear that the gender expectations did not translate into hard-and-fast rules.

Anna's contemporaries, supporters and adversaries alike, responded to her appearances through the lens of gender. Perhaps the most dramatic example of gendered criticism appeared originally in the *Geneva (New York) Gazette* in 1864, under the title "Anna E. Dickinson and the Gynekokracy." This editorial, which the *National Anti-Slavery Standard* reprinted in its column on excerpts from the proslavery press, linked Dickinson with a history of "absurd endeavors of women to usurp the places and execute the functions of the male sex" but concluded that "to the credit of the sex, it should be added, that so far as is known to the writer, she has not been encouraged in this career by respectable ladies. Her sphere is with the men, and all sensible and modest women, who have a regard for the proprieties of the sex, will be content to leave it there."[25]

As noted, other commentators revealed more subtle gender assumptions by concentrating on Dickinson's appearance and clothing or by asserting that her ideas must certainly have been borrowed from male abolitionists. Of course, some of these responses and much of the initial fascination with Dickinson focused as much on her youth as on her gender; thus, suggestions that she was intellectually immature must be read in that context. And, in fact, one might argue that the more striking message from Anna Dickinson's experience in the war years is not the gender (and age) barriers that she faced so much as the ease with which she traversed them. Once she established herself as a national celebrity, she was able to draw large audiences and substantial paychecks for lectures on a wide variety of wartime concerns, including pointed commentaries on the male-dominated worlds of military affairs and party politics. And even if observers were not blind to gender when they heard her speak, the larger truth is that Dickinson's opinions and endorsements received a popular attention that transcended commonly understood gender spheres. Her contemporaries understood that Anna Dickinson was truly unique; we are left to speculate about how her example—perhaps like that of a Frederick Douglass or Harriet Tubman—may have created a subliminal challenge to broader cultural stereotypes and prejudices.

Notes

1. Giraud Chester, *Embattled Maiden: The Life of Anna Dickinson* (New York, 1951); Anna Dickinson Papers, Manuscript Division, Library of Congress, Washington, DC, microfilm (hereafter cited as ADP).

2. Apart from the 1951 Chester biography, Dickinson has received scant attention from scholars. For brief, generally similar treatments of Dickinson's war years, see Elizabeth Cady Stanton, Susan B. Anthony, and Matilda Joslyn Gage, eds., *History of Woman Suffrage*, 3 vols. (1881; reprint ed., New York, 1970), 2:40–50; Judith Anderson, "Anna Dickinson, Antislavery Radical," *Pennsylvania History* 3 (July 1936): 147–63; James Harvey Young, "Anna Elizabeth Dickinson and the Civil War" (Ph.D. diss., University of Illinois, 1941); idem, "Anna Elizabeth Dickinson and the Civil War: For and Against Lincoln," *Mississippi Valley Historical Review* 31 (June 1944): 59–80; Wendy Hamand Venet, *Neither Ballots nor Bullets: Women Aboli-

tionists and the Civil War (Charlottesville, VA, 1991), 37–56 and passim; and Karlyn Kohrs Campbell, "Anna E. Dickinson," in *Women Public Speakers in the United States, 1800–1925: A Bio-Critical Sourcebook,* ed. Karlyn Kohrs Campbell (Westport, CT, 1993), 156–67. The best sources for Dick inson's wartime experiences are her correspondence and extensive scrapbook and miscellaneous papers, all part of the Anna E. Dickinson Papers, ADP.

3. Campbell, "Anna E. Dickinson," 156; Anderson, "Anna Dickinson," 150–51; Chester, *Embattled Maiden,* 14–18.

4. Chester, *Embattled Maiden,* 18–22; *Philadelphia Press,* n.d., reprinted in Dickinson scrapbook, ADP.

5. Chester, *Embattled Maiden,* 17.

6. Ibid., 23–25; *Daily Evening Bulletin,* n.d., Dickinson scrapbook, ADP; *West Jersey Pioneer,* n.d., Dickinson scrapbook, ADP.

7. Stanton, Anthony, and Gage, *History of Woman Suffrage,* 2:42; Chester, *Embattled Maiden,* 26–29.

8. Chester, *Embattled Maiden,* 30–35; Dickinson scrapbook, ADP.

9. Anna Dickinson to Susan Dickinson, April 28, 1862, container no. 1, ADP.

10. *New York Herald,* May 17, 1862, and *National Anti-Slavery Standard,* May 17, 1862, Dickinson scrapbook, ADP; Chester, *Embattled Maiden,* 38–40.

11. Stanton, Anthony, and Gage, *History of Woman Suffrage,* 2:42–43; Chester, *Embattled Maiden,* 42–44.

12. Susan Dickinson to Anna Dickinson, December 6, 1862, and January 17, 1863, ADP.

13. Stanton, Anthony, and Gage, *History of Woman Suffrage,* 2:43–44 (the losing candidate actually tried to get on Dickinson's calendar but only after it was too late); Chester, *Embattled Maiden,* 45–49.

14. *Hartford Press, Hartford Post,* and *Hartford Courant,* all March 1863, Dickinson scrapbook, ADP; Chester, *Embattled Maiden,* 49–58.

15. Venet, *Neither Ballots nor Bullets,* 45.

16. Dickinson scrapbook, ADP; Chester, *Embattled Maiden,* 59–65; Young, "Anna Elizabeth Dickinson and the Civil War," 66–67.

17. Stanton, Anthony, and Gage, *History of Woman Suffrage,* 2:46–47; Chester, *Embattled Maiden,* 64–69.

18. Chester, *Embattled Maiden,* 70–74; Venet, *Neither Ballots nor Bullets,* 46–47. Chester reported that the crowd warmed to Dickinson when she stood up to the pistol-wielding heckler.

19. *Chicago Tribune,* October 25, 1863, through November 11, 1863; *Peoria Morning Mail,* November 14, 1863; Dickinson scrapbook, ADP; Chester, *Embattled Maiden,* 73.

20. Stanton, Anthony, and Gage, *History of Woman Suffrage,* 2:47–48.

21. Chester, *Embattled Maiden,* 74–84; Young, "Anna Elizabeth Dickinson and the Civil War," 68–77; Stanton, Anthony, and Gage, *History of Woman Suffrage,* 2:47–48.

22. Chester, *Embattled Maiden,* 83–84; Young, "Anna Elizabeth Dickinson and the Civil War," 77–79.

23. On Dickinson's postwar life, see Chester, *Embattled Maiden,* 85–293, and Campbell, "Anna E. Dickinson," 158–160.

24. The newspaper accounts of Dickinson's speeches routinely—although certainly not universally—spoke of her tremendous rhetorical power. Her personal correspondence provides tantalizing hints of a similar effect on those around her; see ADP.

25. *Geneva (New York) Gazette,* reprinted in the *National Anti-Slavery Standard,* April 2, 1864. (This clipping is misdated in the Dickinson scrapbook and thus is miscited in several secondary sources.)

8

LaSalle Corbell Pickett
"What Happened to Me"

Lesley J. Gordon

In some ways, one might describe LaSalle Corbell Pickett as a Southern equivalent to Anna Dickinson, for she, too, simultaneously overstepped and affirmed the accepted role of a woman in mid-nineteenth-century America. The wife of the tragically famous but hapless Confederate general George Pickett, she used both her status as his widow and her own considerable literary talents during the decades after the Civil War to remake her own and her husband's past, forging an idealized version. In doing so, she was, perhaps to a lesser degree than Dickinson, moving beyond the conventional role assigned to women in the mid-1800s. Yet at the same time, she validated the cultural forms of her society, for the idealized Sallie Pickett of her retouched memories was far more meek and retiring than the forceful woman who made her husband a hero after the fact and herself "the child-bride of the Confederacy."

Lesley J. Gordon, who presents LaSalle Pickett's story, is an assistant professor of history at the University of Akron and author of *General George E. Pickett in Life and Legend* (1998).

In her 1917 autobiography, *What Happened to Me,* LaSalle "Sallie" Corbell Pickett described a dream she had soon after the end of the Civil War when she and her infant son were traveling by train to Canada to rejoin her husband, ex-Confederate major general George Pickett. The sound of the train had kept her up much of the night, she wrote, reminding her "of the sound of the executioner's axe. All night long it rose and fell through seas of blood—the heart's blood of valiant men, of devoted women, of innocent little children." When LaSalle finally drifted off to sleep near morning, she dreamed that "it was I who had destroyed the world of people whose life blood surged around me with a maddening roar, and that I was destined to an eternity of remorse."[1]

Portions of this chapter have been taken from Lesley J. Gordon, *General George E. Pickett in Life and Legend* (Chapel Hill: University of North Carolina Press, 1998). ©1998 University of North Carolina Press. Reprinted by permission of the University of North Carolina Press.

In this passage and throughout her many published writings, LaSalle Corbell Pickett blended the personal story of her life with a public retelling of war and defeat. In this excerpt, she blamed herself for the suffering and death that all of America, not just her native South, endured in its bloody civil war. But Pickett was no unimpassioned chronicler of events that had occurred decades before, nor was she a helpless victim. As the widow of a famed Confederate general, she claimed a personal role in the dramatic saga of Southern defeat. Despite the passive title of her autobiography, Pickett wrote in a decidedly active and powerful voice. She outlived her husband by five decades, supporting herself and her son with a lucrative career—touring the United States, giving lectures, writing ten books and numerous articles, visiting veteran reunions, and bringing her "firsthand" account to a national audience.

Although Pickett insisted on the veracity of her recollections, scholarly research shows that she fabricated much of her published writings. She lied about her age, lied about her husband's defeats and failures, and lied about her contemporaries. She erroneously presented herself as a child in many of her writings, so that, it would seem, she could better hide the assertiveness and independence she attained as a successful writer and single mother. In writing of the past, she transformed herself into a "child wife," highlighting her husband's strength and masculinity and emphasizing her own delicacy and fragility. Pickett smoothed over embarrassing aspects of the past, using the shield of widowhood to protect her husband's memory and deflect any challenges to her own authority.[2]

Yet there is still "truth" in the emotionally charged words Pickett wrote. Her mix of fact and fiction provides important insights into the war's meaning for a white Southern woman. Underneath her Victorian romanticism and occasional morbidity was a strong-willed woman desperate to make order out of war's chaos. The voice telling these stories spoke of real anguish, true despair, and a steely determination to set things right again.

LaSalle Corbell was eighteen years old in 1861. The first of nine children, she had spent her childhood at her family home in Nansemond County, Virginia. Her parents, John David and Elizabeth Phillips Corbell, were wealthy slaveholders and owned a sizable plantation. War shattered her family's peaceful existence, and Sallie's life, like that of so many of her contemporaries, was never the same.[3]

War first touched LaSalle while she was a student at Lynchburg Female Seminary in Lynchburg, Virginia. She was not attending the elite academy to expand her intellectual capacities; as the eldest daughter of a large Tidewater planter, she was learning how to be a cultivated white Southern lady and preparing to assume the traditional role of devoted wife and mother.[4]

Pickett's published memoirs vividly recalled the early days of secession and crisis. Her autobiography recounted how she and her classmates clustered excitedly in their schoolrooms, believing "that we knew something of war." They cheered at the sight of the first Confederate national flag and felt confident that their brothers, fathers, uncles, and male friends soon would come home, safe and victorious, from the battlefront. They also held a springtime festival to raise money for knapsacks to equip a local rifle company. LaSalle admitted to her postwar readers that she, like so many other Southerners, believed the war would be relatively bloodless and quick. "We saw then," she remembered, "only the bonfires of joy and heard the paeans of victory."[5] Her impression changed when she met a man wounded in battle: "I began to feel that war meant something more than the thrill of martial music and shouts of victory." In retrospect, she stated that "not only soldiers in the field had obstacles to encounter; they loomed in the pathway of the school-girl."[6]

Historians have recently explored the ways in which white elite Southern women such as LaSalle Pickett tried to reinvent themselves during this time of great social crisis. Traditional gender roles no longer sufficed, and new ones were created, tried on, and tested by war.[7] Pickett's wartime recollections showed a young woman eager to play an active role in the conflict, but often frustrated by conventional attitudes and restrictive gender expectations.

In one story, Pickett told of visiting her uncle Col. J. J. Phillips in camp on the day of the famed naval battle between the *Virginia* and the *Monitor* in early March 1862. When her uncle readied a dinghy to join in the action, Pickett begged to accompany him. " 'No, No!' he shouted. 'Go Back.' " Unshaken by his refusal, she took a seat in his small vessel when he turned his back. As her uncle realized that she had defied him, "a look of horrified amazement" came over his face. According to Pickett, he declared, " 'You needn't think I am going to try to keep you out of danger, you disobedient, incorrigible little minx. . . . It would serve you right if you were shot.' " Pickett attested that she had given little thought to the danger she faced, wanting only to get a good view of the fight.[8]

LaSalle Pickett claimed that the Battle of Seven Pines "brought the war closer to me than any other had yet done."[9] In 1862, she went to Richmond to spend her summer vacation, unable to return to her Tidewater home because it was caught behind Federal lines. This time she did not have to go looking for action, for Northern troops came dangerously close to the Confederate capital. Her portrait of a city reeling from its first brush with enemy invasion is riveting. She wrote to readers of *Cosmopolitan*: "If I could lay before you the picture of the Richmond of those battle-days, you would say that I had written the most powerful peace argument ever penned." Emphasizing the terrible sights and sounds the Richmond citizenry witnessed during the two-day battle, she described the Confederate capital "shaking with the thunders of the battle while the death-sounds thrilled through our agonized souls." Carts loaded with the wounded and the dead crowded the streets, and most residences were open to the injured. Women and children found that the horror of war had come directly into their homes: "Women, girls, and children stood before the doors with wine and food for the wounded as they passed." Soldiers and civilians flooded into Capitol Square, anxiously awaiting news of loved ones, and black crepe was draped on doorways and windows. Remembering a mother who lost her son at Seven Pines, Pickett declared, "Sometimes the Richmond of those days comes back to me now, and I shudder anew with terror."[10]

Her writings mixed traditional gendered reactions to war, blending the stereotypical feminine repulsion to fighting with the equally stereotypical masculine fascination with battle. She often depicted herself at the forefront of the action, impervious to the danger surrounding her. It appeared that she could not pull herself from the violence. In one account, she told readers of accompanying George as he inspected the lines. As shells began to explode dangerously close, her husband pleaded with her to leave:

> "No indeed," I said. "I'm not a bit afraid, and if I were do you think I would let Pickett's men see me run?"
> "Come, dear, please! You are in danger, useless danger, and that is not bravery."

Despite his entreaties, she stayed at the front, snatching a pair of field glasses to gaze across the lines and allegedly catching a glimpse of General Grant and his wife.[11]

In another story, Pickett spoke of witnessing the decapitation of a young officer just after he, too, had warned her of the danger she faced in visiting the front. She watched him "riding in that graceful way which the Southerner has by inheritance from a long line of ancestors who have been accustomed to ride over wide reaches of land."[12] Regretting her "obstinate resistance to his appeal" that she take shelter, she was mortified to see his death. "Impulsively I sprang from my horse," she wrote, "and ran and picked up the poor head, and I solemnly believe that the dying eyes looked their thanks as the last glimmering of life flickered out."[13] This was a strange portrait, indeed—an officer's wife standing defiant to the dangers of battle.

Most of LaSalle Pickett's books and articles had a decidedly martial tone to them. In *The Bugles of Gettysburg, Pickett and His Men,* and her serialized *Cosmopolitan* article, "The Wartime Story of General Pickett," she became an official military historian. Perhaps this explains why she unabashedly plagiarized large portions of a staff officer's book for her own writings. Realizing that veterans might question a woman's authority to speak of battle, she inserted a male author's voice for the purely military passages. Pickett insisted to readers that she had a right to publish battle narratives; after all, as a general's wife, she had loyally shared in his victories and his defeats. "My story has been so closely allied with that of Pickett and his division," she wrote in *Pickett and His Men*, "that it does not seem quite an intrusive interpolation for me to appear in the record of that warrior band." She asked, "How could I tell the story, and the way in which that story was written, and not be part of it?"[14]

She believed her wartime romance with George Pickett and their subsequent marriage justified her role as historian of this grand American saga. In her published recollections, she never failed to include details of her whirlwind courtship and the marriage to her "Soldier." It is unclear exactly when their courtship began. LaSalle always maintained that she fell in love with George in 1852 when she first met him on a beach in eastern Virginia. Certainly by the spring of 1863, there was supporting evidence from witnesses of a budding romance. It was apparently during the 1863 Suffolk campaign that things really began to heat up. LaSalle described to readers how George saw her nightly after she went to stay with her aunt some ten miles from his command. "Here when all was quiet along the lines," LaSalle attested, "my Soldier would ride in from his headquarters almost every night between the hours of sunset and sunrise to see me—a ride of about thirty miles."[15]

Two officers corroborated LaSalle's assertions. Col. William Dabney Stuart of the Fifty-sixth Virginia complained to his wife that his division commander was "continually riding off to pay court to his young love, leaving the division details to his staff."[16] And Maj. G. Moxley Sorrel criticized George's "frequent applications to be absent" to see his lover. These nightly rides were long, and the major general did not return to his command until early the next morning. Sorrel sensed that even George's close friend James Longstreet, the corps commander, was irritated with Pickett's constant requests to leave camp, and he recounted how Pickett once asked him (Sorrel) for permission instead. The staff officer declined. He felt he could not justifiably take responsibility for a major general's absence should the division move or be attacked. "Pickett went all the same," Sorrel wrote, "nothing could hold him back from that pursuit." He concluded, "I don't think his division benefited from such carpet-knight doings on the field."[17]

LaSalle Pickett also shared her wartime romance with postwar readers by publishing a collection of letters George allegedly sent her from the battlefront. As already mentioned, scholars have seriously questioned whether her husband actually penned these letters. Comparing them to LaSalle's other published writings and a staff officer's history of Pickett's division, they accuse her of fabricating the letters' contents because the published correspondence contains information George could not have known at the time the letters were purportedly written. Scholars have also pointed to the emotional and romantic tone of the published letters as betraying LaSalle's authorship. Some have wondered if LaSalle heavily edited original letters.[18]

It does seem likely that Pickett constructed the bulk of these missives herself, perhaps basing them loosely on some original love letters George sent her. Her other writings repeatedly stressed her husband's devotion to her, even in the thick of battle. This published collection of wartime letters made her "Soldier" speak for himself and thus bolster her claims. Even the title is telling: *The Heart of a Soldier: As Revealed in the Intimate Letters of Genl. George E. Pickett CSA.*

While Pickett yearned to be at the forefront of battle, these letters show her husband was growing weary of war. In one of the published letters, George declared: "Oh, my darling, war and its results did not seem so awful till the love for you. Now—now I want to love and bless and help everything, and there are no foes—no enemies—just love for you and longing for you."[19] Until the war ended, LaSalle attested that her husband frequently interrupted important military operations to write her. In another published letter, he pleaded to know why she had quipped "never mind" to him at their last meeting. "It troubled me all night," he declared. "I wanted to follow after you and ask you what you meant, but couldn't. I would have jumped on Lucy [his horse] and ridden in to Petersburg and found out if it had been possible for me to leave. I was so troubled about it that I was almost tempted to come in anyhow." He wondered if he had hurt her feelings by telling her she need not come to the front anymore, that he had enough men to do soldiers' work: "Were you aggrieved because your blundering old Soldier told you there was no necessity for your coming out to bring dispatches, any longer, that, thank heaven, the recruits and reinforcements were coming in now and that we could manage all right?"[20]

In the published Pickett letters, George appeared more impatient to marry than LaSalle. In one, he urged: "So, my Sally, don't let's wait; send me a line back by Jackerie saying you will come. Come at once, my darling, into this valley of the shadow of uncertainty, and make certain the comfort if I should fall I shall fall as your husband." According to LaSalle, he suggested that they "overlook old-time customs" and marry immediately in his camp. She hastily explained to her postwar audience that some might disapprove of the impropriety of his proposal, noting that for those who knew of the "rigid system of social training in which a girl of that period was reared," it would not be "strange that a maiden, even in war times, could not seriously contemplate the possibility of leaving home and being married by the wayside in that desultory and unstudied fashion." LaSalle felt bound by "social laws" even if George did not, and she convinced him to wait.[21] But her lover was a professional soldier and high-ranking general and had to go where orders sent him. "Cupid does not readily give way to Mars," she stated to her readers, "and in our Southern country a lull between bugle calls was likely to be filled with the music of wedding bells."[22]

Pickett naturally chose to include a description of her wedding day in her writings, and it was a dramatic one. She alleged that she and George had difficulties just getting to the Petersburg church. Unable to obtain a furlough, George instead received permission for "special duty" to leave the front, and LaSalle and her family had to sneak across enemy lines, traveling by ferry and train to reach Petersburg from Chuckatuck. LaSalle's father, two uncles, and a female chaperone accompanied her; her mother had to stay behind to care for her baby brother. At the church, she reunited with George, his brother Charles, and his faithful Uncle Andrew and Aunt Olivia. Finally, after a brief but dramatic delay in obtaining the marriage license, George and LaSalle married on September 15, 1863. She recalled: "I felt like child who had been given a bunch of grapes, a stick of candy. Oh I was happy."[23]

A honeymoon was out of the question, but the couple allegedly managed a festive reception in the Confederate capital. The Picketts's personal celebration became public: LaSalle claimed that several Confederate luminaries attended the party, including President and Mrs. Jefferson Davis, members of Davis's cabinet, and officers in Lee's army. There was also plenty of food, drink, and dancing. "If people could not dance in the crises of life," LaSalle explained to her postwar audience, "the tragedy of existence might be even darker than it is."[24]

In reality the man whom LaSalle Corbell married in 1863 was deep in a personal and professional crisis. A West Point graduate and brevetted Mexican War veteran, George found himself ill prepared for civil war. His former comrades and the nation he had pledged his life to defend became the hated enemy. As the violence escalated, he grew more disturbed. He complained repeatedly, showed flashes of quick anger, and failed when left with any sort of autonomy on the field. As a brigadier general, he was a zealous and aggressive fighter, but when promoted to division commander in October 1862, he seemed overwhelmed with his responsibilities. At Gettysburg, he watched in stunned disbelief as his division shattered itself in a desperate attempt to break the Union line. George never forgot Gettysburg: He brooded over the loss of his division, blaming everyone but himself. He increasingly felt a demise of control and began to perceive the North as uncivilized and demonic.[25]

Soon after his marriage to LaSalle Corbell, George showed further evidence of this loss of personal and professional restraint. When he failed to reclaim Union-held New Bern, North Carolina, in February 1864, he turned his rage on a group of Union prisoners, former members of the North Carolina home guard. Pickett ordered a hasty court-martial and execution of these men, mocking the pleas of Federal officials and ignoring the anguish of victims' family members. Later, this episode would nearly earn Pickett indictment for war crimes by the U.S. government.[26]

Readers of LaSalle Pickett's books and articles will find no mention of this troubled, angry man. Instead, her Soldier was loving and sensitive, courageous and chivalrous. Her literary George Pickett was not perfect, to be sure, but LaSalle used her morally superior female sex to monitor his weakness for drinking and swearing. But as destruction and chaos raged around them, she said, love and serenity thrived within their union. The wartime marriage Pickett described in her books and articles was, indeed, a haven in a heartless, senseless world.[27]

Pickett's memoirs contain several examples of her efforts to seek "rifts of sunshine to break the gloom."[28] In the bloody summer of 1864, while General Pickett and his men faced grueling siege warfare, LaSalle insisted that "there was no lack of social diversions. In a small way we had our dances, our conversaziones and musicales, quite like the gay world that had never known anything about war except from the pages of books and the columns of newspapers. True we did not feast."[29]

Pickett set the final chapter of her wartime story in Richmond in April 1865. Separated from her husband during the Confederacy's final days of existence, she waited in the Southern capital, anxious for news. On April 2, 1865, the Confederate government abandoned Richmond, and the next day, Union troops entered the city. Pickett described her terror and fear as she found herself alone with her baby son. Her slaves had long gone, and rumors circulated that her Soldier was dead. Fires set by Confederates spread, and frenzied crowds looted stores and warehouses. Broken furniture, shattered glass, and other wreckage filled the muddy streets. LaSalle likened the experience to a "reign of terror": "The yelling and howling and swearing and weeping and wailing beggar description. Families houseless and homeless under the open sky!"[30] The surreal, hellish picture was made complete by the presence of black Union soldiers.

She recalled that "they were the first colored troops I had ever seen, and the weird effect produced by their black faces in that infernal environment was indelibly impressed upon my mind."[31]

An unexpected visitor supposedly came in the midst of the terror. One day after Richmond fell, Pickett answered a knock at her door and saw before her a "tall, gaunt, sad-faced man in ill-fitting clothes, who asked with the accent of the North: 'Is this George Pickett's Place?'" President Abraham Lincoln had presumably stopped by to pay her a personal visit during his tour of the fallen Confederate capital. As pure fantasy, the account illustrates the delusive pathos of Pickett's latter-day recollections, as well as her overinflated sense of self-importance. Nonetheless, she shrewdly played to her postwar audience's renewed feelings of reunion and Lincoln nostalgia. It made a great story.[32]

All of LaSalle Pickett's published memories of her war experience and marriage were carefully presented. Deliberately crafting her literary self and that of her husband for national consumption, she followed the Southern Plantation Tradition initiated by authors such as Thomas Nelson Page and Joel Chandler Harris. When she described the antebellum South, she celebrated "de good ole times 'fo' de wah," putting herself and her husband in a setting that featured paternalistic slaveowners and loyal, passive slaves. Her racist images were eagerly bought up by the white reading public, North and South, at the turn of the twentieth century.[33]

Besides sheer profit and celebrating the Lost Cause, LaSalle Pickett seemed to have had additional personal motives for publicly recounting her wartime experience. As a Confederate general's wife, she could only celebrate her husband; it would have been highly unacceptable for her to write anything negative about him or her marriage. So instead, she cloaked the suffering and difficulties she must have endured in the conventional role of loving wife and mourning widow. She sought to conform to acceptable gender roles by emphasizing her husband's courage and bravery and de-emphasizing her own autonomy and strength. The resulting picture was a contradictory one: Her husband often appeared in her writings as pacifistic and emotional, and she seemed reckless and bold, eager to be in the thick of battle yet sickened by war's destruction and chaos. Pickett struggled to make sense out of it all decades after the war ended. "Years away from that time of anguish and terror," she wrote, "I awaken suddenly with the crash of those guns still in my ears, their fearful sounds yet echoing in my heart, only to find myself safe in my soft, warm bed."[34] Haunted by these images, she wondered if she were "destined to an eternity of remorse."[35]

Few historians have taken LaSalle Pickett or her published works seriously, for she was overtly dishonest about her husband's failings and difficulties and about people she allegedly met and events she allegedly witnessed. Yet should historians question the sorrow she described? Should they doubt the disturbing nightmares that she told readers she continued to suffer years after the war ended? After all, men such as James Longstreet and George McClellan publicly exaggerated and stretched the "facts" of their wartime experiences. Clearly, LaSalle Pickett's recollections of the Civil War pose difficult questions for modern readers to consider. The line between fact and fiction in her writings is often so blurred that it is nearly impossible to separate myth from reality. But her reconstructed memory of her Civil War experience tells us a great deal about the war's lasting meaning to one of its singular participants. It tells us about powerful gender conventions during and after the war. And it tells us of a woman seeking desperately to stake a personal claim for a painfully uncivil past.

Notes

1. LaSalle Corbell Pickett, *What Happened to Me* (New York: Brentano's, 1917), 216. This chapter is drawn from the author's larger study of the Picketts, *General George E. Pickett in Life and Legend* (Chapel Hill: University of North Carolina Press, 1998).

2. Obituaries in the *Confederate Veteran* 39, no. 4 (April 1931): 151, and the *Washington Post,* March 23, 1931, refer to Pickett as the "Child Bride of the Confederacy." She called herself a "child wife" in her autobiography, Pickett, *What Happened to Me,* 189. The age discrepancy appears in U.S. Census Office, 7th Census of the United States, 1850: Population Schedules, Nansemond County, Virginia, and U.S. Census Office, 8th Census of the United States, 1860: Population Schedules, Nansemond County, Virginia. Both census records list Pickett's age as five years younger than she later claimed to be in her autobiographical writings.

3. U.S. Census Office, 7th Census of the United States, 1850: Population Schedules, Nansemond County, Virginia, and U.S. Census Office, 8th Census of the United States, 1860: Population Schedules, Nansemond County, Virginia; obituaries in *Confederate Veteran* 39, no. 4 (April 1931): 151, *New York Times,* March 23, 1931, and *Washington Post,* March 23, 1931.

4. Pickett, *What Happened to Me,* 83; Dorothy T. Potter and Clifton W. Potter, *Lynchburg: "The Most Interesting Spots"* (Lynchburg, VA: Progress Publishing Co., 1976), 1; Christie Anne Farnham, *The Education of the Southern Belle: Higher Education and Student Socialization in the Antebellum South* (New York: New York University Press, 1994), 72–73, 174; Anne Firor Scott, *The Southern Lady: From Pedestal to Politics, 1830–1930* (Chicago: University of Chicago Press, 1970), 71.

5. Pickett, *What Happened to Me,* 89–92; George Morris and Susan Foutz, *Lynchburg in the Civil War: The City, the People, the Battle* (Lynchburg, VA: H. E. Howard, 1984), 10.

6. Pickett, *What Happened to Me,* 89–90.

7. Drew Gilpin Faust, *Mothers of Invention: Women of the Slaveholding South in the American Civil War* (Chapel Hill: University of North Carolina Press, 1996); LeeAnn Whites, *The Civil War as a Crisis in Gender: Augusta Georgia, 1860–1890* (Athens: University of Georgia Press, 1995); Catherine Clinton and Nina Silber, eds., *Divided Houses: Gender and the Civil War* (New York: Oxford University Press, 1992).

8. Pickett, *What Happened to Me,* 99–100.

9. LaSalle Corbell Pickett, *Pickett and His Men* (Atlanta, GA: Foote and Davies, 1899), 170.

10. LaSalle Corbell Pickett, "The Wartime Story of General Pickett," *Cosmopolitan* 56 (January 1914): 178–80. Pickett repeated this same passage in her 1917 autobiography, *What Happened to Me,* 104–8; see also idem, *Pickett and His Men,* 170–74.

11. Pickett, *What Happened to Me,* 143.

12. Pickett, *Pickett and His Men,* 361.

13. Pickett, *What Happened to Me,* 144–45. An abbreviated form of this story is included in her *Pickett and His Men,* 360–61, but Pickett left out any mention of her retrieving the head.

14. LaSalle Pickett, *Pickett and His Men,* 7. For discussion of her plagiarism, see Gary Gallagher, "A Widow and Her Soldier: LaSalle Corbell Pickett as Author of the George E. Pickett Letters," *Virginia Magazine of History Biography* 94 (July 1986): 335–37.

15. Pickett, *What Happened to Me,* 121.

16. Quoted in William A. Young Jr. and Patricia C. Young, *56th Virginia Infantry* (Lynchburg, VA: H. E. Howard, 1990), 74.

17. G. Moxley Sorrel, *Recollections of a Confederate Staff Officer* (1905; reprint ed., Dayton, OH: Morningside, 1978), 153.

18. Gallagher, "A Widow and Her Soldier," 329–44; Glenn Tucker, *Lee and Longstreet at Gettysburg* (Indianapolis: Bobbs-Merrill Co., 1968), 44–45; George R. Stewart, *Pickett's Charge: A Microhistory of the Final Attack at Gettysburg, July 3, 1863* (Boston: Houghton Mifflin Co., 1959), 297–98; Douglas Southall Freeman, *R. E. Lee: A Biography,* 4 vols. (New York: Charles Scribner's Sons, 1935), 4:563.

19. LaSalle Corbell Pickett, ed., *The Heart of a Soldier: As Revealed in the Intimate Letters of Genl. George E. Pickett CSA* (New York: Seth Moyle, 1913), 65–66.

20. Ibid., 125. Italics in original.

21. Ibid., 75–76.

22. Pickett, *What Happened to Me,* 124.

23. Quoted in Arthur Crew Inman, *The Inman Diary: A Public and Private Confession,* ed. Daniel Aaron, 2 vols. (Cambridge, MA: Harvard University Press, 1985), 1:328; wedding details gathered from Pickett, "The Wartime Story of General Pickett," 764, and idem, *Pickett and His Men,* 320–21; also *Richmond (Virginia) Dispatch,* September 22, 1863.

24. Pickett, *Pickett and His Men,* 320–21; see also idem, *What Happened to Me,* 126–29.

25. Douglas Southall Freeman, *Lee's Lieutenants: A Study in Command,* 3 vols. (New York: Charles Scribner's Sons, 1942), 1:158–59, 192, 242–43; Ezra Warner, *Generals in Gray: Lives of the Confederate Commanders* (Baton Rouge: Louisiana State University Press, 1959), 239–40.

26. Freeman, *Lee's Lieutenants* 3:XXXVI; Warner, *Generals in Gray,* 239–40.

27. Pickett, *What Happened to Me,* 136; see also Pickett, *Pickett and His Men,* 326.

28. Pickett, *What Happened to Me,* 141.

29. Pickett, *Pickett and His Men,* 357; see also idem, *What Happened to Me,* 141.

30. LaSalle Corbell Pickett, "The First United States Flag Raised in Richmond after the War," in *The Fourth Massachusetts Cavalry in the Closing Scenes of the War for the Maintenance of the Union*, ed. William B. Arnold (Boston, n.p.: 19–), 19–22, quote from p. 21.

31. Pickett, *What Happened to Me,* 164–65. See also idem, LaSalle Corbell Pickett, "My Soldier," *McClure's Magazine* 30 (March 1908): 563–71. Richard N. Current, ed., *Encyclopedia of the Confederacy,* 4 vols. (New York: Simon and Schuster, 1993), 3:1331.

32. Pickett, *What Happened to Me,* 167–70.

33. LaSalle Corbell Pickett, *Jinny* (Washington, DC: The Neale Co., 1901), 59.

34. Pickett, *Pickett and His Men,* 343.

35. Pickett, *What Happened to Me,* 216.

9

Prince Felix and Princess Agnes Salm-Salm
Civil War Royalty

David Coffey

Europeans watched the Civil War with interest, and some did more than watch. Military adventurers, among them Prince Felix Salm-Salm, came in relatively small numbers to offer their services and win what glory or other rewards they could. By far the greater part of Europeans who took part in the war, however, were individuals already well on their way to becoming Americans. In the nineteenth century, as in the previous two hundred years, America was a beacon of hope and freedom to Europeans, and thousands continued to migrate to the United States, settling primarily in the North. When rebellion in the South threatened to render self-government a failure in their newly adopted land, these new immigrants were quick to join the fight. The Germans were as aggressive in this regard as any of the Europeans, and the Union army in fact contained dozens of all-German regiments.

Most of the men in such outfits were ordinary, good soldiers. But some of the higher-ranking Germans, including military adventurers such as Prince Salm-Salm, were remarkable characters indeed, as the story of the prince and his equally remarkable American wife demonstrates. Their story also shows how a couple could work together for the husband's advancement. The adventures of this unique pair are one colorful facet of American history during the Civil War.

Historian David Coffey, of Texas Christian University, Fort Worth, Texas, is the author of *John Bell Hood and the Battle of Atlanta* (1998) and is currently researching a larger study of Prince and Princess Salm-Salm.

Times of great conflict have always spawned intriguing romantic relationships, and the American Civil War was no exception. Notable wartime romances included Confederate general George Pickett's marriage to young LaSalle Corbell, upstart Federal cavalry hero George Armstrong Custer's successful courtship of the highborn Elizabeth "Libbie" Bacon, and crippled warrior John Bell Hood's sad pursuit of the alluring Southern belle Sally "Buck" Preston. But perhaps the most extraordinary Civil War pairing was that of Prussian prince Felix zu Salm-Salm, a volunteer colonel in the Union army, and his mysterious, American princess, Agnes.

Theirs was a romance born of and sustained by the incredible circumstances of the Civil War—a mutually beneficial partnership that thrived on the periphery of America's greatest struggle. Neither husband nor wife participated to any large extent in the war's major events, but both profited from their wartime experiences. For the prince the war offered the glory denied him in Europe and a chance to polish a tarnished reputation. And Agnes would see that he made the most of his opportunity. Ambitious, aggressive, and strikingly attractive, she used her regal title and powers of persuasion to advance her husband's career, promote the welfare of sick and wounded soldiers, and carve a place for herself among some of America's most influential leaders.

Agnes appeared in Washington, DC, in autumn 1861, drawn to the capital by the spectacle of war. Just who she was—her origin, her history—would be the subject of wild speculation for years to come. Born on Christmas Day 1844 in Swanton, Vermont, she apparently left home as a teenager and traveled widely before settling in Cuba, where, it was rumored, she performed with a circus as an equestrienne. Her obvious riding skills did nothing to refute this rumor. Some accounts identified her as an actress, but she denied ever taking the stage. One romanticized version of her early life even held that she was the child of an English fur trapper and his Indian bride; according to this version, she was stolen by hostile Indians and sold to a disreputable circus manager who took her to South America and later Cuba, where she finally escaped. Agnes delighted in such speculation but refused to set the record straight. "I confess," she wrote, "it affords me even a malicious pleasure to disappoint, in this respect, a number of persons who for years have taken the trouble of inventing the most romantic and wonderful stories in reference to my youth."[1]

Whatever her past, Agnes arrived in Washington from New York City after "having returned from Cuba," where she had lived for "several years." Like thousands of others, she came to witness a review of Federal troops. In the wake of the debacle at Bull Run, President Abraham Lincoln had placed the army and the hopes of the Union in the hands of thirty-four-year-old Maj. Gen. George B. McClellan. During the summer of 1861 the impressive but untested McClellan worked diligently to build the Army of the Potomac, which now bore little resemblance to the battered force that had scrambled away from Manassas Junction. "Military enthusiasm was paramount in Washington," Agnes recalled, and ladies "were not left untouched by the prevailing epidemic." So complete was the effect, she noted, that "Apollo himself would have passed unnoticed if he did not wear shoulder-straps." And she was, she admitted, as "favorably disposed towards the uniform as other ladies."[2]

The numerous army camps in and around the capital offered a major attraction for curious civilians. After witnessing a cavalry review, Agnes and a party of fellow spectators crossed the Potomac into northern Virginia to visit one of the camps. One cantonment, that of flamboyant Brig. Gen. Louis Blenker's "German Division," became the favored destination for General McClellan and civilian visitors alike.[3]

Admired for its martial appearance and grand hospitality, Blenker's camp featured fine food and drink as well as a sizable complement of exotic officers. "German," a label liberally applied to almost any soldier of non-English-speaking origin, in this case described a truly ethnic division composed of Germans, Poles, Hungarians, and other Europeans. Blenker, himself a refugee from the German revolutions of 1848, maintained an extended staff that included fellow refugees, soldiers of fortune, and a number of lavishly attired noblemen—"shipwrecked Germans," as Agnes called them.[4]

At Blenker's tent, Agnes took notice of a late-arriving staffer whom the general presented as "Colonel Prince Salm." She described a man of "middle height" with an "elegant figure, dark hair, light moustache, and a very agreeable handsome face." He appeared bashful and wore a monocle over his right eye. "I felt particularly attracted by the face of the Prince," Agnes recalled, "and it was evident that my face had the same effect on him." Although the prince spoke no English and Agnes knew nothing of German or French, they managed to communicate in "the more universal language of the eyes, which," she admitted, "both of us understood."[5]

Born at Anholt, Westphalia, Prussia, in 1828, like Agnes on Christmas Day, Felix Constantin Alexander Johann Nepomuk, Prince Salm-Salm, was a younger son of the reigning Prince Salm-Salm and, therefore, low on the list of succession. He received a military education in Berlin and as a young subaltern in the Prussian cavalry was seriously wounded while fighting the Danes in Schleswig-Holstein. Accustomed to ready access to his family's wealth, Salm spent carelessly and entertained with extravagance, and when he was cut off from the family purse after his father's death, he ran up huge debts. To escape his creditors, he joined the Austrian army, only to repeat his financial frivolity: A prince simply could not live on a junior officer's pay. When his brother, the reigning prince, refused to cover his mounting bills, Salm looked across the Atlantic to America, where war beckoned.[6]

Carrying letters of recommendation and an aura of Prussian military mystique, Salm arrived in Washington and offered his sword to Federal authorities, who gratefully accepted his services. The irony was not lost on Agnes, who later wrote, "Though republicans, the American people were no enemies to princes. . . . A live prince was an object of great interest to both gentlemen and ladies."[7] His inability to speak English, however, prompted Salm to decline the command of a Kentucky cavalry regiment; he hoped instead for a slot in one of the German regiments. He settled for a colonelcy on Blenker's inflated staff—a precarious position from the start.

Although Blenker welcomed old-country aristocrats, Prussian noblemen, regardless of merit, attracted the contempt of other, more radical Forty-Eighters in the division. This attitude was manifested in political backbiting and charges of corruption leveled against Blenker. To make matters worse the War Department soon cracked down on opulent staffs, leaving Salm's future in the army very much in doubt.[8]

If the Civil War was, as Agnes expressed, a "godsend . . . to shipwrecked Germans," she herself was a godsend to Salm. Recalling their first meeting, she wrote, "When I left General Blenker's camp I left behind an enamoured Prince." She and Salm saw each other often over the next few weeks, and the "sweet malady increased."[9]

In March 1862, Salm accompanied Blenker's command as it moved into western Virginia to join Maj. Gen. John C. Frémont's ill-fated Mountain Department. After a miserable journey, the German Division arrived in time to share the suffering wrought by Confederate major general Thomas J. "Stonewall" Jackson's brilliant Shenandoah Valley campaign. After the Battle of Cross Keys in June, Blenker's division was ordered back to northern Virginia as part of Maj. Gen. John Pope's newly formed Army of Virginia. But on Blenker's return to the Washington area, controversy, political intrigue, and the failure of the recent campaign, although hardly his fault, combined to topple the fiery German. Relieved in June, Blenker awaited a new assignment that never came, which left Salm's military future in limbo.[10]

While Salm toiled in the field, Agnes remained in Washington, but the two carried on a "lively correspondence" in English, with which Salm showed progress. During his absence, she worked diligently on his behalf. "I soon became aware that we could never progress or succeed much in America," she wrote, "without the help of influential friends."[11] Agnes soon proved remarkably adept at acquiring influential friends—friends who would come in handy now that Salm's American career was in serious jeopardy.

Despite the unfortunate turn of events in his professional life, Salm's romance with the American beauty blossomed. On August 30, 1862, as his former division fought a second battle at Bull Run, the colonel married Agnes in a private ceremony at Washington's Saint Patrick's Church. The newlyweds understood that Salm's continued employment depended on his ability to land a state commission and his own regiment (and anything less than a colonelcy was apparently unthinkable). To this end the royal couple traveled to Albany, New York, where Agnes hoped to exert some influence of her own.[12]

She had good reason for optimism. In Albany, she called on U.S. senator Ira Harris, one of the influential friends she had cultivated in Washington. Harris, a well-connected Republican, proved a valuable ally, securing for the princess an audience with Gov. Edwin Morgan. The senator even agreed to accompany her. Incredibly, Salm did not attend the meeting, persuaded that his weak grasp of English would endanger the mission, but Agnes managed quite nicely without him. Although Harris warned her that Morgan possessed "the reputation for being a woman-hater," Agnes won over the governor with a passionate appeal, and in short order, Morgan presented her with a colonel's commission for Salm. Agnes had delivered her husband a regiment, and a German regiment at that—Blenker's own Eighth New York Volunteer Infantry.[13]

In November 1862, Salm left Albany to join his new command in northern Virginia. A few days later, Agnes arrived in camp. But the opening of Maj. Gen. Ambrose Burnside's disastrous Fredericksburg campaign in December meant active operations for the troops, prompting Agnes's return to Washington. Salm's regiment, part of Hungarian-born Brig. Gen. Julius Stahel's First Division, Eleventh Corps, Army of the Potomac, escaped the carnage at Fredericksburg. Shortly thereafter a lull in the fighting allowed Agnes to rejoin her husband in time to celebrate their mutual birthday.[14]

Circumstances dictated the event would be a shabby affair by royal standards (or any other standard for that matter), but the entire division pitched in for the occasion. General Stahel sent a band, and soldiers prepared a finely decorated mud cake. Dining fare consisted of salt pork and hardtack. "With the utmost difficulty," Agnes recalled, "Salm procured four bottles of very vile whisky," to which sugar and lemons were added, producing "a most abominable, abundantly watered stuff." The makeshift party, nonetheless, was a decidedly pleasing affair.[15]

Such merriment became a distant memory once Burnside again took the offensive in a desperate effort to dislodge the Confederates from their Rappahannock River stronghold. Torrential rains began on January 20, 1863, turning the intended troop movement into the infamous "Mud March." Agnes shared the hardships as the army slogged toward a new encampment at Aquia Creek, not far from the Fredericksburg battleground.[16]

The Salm-Salms settled into winter quarters at Aquia Creek, erecting a temporary home of considerable opulence even for the now abundantly provisioned Army of the Potomac. Agnes reported that "Salm procured a large hospital tent, which was decorated very tastefully and even gorgeously; for amongst the soldiers of his regiment were workmen of all trades." The soldier-decorators lined the tent walls with colorful damask; the salon featured carpeting and a "splendid sofa," and Salm added a large mirror that attracted the "admiration of everybody." A separate kitchen tent housed a "negro servant girl," whom Agnes had brought from Washington. "We had our own caterer," the princess confided, and a "wine cellar, which was dug in the ground, contained bottles of the most different shapes and contents."[17]

In late January, Maj. Gen. Joseph Hooker replaced the unfortunate Burnside. Hooker brought with him solid credentials as a fighter and the not-so-welcomed reputation of a heavy drinker and womanizer. Under his command the army's camps assumed an often unmilitarily festive aspect. Liberalized visitation rules brought officers' families from throughout the Union, and soon the camps were, according to Agnes, "teeming with women and children." This naturally contributed to a lively social season: "Scarcely a day passed without some excursion, pleasure party, dinner, or ball," the princess stated.[18]

As resident royalty the prince and princess played a conspicuous role on the winter party circuit, but the master of ceremonies was the controversial Third Corps commander, Maj. Gen. Daniel Sickles. Agnes described one event attended by some two hundred "ladies and gentlemen" that "could not have been better in Paris, for the famous [restaurateur] Delmonico from New York had come himself to superintend the repast." On another occasion, officers from Sickles's corps organized a day of festivities and horse races attended by Hooker and other top brass. During one race, Salm was thrown from his mount and, according to one observer, "came near breaking his neck." The First Corps chief of artillery, Col. Charles Wainwright, noted the large number of women present. Two in particular caught his attention. "Mrs. Salm-Salm and Mrs. Farnum [wife of Col. J. E. Farnum], of course, were on hand," he wrote, adding cryptically that "the camps are full of stories about them both."[19]

Rumors were likely to follow any woman who, married or not, too closely associated herself with General Hooker or General Sickles. Charles Francis Adams Jr., grandson of President John Quincy Adams and a captain in the First Massachusetts Cavalry at the time, echoed the opinion of many soldiers and civilians alike when he wrote that "the Headquarters of the Army of the Potomac was a place to which no self-respecting man liked to go, and no decent woman could go. It was a combination of barroom and brothel."[20] Agnes's physical beauty, combined with her bold, assertive personality and an evident preference for male company, made her a prime target for, if nothing else, guilt by association. She undoubtedly sparked a good deal of innuendo.

Her leading role in the season's crowning event only enhanced whatever reputation she had. In April, before spring campaigning commenced, President and Mrs. Lincoln and their son Tad paid a visit to Hooker's army, and after reviewing the troops the president attended a reception arranged by General Sickles. In an effort to buoy the president's spirits, Sickles persuaded a group of officers' wives to shower Lincoln with affection. According to one account, "The Princess Salm-Salm, a very beautiful woman, led the way. . . . A glance from the princess toward the ladies in her train was all that was necessary." The petite Agnes stood on her tiptoes and, pulling Lincoln's head downward, kissed him on the cheek. "If a squadron of cavalry had surrounded the president and charged right down upon him, he could not have been more helpless."[21]

Mrs. Lincoln, who had not been present at the reception but had apparently heard about the incident, refused to speak to Sickles when he escorted the First Family back to Washington. Over dinner, Lincoln tried to break the ice, saying to Sickles: "I never knew you were such a pious man." When the general insisted that was not the case, Lincoln replied, "They tell me you are the greatest Psalmist in the army. They say you are more than a Psalmist—they say you are a Salm-Salmist." At that, Mrs. Lincoln gave in to her husband's humor and forgave the general.[22]

Indeed, Sickles had become an enthusiastic advocate of Col. Prince Salm, evoking the names of LaFayette and Steuben in a letter to the president that urged Salm's promotion to brigadier general. Sickles actually had little evidence on which to judge the prince and place him in such lofty company, for Salm was yet to lead his troops in battle. Without promotion, though, he would be mustered out of the service when his regiment's two-year enlistments expired in late April—on the eve of the next major campaign.[23]

With no promotion forthcoming, Salm dutifully prepared to accompany his men back to New York. Meanwhile, Agnes went to Washington to plead her husband's case—to no avail. Her departure from camp did not go unnoticed. "We are all sorry that Mrs. *Salm-Salm* has left the army," wrote Lt. Frank Haskell, who would find fame at Gettysburg, adding, "She is a beautiful woman and the presence of *ladies* is so charming in camp, to chasten the morals and manners of the men."[24]

The Salm-Salms moved to New York, where they began the search for a new command. There, they received the news of Hooker's crushing defeat at Chancellorsville. The heavily German Eleventh Corps had been mauled, prompting a general indictment of German soldiers. Nonetheless, the prince managed to obtain the colonelcy of the Sixty-eighth New York Infantry, a depleted, three-year regiment, but he had to bring it up to strength first. Ultimately, it would take him more than a year of frustration before his new commission could be activated. He established a recruiting office, but volunteering had all but stopped in the North. He and a friend hatched a plan to recruit a brigade in Germany, but despite some official support, that prospect never became a reality. His regiment remained a paper tiger.[25]

While Salm concentrated on recruitment, Agnes busied herself in New York. That July, she witnessed in horror the reaction to the newly enacted Federal draft laws. The New York draft riots became one of the ugliest episodes of the war as a mob, largely composed of working-class Irishmen, terrorized the city for several days, focusing their anger and frustration on blacks, government officials, and abolitionists. In the midst of the crisis, Salm offered his services to local officials, and Agnes moved about the city in the company of her Irish servant girl, from whom she borrowed a dress. "To go in the street in my usual dress would have been madness," she later confided, making no effort to conceal her contempt for the "low Irish rabble of New York."[26]

The princess used her time in the metropolis to cultivate new influential friends and dabble in spiritualism. She became a frequent guest in the home of *New York Herald* publisher James Gordon Bennett, whose dashing son and heir, James Gordon Bennett Jr., presented her with a fine black-and-tan terrier, which she named Jimmy in his honor. (Jimmy, raised on fried oysters and roasted veal, would be her constant companion for many years to come.) She also found time to experiment with the spiritualist movement that swept the city, but her interest stemmed more from a sense of mischief than from genuine curiosity.[27]

Meanwhile, when Salm's recruiting efforts stalled, Agnes again rose to the challenge. She contacted "dear old" Senator Harris, who suggested that the provost marshal general in Washington might have unassigned troops available. Without disclosing the true nature of her journey, Agnes traveled to the capital on the pretext of visiting her sister. Arriving in Washington, she immediately called on Col. James B. Fry, who agreed to detail the few hundred men he had at his disposal to Salm's Sixty-eighth New York. Still short of her goal, she then persuaded Fry to help her raise the rest of the troops her husband needed. To that end, he introduced her to Illinois governor Richard Yates. Yates offered a company of Illinois troops but refused to have it commanded by a New York officer, and, according to Agnes, he therefore proposed that he give *her* command of the company. She wrote: "I received from him a captain's commission and captain's pay, which, he said, would assist me in defraying the expenses I incurred in assisting the sick and wounded soldiers, in whose treatment I was much interested."[28]

Agnes had come through again. The new regiment contained the reenlisted men of the old Sixty-eighth as well as some from Salm's former command, the Eighth, and a rough mixture from several other units. The newly designated Sixty-eighth New York (Veteran) Infantry assembled at Nashville, where, on June 8, 1864, Salm was mustered into service as its colonel. With Maj. Gen. William T. Sherman's march on Atlanta in full swing, the Sixty-eighth moved to Bridgeport, Alabama, to protect Sherman's all-important rail communications between Nashville and Chattanooga. It was an unglamorous assignment shared by the thousands of troops who supported Sherman's main effort in Georgia.[29]

Salm's appointment angered the Sixty-eighth's veteran officers, who expected promotions as a reward for reenlisting. Instead, they got an unproven colonel who was also a cash-strapped prince. To make matters worse the commander brought with him several men to whom, one disgruntled officer charged, "he was under great obligations." Salm "could only reward them by commissions in the 68th," he added. Capt. Frederick Otto Von Fritsch, himself a German nobleman, suggested that Salm "would have been a perfect gentleman and a most charming companion if possessed of sufficient means, but situated as he was, he did many things which he would not have done had he been well off."[30]

After a brief rendezvous with the prince in Nashville that July, Agnes returned to Washington to await his call to join him in camp. The summons finally came, and in October 1864, she headed westward. She found his command stationed on a large, flood-prone island in the Tennessee River, near Bridgeport. If Salm stirred negative feelings in the regiment, the princess had the opposite effect. Captain Fritsch recalled his first meeting fondly: "She then shook hands with me and gave me one of the most charming, bewildering of smiles, with which she conquered all men, and I deeply regretted that she did not add an embrace and a kiss besides."[31]

Fritsch also offered a most insightful description of Agnes:

Besides her great beauty, the Princess was known for her remarkably free and easy manners, her determined ways and daring horsemanship, and of course other ladies considered her a mere adventuress; but in reality she was only a very shrewd woman, whose motto was the same as that of the Jesuits: "The end justifies the means." She was never vulgar, but blushed easily, and often showed that at heart she was a most respectable little woman. Naturally, she made use of her charms, and bestowed her favors on those who could promote her husband's interests. Proud and politely cold with ordinary men, she was seductive only with influential people and a few personal friends.[32]

As Bridgeport offered little opportunity to woo influential people, Agnes turned her energies to another passion—the care of sick and wounded soldiers. During her stay on the island and in nearby Bridgeport, she worked to improve conditions at local hospitals, often traveling to Nashville or Chattanooga to gather supplies. She did not nurse the men, nor did she, as was often reported, tend the wounded on the battlefield. Rather, she acted as benefactor, using her title and tenacity to acquire what others using normal channels failed to provide. It was the beginning of a new career for the American princess.[33]

The island posting was not without diversions. In one instance, Captain Fritsch conducted a "sham defense" of a blockhouse for invited guests to honor Agnes. Another time the Salm-Salms visited Lookout Mountain, the site of a great Union victory less than a year before. "After having feasted our eyes to our hearts' content," Agnes recalled, they shared an "exquisite breakfast . . . together with a good supply of champagne, which made us all very merry."[34]

In December the prince finally received a chance to participate in a major campaign when Maj. Gen. James Steedman detailed Salm to his staff. Steedman commanded the District of the Etowah in Maj. Gen. George H. Thomas's Department of the Cumberland, and Thomas ordered Steedman to gather portions of his far-flung command to help repel Confederate general John B. Hood's advance on Nashville. The Battle of Nashville became one of the most lopsided Union victories in the war. Salm's efforts drew Steedman's praise and earned him the command of a provisional brigade, which he led in pursuit of Hood's retreating army. Throughout the winter and into the following spring, Salm's unit harassed isolated rebel detachments and guerrilla bands in Tennessee, Alabama, and Georgia, fighting small engagements at places such as Elrod's Tanyard, Hog Jaw Valley, and Johnson's Crook. The prince led most of the raids in person and acquitted himself well in many minor actions.[35]

General Steedman had recommended Salm's promotion, but as winter passed, the prince remained a colonel. The matter became a cause unto itself. In February 1865, Agnes left for the East to secure for her husband his coveted brigadier's star. In Washington and Albany, she pulled every string she had—courting General Hooker, General Fry, Senator Harris, the newly elected Senator Yates, and the governors of New York, New Hampshire, and Massachusetts. But the War Department, bombarded by thousands of such requests, moved slowly. Finally, on April 13, Yates came through, and Salm at last received the brevet rank of brigadier general U.S. Volunteers—a largely honorary reward for his service in the Nashville campaign.

(More than thirteen hundred men received brevets to general officer but never attained the substantive rank.)[36]

The diminished nature of Salm's promotion failed to register on Agnes, who proudly wired the good news to *"General* Felix Salm" at Bridgeport. Reflecting on her valiant services to her husband, she wrote, "I procured for him the command of the 8th, and raised for him the 68th Regiment; now he had become a general through my exertions."[37] As incredible as it seems, such was the extent of her influence.

While still in Washington on the morning of April 15, Agnes learned of Lincoln's assassination. Over the next few days, she attended to various concerns and, never one to bypass an opportunity to make powerful friends, gained an audience with the new president, Andrew Johnson. In May, she headed westward to join her husband, now stationed at Dalton, Georgia. But even as the war wound down, things remained interesting for the princess.[38]

Agnes's sister Della, whose husband, Capt. Edmund Johnson, commanded a company in Salm's regiment, expected a second child in July. "I felt very envious," Agnes recalled, "for I had no child, which made me quite unhappy." Curiously, Della offered the new child to Agnes "should it be a boy." Good as her word, on giving birth Della presented to her sister a baby boy, whom Agnes named Felix. This arrangement, however, lasted only a short time.[39]

Also that July, Salm's brigade moved on to the ravaged city of Atlanta, where the prince assumed command. The hospitals there overflowed, and Agnes pitched in by "going now and then to Augusta, or even to Nashville, to fetch provisions," often riding on a locomotive's cowcatcher. From Atlanta, the Salms moved on to Savannah, where at Fort Pulaski, the prince and the Sixty-eighth were mustered out of service on November 30, 1865. An amazing war was over, but new, even more amazing events loomed.[40]

Prince Salm, ever looking for a war, defied U.S. policy by traveling to Mexico to join the forces of Emperor Maximilian even as Federal troops massed on the Rio Grande as a formidable warning to the French-supported regime to leave the region. Agnes followed. When the republican forces of President Benito Juárez captured the hapless monarch, Salm shared his fate. Agnes garnered international renown for her efforts to save the emperor from a Mexican firing squad, but though she failed in that, she did manage to gain her husband's release. From Mexico the prince and princess sailed for Europe, where Salm again entered the Prussian cavalry. Agnes intensified her interest in medical care, and she accompanied the Prussian army when it went to war against France in 1870. The unlikely career of Prince Salm-Salm came to an end at the Battle of Gravelotte that August when he fell in a hail of French bullets.[41]

Agnes worked tirelessly throughout the Franco-Prussian War on behalf of wounded soldiers. For her efforts, she was nominated for the prestigious Iron Cross, Germany's highest military honor but a decoration unfortunately reserved for men only. Later, she settled into a quiet existence at Karlsruhe, Germany, and wrote a lively account of her adventures, *Ten Years of My Life,* published in 1875.[42]

In 1899, she returned to the United States to present the flags of the Eighth and Sixty-eighth to their surviving veterans. A reception held in her honor in New York City attracted former generals Carl Schurz, Franz Sigel, and Julius Stahel. Also present were Agnes's sister Della, her husband, and their son, Felix Salm-Salm Johnson. On this occasion, a *New York Times* reporter described Agnes as "dressed in a black silk gown with a long train and a small black hat fringed with pink roses. There was a red ribbon over her shoulder, and on her breast were medals of gold which had been presented to her for bravery on the field of battle."[43] The princess died at her Karlsruhe home in December 1912.

Notes

1. *Dictionary of American Biography*, s.v. "Salm-Salm, Agnes"; *New York Times,* December 22, 1912; John Tyler Butts, ed., *A Gallant Captain of the Civil War: Being the Record of the Extraordinary Adventures of Frederick Otto Baron Von Fritsch Compiled from His War Record in Washington and His Private Papers* (New York: F. Tennyson Neely, 1902), 113; Princess Felix Salm-Salm, *Ten Years of My Life,* 2 vols. (London: Richard Bentley and Son, 1876), 1:4. There are conflicting reports of her date and place of birth; available evidence favors December 25, 1844, and Swanton, Vermont.

2. Salm-Salm, *Ten Years of My Life,* 1:5–7.

3. Ibid.; William L. Burton, *Melting Pot Soldiers: The Union's Ethnic Regiments* (Ames: Iowa State University Press, 1988), 86–87.

4. Shelby Foote, *The Civil War, A Narrative: Fort Sumter to Perryville* (New York: Random House, 1958), 272; Burton, *Melting Pot Soldiers,* 86–87, 169–71; Salm-Salm, *Ten Years of My Life,* 1:7–14.

5. Salm-Salm, *Ten Years of My Life,* 1:15–16.

6. Ibid., 16–17; Stewart Sifakis, *Who Was Who in the Union* (New York: Facts on File, 1988), 350.

7. Salm-Salm, *Ten Years of My Life,* 1:18–19; *Harper's Weekly,* May 9, 1863; U.S. War Department, *The War of the Rebellion: Official Records of the Union and Confederate Armies,* 128 vols. (Washington, DC: U.S. Government Printing Office, 1881–1901) (hereafter cited as *OR*), series 3, vol. 1, pp. 528–29.

8. Burton, *Melting Pot Soldiers,* 87.

9. Salm-Salm, *Ten Years of My Life,* 1:14, 19–20.

10. Foote, *The Civil War,* 272; Sifakis, *Who Was Who,* 37.

11. Salm-Salm, *Ten Years of My Life,* 1:23, 25.

12. Ibid., 20–22.

13. Ibid., 26–29.

14. Ibid., 30, 33–34; *OR,* series 1, vol. 21, p. 935.

15. Salm-Salm, *Ten Years of My Life,* 1:35–36.

16. Ibid., 36; Mark M. Boatner III, *The Civil War Dictionary,* rev. ed. (New York: Vintage Books, 1988), 573.

17. Salm-Salm, *Ten Years of My Life,* 1:36–38.

18. Ibid., 38–39.

19. Ibid., 39–40; Regis de Trobriand, *Four Years with the Army of the Potomac* (Boston: Ticknor and Co., 1889), 428; Charles S. Wainwright, *A Diary of Battle: The Personal Journals of Charles S. Wainwright,* ed. Allan Nevins (New York: Harcourt, Brace and World, 1962), 175.

20. Charles Francis Adams, *Charles Francis Adams, 1835–1915: An Autobiography* (New York: Russell and Russell, 1916), 161.

21. Julia Lorrilard Butterfield, ed., *A Biographical Memorial of General Daniel Butterfield Including Many Addresses and Military Writings* (New York: Grafton Press, 1904), 160–61.

22. W. A. Swanberg, *Sickles the Incredible* (New York: Charles Scribner's Sons, 1956), 175–76.

23. *OR,* series 1, vol. 51, pt. 1, pp. 998–99.

24. Salm-Salm, *Ten Years of My Life,* 1:49; Frank L. Byrne and Andrew T. Weaver, eds., *Haskell of Gettysburg: His Life and Civil War Papers* (Madison: State Historical Society of Wisconsin, 1970), 85, italics in original.

25. Salm-Salm, *Ten Years of My Life,* 1:53–60.

26. Ibid., 63–68.

27. Ibid., 69–70, 71–79.

28. Ibid., 80–84.

29. Frederick Phisterer, comp., *New York in the War of the Rebellion, 1861 to 1865,* 3d ed., 5 vols. (Albany, NY: D. B. Lyon Company, State Printers, 1912), 3:2673.

30. Butts, *A Gallant Captain,* 106, 111, 115–17.

31. Ibid., 112–13; Salm-Salm, *Ten Years of My Life,* 1:102–4, 111–12.

32. Butts, *A Gallant Captain,* 114.

33. Salm-Salm, *Ten Years of My Life,* 1:113–14.

34. Ibid., 122–25; Butts, *A Gallant Captain,* 118–19.

35. *OR,* series 1, vol. 45, pt. 1, pp. 58, 1126; *OR,* series 1, vol. 49, pt. 1, pp. 10–12, 33, 39.

36. Salm-Salm, *Ten Years of My Life,* 1:138, 142–45; Ezra J. Warner, *Generals in Blue: Lives of the Union Commanders* (Baton Rouge: Louisiana State University Press, 1964), 581–95. The brevet rank was so abused during the Civil War that it was later abolished.

37. Salm-Salm, *Ten Years of My Life,* 1:145–48, italics in original.

38. Ibid., 150–53.

39. Ibid., 154–55.

40. Ibid., 157, 162, 165; Phisterer, *New York in the War,* 3:2673.

41. Sifakis, *Who Was Who,* 350. See also Salm-Salm, *Ten Years of My Life,* vol. 2.

42. Salm-Salm, *Ten Years of My Life,* 2:237.

43. *New York Times,* April 5, 1899, May 15, 1899, December 22, 1912.

10

Lucy Virginia French
"Out of the Bitterness of My Heart"

Connie L. Lester

For some Americans of the Civil War era, the issues between North and South were simple and straightforward, but for others, they were complex and muddied. Most citizens of the upper South states fell into the latter group. Indeed, Tennesseeans were among the most conflicted of Americans in the Civil War generation, for the greater part of them valued both slavery *and* the Union. When forced by circumstances to choose between the two, a slim majority opted for slavery and secession and took the state out of the Union and into the Confederacy. Most, though by no means all, felt they owed loyalty to the state as it fought against the Union.

Moreover, Tennessee saw a disproportionately large share of the Civil War's fighting and still more of the disruption caused by the passing of armies. War was not a distant irrelevance to Tennesseeans; they lived in the midst of it. The story of Lucy Virginia French, an articulate woman of that era, has much to tell us about the conflicts facing Civil War Tennesseeans, as well as the way in which war hardens attitudes and embitters those who experience it, particularly if they must be more or less passive victims. French's story is presented by Connie L. Lester, an assistant professor of history at Middle Tennessee State University, Murfreesboro, Tennessee, and previously an associate editor of the *Tennessee Encyclopedia of History and Culture* (1998).

Through their actions during the emerging sectional crisis of the antebellum period, Tennesseans, like their neighbors in the other upper South states, expressed their belief that slavery and the rights of Southern slaveholders could best be protected within the Union and the constitutional framework. Even as the national parties dissolved over the issue of slavery, Tennessee voters continued to operate within a two-party framework, thinking that their differences could be resolved through the political process without destroying the government. In the election of 1860 Tennessee voters cast their ballots for the "national" candidates, Stephen A. Douglas and John Bell. Bell carried the state, and the combined votes for Douglas and Bell totaled more than 81,000, compared to the 65,000 garnered by John Breckinridge of the more extreme Southern wing of the Democratic Party.

In the days following the election, as the lower South states seceded from the Union and organized the Confederate States of America, most Tennesseans remained unpersuaded by the impassioned agitation for disunion. In January 1861 prosecessionist governor Isham G. Harris called an emergency session of the Tennessee General Assembly, in which he outlined the grievances suffered by the state as a result of "systematic, wanton, and long continued agitation of the slavery question."[1] He proposed a state convention, sanctioned by the state's electorate, to determine whether Tennessee should secede. On February 9, 1861, Tennesseans rejected a state convention by a vote of 69,000 to 57,000. Although the electorate seemed willing to await further developments, Harris nevertheless continued his pro-Confederate campaign and began preparations for a provisional army in anticipation of secession.

The firing on Fort Sumter and Lincoln's call for volunteers to put down the rebellion changed the minds of most Tennesseans and drew the state into the Confederacy. In a second referendum on June 8, 1861, voters demonstrated that they no longer expected protection in the Union, for they approved secession by a vote of 105,000 to 47,000. The vote also revealed significant divisions within the state. Voters in Middle Tennessee (25 percent slave) and West Tennessee (40 percent slave) overwhelmingly favored secession, with some counties even claiming unanimous support for disunion. But East Tennesseans (15 percent slave) again rejected the action and threatened to secede from the state. The quick deployment of pro-Southern troops by Governor Harris prevented the eastern counties from carrying out their threat, but that portion of the state remained strongly Unionist throughout the war.

Tennessee's Civil War and Reconstruction history mirrored the divisions so evident across the South at the time of secession. The last state to join the Confederacy, it became the first to reenter the Union. In the interim, more major battles were fought on Tennessee soil than in any other state except Virginia, and some of these contests—Shiloh, Stone's River, Chattanooga, Franklin, and Nashville—were among the bloodiest of the war. Tennessee also sent more soldiers (approximately 186,000) to the Confederate armies than any other Southern state. At the same time, however, it provided more Union troops than all the other Southern states combined (31,000 soldiers, a pro-Union militia of 15,000 whites and 4,000 African Americans, and another 7,000 men who left the state to enlist).

The statewide divisions also resonated through local communities and within Tennessee families. Most men of fighting age in Middle and West Tennessee marched away in gray, but a few in virtually every county joined the Union forces. After secession, Unionists in Middle and West Tennessee either retreated to their farms and plantations to await the outcome or joined their neighbors in support of Confederate nationalism. Once Union occupation came, a number of pro-Unionists (most notably William Bowen Campbell) reemerged to take positions in the military government of the state. Finally, some areas of the state that were not dominated by either army erupted in lawlessness as "bushwhackers" and thieves fought in their own self-interest. Thus, to understand the war in Tennessee, we must study the many people whose views fell between those of the radical supporters of either the Union or the Confederacy. For these men and women, support for either cause was tempered by their experiences with loss—loss of friendships, loss of economic stability and social order, loss of a sense of well-being and health, and, for many, the loss of life itself.

One such person was Lucy Virginia French. The diary she kept from January 1862 to August 1865 offers a thoughtful and articulate presentation of the ambivalence that accompanied secession and war and the rise of Southern nationalism, as well as a poignant chronicle of the breakdown of the ties that supported antebellum Southern life. The daughter of a wealthy Virginia family, French taught school in Memphis and achieved modest fame as a poet and writer before her 1853 marriage to Col. John Hopkins French of McMinnville, Tennessee. A wealthy breeder of fine horses, Colonel French was older than his wife and offered her a genteel future in Tennessee's antebellum society. Lucy French continued to write after the birth of her three children, a boy and two girls. In 1856, she published a book of poems, *Wind Whispers*, and a drama, *Iztalilxo*.

Throughout the war, French received visitors from the ranks of both armies who were anxious to meet the poet and author. Her residence, Forest Home, was located in Warren County on the eastern edge of Middle Tennessee and at the periphery of much of the fighting: She reported hearing the sounds of artillery during the Battles of Stone's River, Franklin, and Nashville. Although seemingly isolated, she remained well informed about military and political activities through her contacts with many of the major participants. She begged visitors and friends to send her accounts of their own experiences, hoping to incorporate this eyewitness information into a history of the war. French never published a historical account, but her war diary provides a vivid description of the effect of military and political decisions on community and family life. Her access to information, astute powers of observation, and literary skills enabled her to write a compelling account of the changes produced by war and offer insight into the sources of Southern nationalism that survived the war and Reconstruction as the mythology of the Lost Cause.

Lucy Virginia French did not support secession. Like many Tennesseeans, she and her husband steadfastly upheld Unionism during the turbulent weeks following the election of Abraham Lincoln. Her efforts went beyond personal support as she marshaled Southern and Northern women to sign a peace memorial that was read to the U.S. Senate by Stephen Douglas and printed in the *Nashville Patriot.* On New Year's Eve 1860, French and her family and friends celebrated the coming year with a "Union party," and she recorded the year's end "with 'Union' on heart and lip."[2]

Although French soon embraced Southern nationalism, she never entirely rejected her earlier patriotism and repeatedly referred to that 1860 Union party as a touchstone of devotion to the United States. She first acknowledged and explained her conversion to Southern nationalism during a confrontation with a Union soldier who had asserted that "the South had brought this army with its consequent troubles upon herself." French countered by briefly tracing Tennessee's road to secession and declared that the state's citizens loved the Union until driven into exile and rebellion, adding, "Now here you are with your armies to drive her back again."[3] Like many Southerners, her resistance grew with the presence of Federal troops.

Nevertheless, her earlier Union patriotism resurfaced on several occasions. In July 1862, following Nathan Bedford Forrest's successful raid on nearby Murfreesboro, French recorded her first sight of captured Federal soldiers. A long procession of wagons and prisoners passed before her gate throughout the day and into the night, filling her with joy over the Confederate success. She admitted, however, that she shed tears at the sight of the "stars and stripes a *captive banner.*" She confessed, "I felt badly to see it thus . . . it was the old flag I had loved so long."[4] She expressed her anger and bitterness at the "trouble this vile thing 'Secession' had brought upon us" and proclaimed, "I was sincere then [as a Unionist] and I am sincere still but oh how changed in sentiment." A proud Unionist initially, she was "glad I am not now,—though I am not a *secessionist* now nor ever will be."[5]

French's support for the Confederacy intensified as the result of personal encounters with Union soldiers rather than through her identification with secession and antebellum Southern radicalism. Initially, Union officers followed a policy of conciliation, hoping to produce a change of heart in the presumably misguided civilian population. The failure of that policy led to a more aggressive and less tolerant approach in which all Southern sympathizers were labeled "secesh." As part of the antebellum elite, French expected a degree of deference that Union soldiers were unwilling to give her. She was filled with resentment and bitterness by their lack of respect for her family, their property, and their obvious position in the community; the material losses that resulted from troop movements and confiscations or thefts; the arrest of friends; and her perception of American troops as "miserable wretches . . . brutal looking . . . so impertinent . . . and so insufferable in every way." At war's end, she declared, "I don't think I should be half so Southern if it were not for the stupid troops." She went on to explain that whenever she managed to achieve a feeling of goodwill toward the North, the sight of "these blue things" filled her with rebellion. "How I do hate them!" she wrote, "and how I want to let 'em know it to the full."[6] The transformation of French's loyalties followed the disintegration of communal, familial, and personal ties that called into question political authority, the efficacy of the law, and the limits of human morality.

Throughout the war, French maintained a strong sense of skepticism, if not cynicism, toward political and military leaders on both sides of the conflict. A political foe of the secessionist governor, Isham Harris, she condemned his flight to Memphis in anticipation of the February 1862 fall of Nashville as a disgrace, the result of his "inefficiency and cowardice." She also joined many others in criticizing Confederate general Braxton Bragg following the Battle of Murfreesboro in January 1863, repeating the views of her neighbors that Bragg had chosen a poor position. She blamed the Confederate loss on his failure to renew the fight the following day, a delay that allowed the Federal troops to reorganize. In the wake of Bragg's losses at Stone's River and his subsequent retreat, French believed, incorrectly, that the Army of Tennessee remained in the state only at the insistence of the soldiers themselves, who "swore to his face that they [would] not leave their homes to the invaders."[7] Such overt rebellion within the ranks boded ill for the army and the fortunes of the South. In French's view, it was an unsettling example of what she came to perceive as an unexpected consequence of war—the rise in the power of "the masses."

As the Army of Tennessee retreated from Stone's River and established winter quarters, French was offered a closer view of Confederate officers at numerous social events in her community. During the Christmas celebration in Murfreesboro the previous December, thirty-six-year-old Gen. John Hunt Morgan, the dashing cavalry commander, married seventeen-year-old Mattie Ready in a ceremony unexcelled for military pomp. In late January 1863 the newlyweds took up residence in McMinnville, and the women of the town attempted to make the couple feel welcome with dinners, balls, and benefit concerts, despite criticism by some who felt displays of gaiety were inappropriate during wartime.

French declared her disappointment with the results of the first event, a benefit concert for the Confederate wounded. On this occasion officers filled the house, but their determination that "everybody near them should know that they were Cols." and their loud talk about my regiment and my regiment and my regiment until they thought everybody near them should know of their *officership*" disgusted her. Squeezed "jam up" between the men, she was aware that they passed "coarse remarks upon the girls and wish[ed] the bore would stop and the ball commence so that they could get brandy." She soon became "sick with the fumes of their breath—disgusted with their conversation—and indignant at their ingratitude." The officers followed up their earlier rude behavior with an evening of flirting, displaying elegant manners designed to impress the very women they had mocked. Although French conceded that "it always hurts me to find people worse than I imagine them to be," she continued to expect an elegance of manners in Southern officers that the realities of war undermined.[8] In particular, she took exception to the heavy drinking she noted among both officers and their men.

French found Morgan's officers and men generally of suspect character. When Bragg sent reinforcements in early March, she described them as "rough looking troops" and believed they were intoxicated. Although she held Gen. Joseph Wheeler's cavalry in higher esteem, she admitted later that month that his staff was "very drunk" when they left to investigate Federal troop movements. In addition to drunkenness, Morgan was upbraided by both French and the *Chattanooga Rebel* for acts of arson, thefts, and unreasonable confiscations committed by his cavalry in the nearby Sequatchie Valley. As area farmers viewed the destruction the troops wrought, they declared they would be just as happy under Yankee occupation, a view French did not endorse.[9]

Lucy French held an even dimmer view of Northern leaders. Her criticisms of Yankee behavior revealed a distinct class consciousness not found in her judgments of Southern officers, as she routinely described the "plebian [sic]" activities and manners of Union officers and public officials. On several occasions Federal officers dined at the French home or stayed overnight—often at the insistence of the family, who viewed their official presence as a guarantee against theft and vandalism by enlisted men. French made no effort to hide her disdain for the officers whose attempts to "put on the courtesy and easy dignity of Southern gentlemen" fit them like "a stiff suit of new clothes to a 10 year old boy." She described one Union general and his wife as "people in the middle walks of life—clever enough in their way" but clearly inferior in class to General Morgan and his wife.[10]

French saved her most vitriolic comments for Andrew Johnson, the onetime tailor from east Tennessee who had served before the war as governor, congressman, and U.S. senator and who now, by virtue of Lincoln's appointment, was military governor of the state.

In the view of most Tennessee Confederates, the appointment of the East Tennessee Unionist unleashed a period of tyranny and gave him free rein to attack his political enemies among the state's "aristocracy." Johnson replaced elected Southern sympathizers with loyal Union appointees and controlled Nashville newspapers by closing opposing presses. French reported his well-known alcoholic excesses and gleefully expressed the view that Johnson "made an ass of himself."[11]

On Johnson's election to the vice presidency, she vented her hatred toward the "Tennessee Tailor." Calling Johnson's inaugural speech "the climax of absurdity and plebianism [*sic*]," she accused him of confirming nothing but his own low birth. She accepted his "shoddy" performance as appropriate to the people over whom he ruled. With the death of Lincoln and Johnson's elevation to the presidency, French accused him of carrying out his "leveling" war on the aristocrats with a vigor that threatened impoverishment. Although popular mythology supported her assessment of Federal control, recent scholarship suggests that Tennessee's upper class, though reduced in wealth, remained firmly in control of the political and economic future of the state.

If the war did not displace the antebellum power brokers, it did undermine the bonds of community and family. It took men away from their homes and families, leaving women to manage farms, plantations, slaves, and households. In this regard, French proved an exception, for "Darlin'" (her name for Colonel French) remained at home throughout the war. Although she rejoiced that he was too old for military service, she was often separated from the colonel by business and the circumstances of war. Thus, like other Southern women, French faced potentially dangerous situations alone or with only her minor children and her female household slaves for support, and she increasingly viewed herself as a planner and the mainstay of the family's future. Indeed, with her husband's blessing, she moved to Beersheba Springs in the spring of 1863 to be alone and work on her writing, hoping to sell a manuscript and replenish the family's diminishing fortune.

French's experience and that of other women across the South altered the social perceptions of gender in important ways. Although few of these women emerged from the war as suffragists, their actions in defense of home and in support of Southern nationalism gained the respect of Confederate men and even a grudging admiration from Union soldiers. In the postwar period these same women took a leading role in perpetuating the myth of the Lost Cause—a potent reminder of their own part in the war.

Female support for the war drew public attention almost immediately. Soon after the fall of Nashville in 1862, French added a clipping from the *Knoxville Register* to her diary. In it the paper's editor praised the "Spirit of the Ladies" of Nashville, who reportedly refused to renew acquaintances with old friends who had joined the Union army. The editor predicted such defiance would "nerve [men's] arms in the hour of battle" and bring victory to the Southern cause.[12]

Within months, French also stood defiantly against Union soldiers, initially attacking them for what she perceived as the invasion of an otherwise peaceable land. As the cost of war escalated, she planted herself in the doorway of her home to prevent marauding soldiers from entering to steal her possessions and vandalize her property, and on several occasions during particularly chaotic times, she stood guard with a loaded gun through the night. Like other Southerners, she buried the family's silver and other valuables, moved beloved pieces of furniture to the more secure homes of friends, and kept her jewelry in pouches sewn to the hoops of her skirts.

A year after clipping the editorial praising Nashville's women, however, French recorded a very different view of the city's females. She labeled the occupied capital a city "full of bad women" who lived in hotels and private homes pretending to be the wives of Union officers. In addition, she said, the town harbored "female spies and detectives" who reportedly entrapped honest Southern men by appealing to their charitable nature and rewarding their generosity with arrest for supporting the Southern cause.[13]

In French's view the most inexcusable example of the flaunting of public morality occurred in 1864 during her stay at Beersheba. One April afternoon the resort was visited by a mounted party of thirty Union soldiers accompanied by five McMinnville women. The unchaperoned group stayed ovenight and returned home by horseback the next day. "What in the name of common sense and common decency" could the mothers of the young women have thought? French wondered. She knew the women sensed the condemnation of their "improper" behavior, but no one dared criticize their conduct. French took further offense when the young ladies later paid a social call at Forest Home as if unaware of her disapproval. Fearing future retaliation, French again kept her silence.[14]

The breakdown of sexual mores paralleled a general fraying of community and familial ties. The tensions associated with life so near the major battlefields, the disruptions that accompanied massive troop movements and periodic skirmishes, the loss of material possessions, the inability to plan for the future, the overall decline in health, the separations from loved ones, and the deaths of friends and family combined to create a sense of hopelessness, exhaustion, and lethargy. Many found it difficult to carry out routine daily tasks, and petty annoyances and minor character flaws assumed greater importance under the stresses of war. Suspicion and jealousy increasingly controlled the actions of men and women of otherwise generous and caring natures.

French initially worried that the war would isolate her from newspapers, books, and correspondence with friends and family. In the early days of the war, she fretted over these inconveniences, but she soon found ways to route letters to both Northern and Southern friends—communicating by mail became much slower but was not impossible. Likewise, she obtained both Northern and Southern newspapers but despaired of reading the truth in either. She noted the early effects of the Federal blockade—"calicoes, domestics, linseys, etc. are at ruinous prices"—but cheerfully anticipated that her own family would "make out" until the blockade was lifted. French reported that life went on as usual and ended her entry with the assurance that "we are well and quite social and happy among ourselves."[15]

In time, however, her cheeriness gave way to the pressing concerns of life in a war zone. By the end of the conflict, she confessed to an "insurmountable weariness" and bitterness of the heart. Although she believed she had always "tried to do my duty," she said she had lost "until there is little now left to lose." She further confessed, "I do feel so much discouraged—so weary—so worn out with hoping and working, and all to no purpose." The events that brought French to such feelings of despair tore at every facet of Southern life.[16]

With the collapse of the Tennessee state government in February 1862, courts closed and county governments were suspended. Churches soon stopped holding regular services, and schools ended classes, leaving many children without access to education for extended periods. French, a former teacher, taught her children at home and kept up their religious education with Bible lessons and prayers. Yet even that proved impossible at times. In the fall of 1864, for example, French promised to "have the children commence with their lessons again," admitting "they have done no studying now for some time." Even when schools opened, as they did briefly during the Confederate occupation of McMinnville in 1863 and again after the war, parents worried about exposing the children to the presence of soldiers as they traveled to and from school.[17]

As the institutions of community life disintegrated, people became more cautious and watchful in their behavior and less confident of associations that had sustained them in the past. Soon after the war began, French observed that "there are informers among us who keep [the Federals] thoroughly posted." As a result, a "perfect reign of terror" had been imposed by the occupying army, and French feared that she might soon have to burn her journal to keep it from falling into the wrong hands and incriminating her. During such "feverish times," with the "community split to pieces," she concluded that "the best place for a quiet woman" was at home.[18]

The war also affected the health of men and women caught in the path of armies, for the stress of living near a battle zone and dealing with competing armies produced a weariness and a decline in overall well-being. In her diary, French recorded an endless succession of medical complaints as her health steadily worsened, and her chronic migraine headaches grew more intense until she found little relief even in repeated doses of laudanum and brandy. For days at a time, she was unable to leave her bed to write, teach her children, or supervise the household. Consultations with physicians produced the expected diagnosis—"nervous excitement" brought about by the war—but no prognosis for recovery.

The communicable diseases that accompanied the armies posed a more serious threat. Early in the war, French and her children received smallpox vaccinations as a deterrent to that dreaded disease, but in August 1863, she reported "a great deal of sickness in McM[innville]," where "scarlet fever" and "flu" had reached epidemic proportions. The presence of so much illness caused the town to "smell to Heaven" with a "nauseous scent" detectable for more than a mile outside the city limits. Not surprisingly the health of the family's slaves suffered to a greater degree, and two of the five slaves named in French's diary died during the course of the war.[19]

In addition to illness, French and her fellow Tennesseeans faced food shortages as armies foraged and confiscated meats and vegetables intended for home consumption. On more than one occasion, she wondered how her family would survive the winter: "Our place shows what it is to live near the track of an army," she wrote in 1862. "Fences, gates, etc. are no more, cornfields bare or trodden under foot—livestock, all or nearly all disappeared—gardens and flowers withered and gone." In addition to the pillaging and confiscations, lawless men of "neither or both armies" roamed the countryside, robbing and burning. Reports of house fires in nearby White and Van Buren Counties filled French with concern about the safety of her own home and family. But she stoically declared, "I should not be surprised at any time [to] have our house burned over our heads, and if it were to happen, I think I could bear it resolutely."[20]

The most shocking examples of lawlessness and the breakdown in social restraints occurred in Beersheba during the summer of 1863 as Union and Confederate armies moved toward Chattanooga, briefly leaving the area without any form of authority. The mountain gulphs around Beersheba and nearby Altamont provided sanctuary to bands of "lawless desperadoes"—men who used the cover of war to attack and rob their neighbors. The few males remaining in Beersheba slept with shotguns and revolvers close at hand, and the tiny community posted a guard to warn against attacks. The bands of outlaws had threatened John Armfield, the resort founder and owner of the hotel, and French reported periodic robberies on unoccupied outlying cottages. Generally the thieves helped themselves to blankets, bedding, china, and clothing but little of significant value. After expressing some concerns for her safety soon after her arrival, French declared that she slept through the nocturnal raids.

By mid-July, Bragg and the Army of Tennessee were in another "advance backward," and the mountains were full of deserters. To add to the concerns of the Beersheba residents, news of the fall of Vicksburg arrived on July 19, and soon afterward the men of the community, including Armfield and Colonel French, were called to McMinnville to take the oath of allegiance to the United States. French predicted that their community would be "abandoned to fate." Within a week, her prediction proved correct as Beersheba came under attack not by the renegades and desperadoes but by the poor mountaineers. The attackers focused on sacking the cottages and hotel, reminding French of the Reign of Terror and the mob of Paris. Although they never physically harmed the residents, "the masses had it all their own way on this memorable day—the aristocrats went down for nonce, and Democracy—Jacobinism—and Radicalism in the meanest form reigned triumphant!" The scene she described in detail bore a striking resemblance to other examples of class warfare.[21]

"Gaunt, ill-looking men and slatternly, rough barefooted women" hauled out furniture, matting, and carpets, French wrote of the scene, and "the women [were] as full of avaricious thirst as the ruffianly men." Successful plunderers sat on their piles of loot and glared defiance at all who approached their treasures; one old woman even *"crooned a hymn"* as she guarded her booty. A younger woman carried an armful of dresses from a cottage, dropped them at a fence corner, and tried them on with the help of an "overgrown boy." Another woman ran from the cottage of Episcopal bishop James Otey with her arms full of "very profound theological [books and] pamphlets of Church proceedings," declaring her intention to encourage her children to read.[22]

French's detailed description illustrates several characteristics of wartime Tennessee. For example, it reveals how areas under the control of neither army were at greater risk from the unlawful acts of deserters, renegades, and common thieves. The lack of institutional controls also exposed the class antagonisms that had long simmered between the wealthy "aristocrats" and the poorer subsistence farmers. French clearly interpreted the sacking of Beersheba in class terms and understood the ramifications of the event.

She saw the act as a repudiation of the paternalistic endeavors of Armfield, a man who had worked to "build up" the mountain people. She also recognized the "demoralizing effect" the event had on slaves who witnessed the thefts and revelry, and she worried "what its effect would be upon an army; if allowed to revel in the license which has marked the proceedings this day."[23]

The armies never succumbed to the loss of discipline that French feared, but their activities were more costly in terms of the destruction of material possessions. Bettie Ridley Blackmore told French that Fair Mont, the Stone's River home of a family friend, had been burned, and she asserted that within a four-week period in early 1863, "17 Gins and several dwelling houses had been burned by the Federals in a circle of seven miles." But though arson accounted for much of the destruction of the Tennessee countryside, confiscations also took a toll. By the end of the war, Colonel French had lost all his fine horses but one, a gray mare that remained at Beersheba. Most had been confiscated, but some younger ones had escaped, and they ran wild in the surrounding meadows and woods, useless to everyone. French reported that "all the horses and mules in the country have 'gone up'—scarcely a farmer that has one left." Such losses could not be easily recouped, and they compounded the difficulties of sustaining area families. In a period when human and animal muscle still provided the energy for most work, the loss of mules and horses, combined with the loss of shelter, left many Tennesseeans destitute.[24]

Arsonists spared Forest Home, but the house needed numerous repairs, and French quickly grew impatient with her husband "Col. Knock-around," who seemed more intent on daily excursions to town to learn the latest war news than providing for the comfort of his family. The colonel's lethargy brought an unusual outburst from French, reflecting the tensions that war placed on marriages. "I often wonder what men are made for!" she wrote. "To keep up the species I suppose—which is the only thing they are 'always ready' and never slow about doing! For my part I am quite wearied and worn out with their general no-accountability—and wish they were all put into the army, where they could kill each other off—the less of them the better!" Although she admitted that the accumulated bitterness of "years of hardship, privation, and sorrow" had provoked her outburst, she nevertheless continued to question her husband's willingness and ability to fulfill his role as protector and provider, believing him to have become a spinner of grand schemes rather than a doer of necessary work.[25]

Perhaps her doubts stemmed from her renewed correspondence with family members living in west Tennessee, for letters from her sister, Lide, depicted a life of travel and pleasure now lost to French.

Lide confided, with no apparent recognition of her sister's circumstances, that she and her husband had survived the war with their wealth intact. French attributed this good fortune to the Memphis couple's cotton speculation. She knew her brother-in-law, Henry French, was guilty of that illegal practice—and had even been arrested for it by the Confederates. Arrest did not end his speculative ventures, though, and he, too, ended the war with few losses. Beyond that, everyone at Beersheba had heard the story of Adelicia Acklen and her cotton deals. The determined widow of slave trader Isaac Franklin and subsequently the wife of Joseph Acklen, Adelicia had moved her cotton, with the help of both Confederate and Union soldiers, to New Orleans, where it had run the blockade; at the end of the war, Acklen was one of the wealthiest women in the South. Such examples of "success" moved French to "very bitter thoughts." She herself had been dutiful, but those who had been "mean and inconsistent, nay even wrong [were] successful in life."

By war's end, Lucy French was weary, hopeless, and desperate. Her despondency might have led her to reject Southern nationalism, but she, like many other Tennesseans, ultimately blamed the North for her difficulties. Certainly material losses and bitter experience with Union soldiers encouraged a continuing adherence to everything Southern. But French's diary offers a more compelling explanation for Southern nationalism and the Lost Cause ethic that succeeded it: a powerful sense of obligation to the soldiers who had fought and gained nothing and a belief that their sacrifice could only be validated through remembrance and public honor.[26]

French's diary contains several descriptions of the experiences of ordinary soldiers in the Army of Tennessee. Her most poignant entry centered on the Battle of Stone's River, perhaps the event that truly shaped her Southern nationalism. At daylight on December 31, 1862, French wrote, she first heard the sound of "very heavy cannonading" from the direction of Murfreesboro. Dozens of local men hurried to the site of the battle, some forty miles to the northwest, and "everything in the shape of a soldier went" as well. A "continuous roar of artillery" filled the morning hours, leaving French nervous and edgy, concerned for the outcome of the battle and the possibility that she and her family would need to flee to safe sanctuary farther south. In the afternoon the sounds of battle tapered off, and that night, word arrived of a Southern victory. French received the news gratefully but with an awareness that even as she celebrated, men were suffering and dying. She vowed to join other "noble Southern women" and "do everything in my power" for the wounded, some of whom would surely be brought to McMinnville. Having made her promise, French turned her attention to mundane household matters (specifically, the purchase of new furniture) before finally offering a brief reflection on the deaths of several acquaintances in earlier skirmishes and battles. On that New Year's Eve in 1862, French's worries seemed superficial and without personal connection to the conflict beyond a concern for her personal safety.[27]

On the following evening, she learned of the death of Capt. D. C. "Cap" Spurlock, a family friend. Hurrying to the home of his parents to offer condolences on the death of a second son (the first died at Perryville), French was filled with grief as she viewed the bloodied body of her friend. In the heat of the battle on the north side of the railroad near the Cowan house, Spurlock had been leading a charge when a bullet entered "just below his left nostril and passed through his head stopping just below the skin." The battle continued over his body throughout the afternoon, with his men returning under cover of darkness to retrieve the corpse. Earlier in the day, Spurlock had visited with his mother and father, who made the trip to Murfreesboro to bring him Christmas gifts. The distraught parents brought their son's body home in the very wagon that hours before had conveyed the Yuletide joy.[28]

French described a painful scene—the frantic mother, the "still silent agony of the aged father," and a young friend, Sophia Searcy, who "stood for hours beside the coffin, weeping." She wondered if Searcy remembered her earlier defiant words, when she had proclaimed, "Let the war come—we are ready." But then French questioned, "Were any of us ready to part with 'Cap'?"[29]

The distant sound of renewed cannonading accompanied the minister's prayers and the "voices tremulous with tears raised [in] hymns around the soldier's coffin. All the way to the graveyard—and while we laid him down to his last rest—and as we returned—it came rolling up from the northwest—a fitting requiem for the gallant dead." The earlier victory had turned to defeat, and French began to understand the true cost of war. For her, the retreat of the Army of Tennessee from its position on Stone's River called into question the value of Cap's sacrifice and demanded some form of validation.[30]

As the war ended and soldiers returned to their families, French reflected on the future of the South and the men who had fought the war. By 1865 their army was a poorly led body of hungry, ragged men, but, she believed "their constancy deserved a better fate." As she thought about those who died and "slept among strangers in unknown graves on dreary battlefields," she asked, "For what? Did God permit this war? Shall we ever find out why it was allowed?" Such questions emerged in private throughout the defeated South, but public discussions of the war reflected a different view, one that French expressed when she asserted, "We are just as proud of [the returning soldiers] as if they had been successful—for they deserved it!"[31]

After 1865, pride in the war records of friends and family became the validation for the sacrifices so many made, and sanctification of the Confederate experience was the mortar used to rebuild the white community into a semblance of harmony—with the aristocracy once more in control and the lower classes bound to them in a brotherhood of sacrifice and loss. Unfortunately for the future of the South, it was not a community built on joyful expectation but one that emerged, in French's words, "out of the bitterness of [the] heart."[32]

Notes

1. Robert H. White, ed., *Messages of the Governors of Tennessee, 1857–1869*, 12 vols. (Nashville: Tennessee Historical Commission, 1959), 5:355.

2. Diary of L. Virginia French, December 31, 1860, Tennessee State Library and Archives, Nashville, Tennessee.

3. Ibid., June 12, 1862.

4. Ibid., July 12, 1862.

5. Ibid., June 12, 1862, and January 19, 1863.

6. Ibid., August 20, 1862, and May 14, 1865.

7. Ibid., February 22, 1862, and January 11, 1863.

8. Ibid., February 8, 1863.

9. Ibid., March 10, March 22, and February 8, 1863; *Chattanooga Rebel*, January 31, 1863.

10. Diary of L. Virginia French, April 16 and September 20, 1863.

11. Ibid., September 14, 1862.

12. Ibid., April 2, 1862.

13. Ibid., January 13, 1863.

14. Ibid., April 17, 1863.

15. Ibid., January 5, 1862.

16. Ibid., August 20, 1865.

17. Ibid., September 25, 1864.

18. Ibid., June 29, 1862.

19. Ibid., August 16, 1863.

20. Ibid., September 3, 1862, and July 7, 1864.

21. Ibid., July 12, July 19, and July 26, 1863.

22. Ibid., July 26, 1863.

23. Ibid.

24. Sarah Ridley Trimble, ed., "Behind the Lines in Middle Tennessee, 1863–1865: The Journal of Bettie Ridley Blackmore," *Tennessee Historical Quarterly* 12 (March 1953): 49; Diary of L. Virginia French, November 6, 1864.

25. Diary of L. Virginia French, September 25, 1864.

26. Ibid., June 1, 1865.

27. Ibid., January 1, 1863.
28. Ibid., January 4, 1863.
29. Ibid.
30. Ibid.
31. Ibid., May 10 and May 14, 1865.
32. Ibid., August 20, 1865.

11

Charles Grandison Finney
"Our Horrid War"

Allen C. Guelzo

Religion as a facet of culture and society in the Civil War era has received less attention from scholars than many other topics. Yet religion was immensely important to Americans in the 1860s. Their diaries and letters are full of references to God, to what they thought His position was in the crisis, and to what they hoped He would do in response to it. The rival presidents, Lincoln and Davis, proclaimed national days of fasting and prayer at frequent intervals. As Lincoln once noted, their peoples prayed "to the same God," albeit with very different petitions.

For many Northern Christians, the war represented the culmination of years of agitation against slavery. Few voices had been louder in the long struggle than that of evangelist Charles G. Finney, whose story is presented by Allen C. Guelzo, Grace F. Kea Professor of American History at Eastern College, Saint Davids, Pennsylvania, and author of several books, including *Redeemer President: Abraham Lincoln and the Ideas of Americans* (forthcoming 2000). Finney's experience during the war reveals the difficulty as well as the desirability of charting and following a consistently moral course in times of unprecedented challenges.

When the American people entered into the long crisis of the Civil War, religious interest and allegiance had reached near-historic highs. Successive waves of a privately organized evangelical Protestant revival swept the American Republic from 1812 to 1828 and again in the 1850s. Between 1780 and 1860 the rate of growth of Protestant Christian congregations outpaced the growth rate of the population itself: Congregationalists expanded from 750 congregations in 1780 to 2,500 in 1860, Baptists mushroomed from 400 congregations to 12,150, and Methodists grew from 50 congregations to nearly 20,000.[1] Along with the rising numbers went an increasingly powerful cultural influence. What American Christianity lost in terms of governmental recognition in the new republic, it more than gained back by the hold it acquired—through teaching, metaphor, and a fund of quotations and illustrations—over the American people at large. "Never again in American history," wrote Alfred Kazin, "would there be so much honest, deeply felt invocation

153

of God's purpose" as there was on the eve of the Civil War; "never afterward would Americans North and South feel that they had been *living* Scripture."[2]

Few figures in this faith-encumbered landscape were more prominent in the minds of Americans than Charles Grandison Finney. In an era when the Protestant clergy formed America's intellectual class and popular preachers such as Henry Ward Beecher held immense urban congregations enthralled, Finney was still the most controversial of names and the most eloquent of all. Born in 1792 in Connecticut, he abandoned law to become an itinerant preacher among the scattered Presbyterian congregations of upstate New York, and he won national attention for a dramatic series of revivals that he managed in the new towns and settlements along the Erie Canal. He made his New York City debut as a preacher in 1829 and moved there in 1832 to become pastor of the Chatham Street Chapel and, in general, to become the point man for a coalition of righteous New York reformers. But Finney turned out to be less happy as a reformer than he had been as a preacher. In 1835, he accepted the invitation of the infant Oberlin Collegiate Institute in Oberlin, Ohio, to become its professor of theology, spending half the year in New York and the other half at Oberlin. By 1837, he gave up on New York completely and made Oberlin his base, where he became pastor of the Oberlin Congregational Church and later (in 1851) president of Oberlin College.

It was not that Finney lacked either the intelligence or the commitments of a reformer. If anything, he had embraced the most ethically demanding system of moral reform in America—the system of the New Divinity, which had been forged in the fires of America's first great wave of religious revival, the Great Awakening, in the 1740s by the disciples of the greatest New England philosopher and preacher, Jonathan Edwards. What Edwards and the "New Divinity Men" taught Finney and hundreds of his contemporaries in western New England (and the New England diaspora in upstate New York and the Western Reserve of Ohio) was the most ultra version of Puritan Calvinism—that every person was born with a set inclination toward sin, that escape from the slavery of sin was possible only by a gracious act of God, and that no efforts by sinners themselves to deal with sin had any hope of achieving deliverance apart from God's intervention.

This might not seem like a particularly hopeful set of doctrines to preach, much less to use as a basis for reform. But Edwards had given this inherited Calvinism an evangelical twist by insisting that although everyone might be born to sin, this did not mean that everyone was helpless in it. People might lack the *moral* ability to turn and convert themselves to God before God implemented His choice to turn and convert them, yet they still possessed the *natural* ability to repent. On the grounds of that natural ability, the doctrine held, sinners should not only be held personally accountable for their sins; they were also obligated to put forth the last extreme of that natural ability in order to repent and be converted. Preachers of the New Divinity thus found a mechanism for simultaneously preaching the absolute and unconditional sovereignty of God and the immediate obligation of the sinner to "create for himself a new heart."

Finney took up this message after a dramatic conversion experience of his own in October 1821. "What is perfection?" he asked. "It is to love the Lord our God with all our heart and soul and mind and strength," he answered, "and to love our neighbor as ourselves." To do this required God to move spiritually on one's heart, but it did not excuse the sinner from exerting a full natural ability to repent. "It is a simple matter of fact that you possess natural ability, or power, to be just as perfect as God requires," Finney preached, pushing Edwards's teachings on natural ability to their extreme.[3] "The mass of theologians regard moral depravity . . . as physical," as something the sinner cannot help, no matter what is willed, Finney said, but he argued that, in precisely the opposite terms, "he [the sinner] is able to do his duty, but he is unwilling."[4]

It was not that people did not know what they should do but that they lacked the desire to put that knowledge into action, he said, and the more religious knowledge they acquired, the more guilty they actually made themselves by refusing to act. "That dear little boy who comes from his Sabbath school knows all about the gospel," Finney explained. "He is almost ready to be converted, but not quite ready; yet that little boy, if he knows his duty and yet will not do it, is covered with more guilt than all the heathen world together."[5] As long as a sinner possessed natural ability, there was no excuse for failing to repent, completely and at once. "Sinner!" Finney addressed his listener, "Instead of waiting and praying for God to change your heart, you should at once summon up your powers, put forth the effort, and change the governing preference of your mind."[6] Perhaps such a sinner, lacking a God-given moral ability to match, might fall morally flat, but better that than not to try at all and thus be doubly condemned.

The best course of all was to convert and thereby receive divine forgiveness. And in that case, the only appropriate response was to plunge oneself as fully and unreservedly into the service of God as one had been plunged into the full exercise of natural ability. "All *things* [are] to be done for *his glory & kingdom*," Finney declared. "Whatever is not done *for him* & from *love to him* is *sin*."[7] Converts should aim at nothing less than "PERFECT HOLINESS." After all, he said, "obedience to God's commands implies an obedient state of the heart, and therefore nothing is obedience that does not imply a supreme regard to the authority of God." Or as his New Divinity models had put it, "All religion consists in disinterested benevolence."[8] The essence of sinfulness for Finney was "selfishness," since "the selfish heart is a preference of self-interest to the glory of God and the interests of his kingdom." The opposite of this utter preoccupation with oneself was the equally utter denial of oneself and "an *honest and disinterested* consecration of the whole being to the highest good of God and of the universe," even at the cost of one's self-satisfactions and desires.[9]

This confrontational and demanding message, delivered more in the style of a prosecuting attorney than a clergyman and accompanied by Finney's hypnotic ice-blue-eyed stare, shook hundreds of frontier New Yorkers out of their pews and onto their knees between 1824 and 1827. Invitations from groups of concerned laypeople began to pour in from Buffalo and Rochester and then from Boston, Philadelphia, Louisville, and Cincinnati, until finally the wealthy evangelical philanthropists Arthur and Lewis Tappan wooed Finney to New York City to become the pastor of the Chatham Street Chapel in 1832. There, surviving a bout with cholera, he found himself preaching in "the heart of the most irreligious population of New York . . . a place of resort highly discreditable to the city."[10] But he still managed to draw in hundreds of converts and then to begin training lay preachers, while also superintending a national weekly newspaper, the *New York Evangelist*. Increasingly he began to confront what he had only rarely encountered before going to New York—the social diseases of a major urban center in the first throes of mass industrialization. If service to God meant absolute disinterested benevolence, no true convert could rest while such evils were unreformed. "The promotion of public and private order and happiness," Finney insisted, "is one of the indispensable means of saving souls."[11]

Among those societal diseases was slavery. Although New York had technically abolished slavery early in the century, New York City was emerging as a major commercial entrepôt for the whole nation, and transit laws permitted merchants from the South to bring their slaves through the city without endangering their enslaved status. New York bankers provided the loans that supported the Southern plantation economy, and New York shippers traded slave-grown Southern cotton to Europe.

Slavery struck Finney almost automatically as an abomination; in fact, he recalled that "[by the time] I first went to New York I had made up my mind on the subject of the slavery question, and was exceedingly anxious to rouse public attention to the subject."[12] However, rousing such attention was precisely what all but a handful of American church organizations, most of whom had large and influential Southern constituencies, hoped to avoid, arguing that slavery was a political subject and that churches had no business mixing politics and religion. Finney disagreed strenuously. He contended that slavery was, at least symbolically, the absolute opposite of natural ability, since a slave had no natural ability to do anything freely, perhaps not even to pursue religious conversion. "To enslave a man is to treat a man as a thing—to set aside moral agency; and to treat a moral agent as a mere piece of property," he said.[13]

Slavery was also the utter opposite of the demand to exercise "disinterested benevolence" he noted, because slaveholding was nothing less than the theft of an individual's labor for the benefit and comfort of the slaveholder. "Revival in the United States will continue and prevail, no farther and faster than the church takes right ground upon this subject," Finney predicted, and in November 1834, he announced that he would refuse communion at the Chatham Street Chapel to known slaveholders. "In that vast congregation some slaveholders of professed piety were almost always present, and the rebuke was being solemnly felt," he recalled. "The example was exerting a decidedly good influence."[14]

Finney said that he "so often alluded to slavery and denounced it, that a considerable excitement came to exist among the people."[15] As far as his backers, the Tappan brothers, were concerned, the excitement was all to the good, since they and many of Finney's other backers were deeply committed to the new American Anti-Slavery Society (the local New-York Antislavery Society was actually formed at the Chatham Street Chapel). But the merchant classes in the city were not so enthused, and New York City workers saw Finney's opposition to slavery as a covert plan to bring cheap free-black labor into competition with them.

In 1835 Finney's sponsors began constructing a newer and larger church for him, the Broadway Tabernacle, where he was installed as pastor in April 1836. But the building was barely finished (the interior, in fact, was still unfurnished) when a story was set in circulation "that it was going to be an Amalgamation church, in which colored and white people were to be compelled to sit together, promiscuously mingled together all over the house." An arsonist set the tabernacle ablaze, and "the firemen were in such a state of mind that they refused to put it out, and left the interior and roof to be consumed." After this incident, Finney suffered a breakdown and left for "a voyage to sea."[16]

Far more significant were the trips Finney had begun taking to Ohio. In 1834 the student body at Lane Theological Seminary in Cincinnati was split by a debate over slavery, and the antislavery students left to become the core of a new school in the northern Ohio town of Oberlin. The Oberlin settlement had been founded in 1833 by a colony of antislavery New Englanders, and a small college was quickly organized; the Lane rebels greatly expanded the college's student body, and in an effort to improve the faculty, Oberlin's founder, John Jay Shipherd, recruited Finney to teach systematic theology as a visiting professor. Oberlin had much to recommend it to Finney. The civic atmosphere was almost a re-creation of the small New England towns he had known in his youth, and the college had committed itself both to opposing slavery and to admitting free blacks as students alongside whites. Finney had originally agreed to the visiting arrangement with the assumption that he would remain a New York City pastor for half the year. But the destruction of the tabernacle and the continuing resistance in the city to the rising antislavery movement disheartened him, and in April 1837, he resigned from the pastorate of the Broadway Tabernacle to take up full-time work at Oberlin. He could now practice revival and reform without fear.

From the first, Oberlin College enjoyed a reputation for evangelical progressivism, not to say radicalism. Not only were free blacks admitted on a par with white students but women students were also admitted to a "female department," sharing the college program and classrooms on an equal basis with male students for the first time in American higher education. The college curriculum, together with the town's Congregational church, stoked a revivalistic atmosphere of "wild ultraisms" and "indecent dogmatism" and, perhaps what was worst of all in the eyes of Oberlin's neighbors in Lorain County, "politico-religious teaching" on slavery.[17] Oberlin theological students who sought ordination in the mainline denominations "heard abusive epithets and ungenerous insinuations thrown out against our institution," and the town itself was denounced as "a 'nigger' town."[18] But Oberlin made no apology for its radicalism. The college happily sheltered runaway slaves from south of the Ohio River, and in 1858 a group of Oberlin faculty and students "rescued" John Price, a fugitive slave who had been arrested by hired slave catchers and taken to nearby Wellington for removal to the South. The Oberliners caught up with Price and his captors, freed Price from the Wellington hotel room where he had been imprisoned, and spirited him off to safety in Canada. Twenty of the rescuers were arrested and tried for violating the federal Fugitive Slave Law. But after a complicated trial, a compromise settlement was reached, and the "Oberlin rescue company" was returned home and enthusiastically greeted by fellow Oberliners.

Like many other nineteenth-century radicalisms, however, Oberlin's progressive patina overlaid a deep and often pessimistic conservatism. The fundamental contention behind the organizing of the original Oberlin colony was that "the church must be restored to gospel simplicity & devotion," not that it needed liberalization.[19] The town itself was based on a closed charter reminiscent of the town covenants of the Massachusetts Bay Colony, which required inhabitants to contribute to missionary causes, to give up "strong and unnecessary drinks" (which included not only alcohol but also tea and coffee), and to eschew "expensive and unwholesome fashions of dress, particularly tight dressing and ornamental attire."[20] There were no saloons, no theaters, and no smoking—even the small shops that sprang up along Oberlin's main street closed for Thursday prayer meetings.[21] In addition the women students whom Oberlin welcomed into coeducational classrooms found that their college degrees were really intended to make them more effective wives for Oberlin theological students, and when Antoinette Brown enrolled in the college's graduate theological studies program in 1847, she was not permitted to graduate.[22] "They hate . . . women's rights," wrote one surprised female student. "I was never in a place where women are so rigidly taught that they must not speak in public."[23] And while black students might study and live alongside whites in the college, the permanent black population of Oberlin was largely consigned to a segregated "Little Africa" and to manual-labor occupations.[24]

In large part Finney was attracted to Oberlin, and eventually made it his permanent base because he, too, spread a progressive surface over a strongly conservative core of attitudes. It was not only the race-baiting mobs in New York City that eventually convinced him to abandon the Broadway Tabernacle for the half-cleared woods of northern Ohio. It was also the whole commercial transformation of the city, which set off in Finney deep, nostalgic yearnings for the virtuous, rural, New England–style towns of his youth. "The whole course of business in this world is governed and regulated by the maxims of supreme and unmixed selfishness," he cried in dismay over the rapid incorporation of the American economy into the network of transatlantic capitalist markets. "The whole system recognizes only the love of self . . . to BUY AS CHEAP AS YOU CAN, AND SELL AS DEAR AS YOU CAN—TO LOOK OUT FOR NUMBER ONE."[25] He had hoped that he could sway "hundreds of businessmen" in New York, but it soon began to appear that "their heads & hearts [were] stuffed with everything but religion . . . confused & perplexed with the details & statistics of filthy lucre."[26] At one point in 1834, Finney was so downcast over his work in New York City that he even thought of quitting the ministry entirely and retiring to the quiet of an up-country New York farm.[27]

Oberlin offered him precisely the sort of compromise that allowed him to salvage his vocation and eventually experiment in re-creating the tightly knit communities he remembered before the

Erie Canal had transformed western New York into a highway of commerce. But in the process Finney's driving passion became the restoration of a virtuous past rather than the discovery of a progressive future. He railed against "the reading of light and trifling publications" such as "Byron, Scott and Shakespeare, and a host of triflers and blasphemers of God and despisers of the Holy Spirit," and even Oberlin's straitlaced students occasionally found him overbearing and intrusive.[28] Finney "had piercing eyes, seemingly with power to read one's inmost thoughts," one Oberlin alumnus recalled, and "his readiness to question the unconverted, added to this insight, would often lead such students to cross a road or go a roundabout way in order to escape meeting him."[29]

In his role as professor of theology at Oberlin and then as president of the college and pastor of the Congregational church, Finney gave no more encouragement to women's rights than his colleagues. When the antislavery, women's rights activist Abby Kelley Foster tried to arrange a lecture at Oberlin in 1846, Finney and the rest of the faculty blocked her appearance as "undesirable and unadvisable," and he accused Antoinette Brown of "atheism, or something very near it."[30] "All *unconverted abolitionists* are slaveholders in heart and so far as possible in life," he declared. "There is not one of them who would not enslave every slave at the South . . . and God himself as far as he could."[31]

Finney was more consistent, not to say public, in his denunciations of "the sinfulness of slavery & the duty of immediate emancipation" than his critics often suggest. He publicly attacked the Fugitive Slave Law in 1851, urging that "no one engage in the execution of the accursed law," and in 1856, he attended the National Kansas Committee's convention in Buffalo, New York, as an honorary representative of Kansas's beleaguered Free-Soil settlers.[32] But even there, he struggled to separate his labors as a revivalist from his opinions as an abolitionist. And at the Chatham Street Chapel, although he threatened to excommunicate slaveholders, he was determined not to "turn aside [and make abolition] a hobby, or divert the attention of the people from the work of converting souls."[33] He surprised his sponsor, Lewis Tappan, by canceling Tappan's plans to end racially segregated seating in the chapel in 1836, and he argued with Lewis's brother, Arthur, that racial prejudice, "a silly & often a wicked *prejudice*," was still not necessarily sinful. "A man may entirely from *constitutional taste* be unwilling to marry a colored women or have a daughter marry a colored man & yet be a devoted friend of the colored people."[34] (And of course he could do this because, by the canons of Edwardsean theology, sin was a matter of *natural* ability, and as long as one did not actually act on one's *moral* perversions, there was no sin.)

Finney might play host to antislavery societies in both New York and Ohio and he might denounce slavery as "this great abomination,"[35] but he firmly believed that preaching conversion came first, and he stubbornly refused to subordinate the one to the other. To Theodore Dwight Weld, he explained that slavery could be abolished in two years if "the publick [*sic*] mind can be engrossed with the subject of salvation and make abolition an appendage."[36] Nothing, he told Arthur Tappan, should be allowed to usurp the pride of place given to the preaching of conversion: "Introduce Baptism, Election, or any other doctrine that does not bear on the question of immediate acceptance of Christ & you either kill or retard the work."[37] In fact, Finney would frequently remove himself from Oberlin whenever it seemed that abolition might be obscuring revival. At the height of the fracas over the Oberlin "rescue" in 1858, for example, he left for New York and sailed off on a two-year mission to England, and he never made any reference to the rescue in his memoirs.

Many of the more radical abolitionists, such as William Lloyd Garrison, read this behavior as lukewarmness on Finney's part, and they warned their friends "against contributing to the support of the Oberlin Collegiate Institute."[38] But Finney's record on slavery was actually far superior to that of most American clergymen and churches in the 1850s. Charles Hodge of Princeton Seminary, the greatest of the Presbyterian Church's theologians, believed that Christianity so plainly taught "that slaveholding is not in itself a crime, that it is a mere waste of time to attempt to prove it"; therefore, he said, "it is plain that the church has no responsibility and no right to interfere with respect to the slave laws of the South."[39] New England Baptist theologian and Brown University president Francis Wayland was more troubled than Hodge by the immorality of slaveholding, but as long as slavery was legal under the Constitution, he was convinced that "as citizens of the United States, we have no power whatever either to abolish slavery in the Southern States; or to do any thing, of which the *direct intention* is to abolish it."[40] Southern ministers such as James Henley Thornwell, Frederick A. Ross, and Benjamin Palmer were actually persuaded that slavery was good for the slaves. And rather than tolerate criticism of slavery, Southern Methodists and Southern Baptists split their denominations in half in the 1840s. In that context, the marvel was that Finney remained as radical as he was.

The arrival of the Civil War, in his sixty-ninth year, left Finney freer than he had ever been to combine the politics of abolition with the preaching of conversion, since slavery now threatened the very life of the American Republic. But he was as suspicious of Lincoln's antislavery credentials as the radical abolitionists had been of his own: "His ground on the score of humanity towards the oppressed race was too low," reported Finney's newspaper, *The Oberlin Evangelist,* shortly after Lincoln's nomination in 1860. "It did him no honor."[41] (Finney was so consistently critical of Lincoln that one of the women students' societies adopted the resolution "that Pres. Lincoln is not so bad a man as Pres. Finney thinks he is".)[42] Finney was nonetheless gratified to see the secession crisis trigger waves of repentance and conversion among the Oberlin students. "The whole town seems moved at the presence of God and such a breaking down and humbling of the church I have never seen in Oberlin," wrote Finney's wife, Elizabeth Atkinson Finney, at the end of December 1860. "The country seems in great commotion just now, but we trust our God has commanded the work of restraining our slaveholders and that he will subdue them and let the captives go free."[43]

Even as she wrote, South Carolina was announcing its secession from the Union, which was soon followed by the formation of a new Southern slaveholding Confederacy and the attack on Fort Sumter in Charleston harbor. Within a week of the surrender of Sumter, forty-eight Oberlin students volunteered to form the town's first military company, and off they went to the war to become Company C of the Seventh Ohio Volunteers. Jacob Dolson Cox, Finney's son-in-law and once an Oberlin theological student, was commissioned as a brigadier general and served throughout the war, eventually marching with Sherman through Georgia. Another Oberlin company was enlisted in the fall of 1861 as Company H of the Forty-first Ohio Volunteers, and a scattering of other Oberlin students joined the Eighty-seventh Ohio, the 103rd Ohio, the 150th Ohio, and the Second Ohio Cavalry. Several of Oberlin's black students and alumni, led by John Mercer Langston (the uncle of the poet Langston Hughes), joined the first Northern black regiment, the Fifty-fourth Massachusetts. All told, approximately 800 Oberliners served in the Union army during the war.[44]

For his part, Finney turned his classroom in the college and his pulpit in the Congregational Church into a drum ecclesiastic. He was impatient with Lincoln's determination, through the first year of the war, to limit the conflict merely to the restoration of the union rather than the conquest of the South and the abolition of slavery. "Watch and pray," he told the college early in 1862. "Our *nation* does not yet repent . . . our *rulers* do not *fear* God [and] the *national* interpretation of our *Constitution commits* the *nation* to *injustice.*"[45] To a friend in England, Finney confided, "We are afraid that *secretly* the *government* (not the people) of France & England wish to see our Republick [*sic*] broken up & that they will take advantage of this great rebellion to try to secure our overthrow."[46] But Finney remained sure that, inevitably, "God has . . . turned all their selfishness triumphantly against them & worked on to bring about emancipation."[47] Beyond that, his principal concern was that Lincoln would prove to be the most significant stumbling block in the path to emancipation. In July 1862, Finney sponsored a mass meeting in the college chapel, which formally petitioned Lincoln "to proclaim universal emancipation, and to enforce the same to the full extent of his executive ability." He also joined with other Radical Republicans in demanding "a more radical man" than Lincoln "to finish up this war."[48]

Even when Lincoln finally issued the Emancipation Proclamation and shifted the course of the war toward the abolition of slavery, Finney remained implacable. "*Christianity* is *radically reformatory*," he reminded Oberlin in 1863. "Christ has undertaken the work of *counter-revolution* . . . to *create all things new* in the *moral order* of *things*."[49] His response to Lincoln's call for a national thanksgiving day in November 1863 was to warn that there was as yet little for which to give thanks. "Let us not deceive ourselves & *rejoice* in our boastings," Finney insisted. "The *north* are not *yet just*. . . . The south *must be reformed* or annihilated. . . . The colored man is still *denied* his *equal rights*" and "is *most intensely hated & persecuted* by a *majority*." Simply put, he said, "in no *publick* [sic] *proclamation either* north or *south* is *our great national sin recognized*."[50]

In the end, Oberlin voted for Lincoln again in 1864. But at the conclusion of the war in April 1865 and after Lincoln's assassination on Good Friday, April 14, Finney was as unreconciled to the president as ever. On Easter Sunday, he preached in both the morning and the afternoon, calling down judgment on the South but also explaining that God's purpose in Lincoln's death was deliberate. "The President was an amiable man, tender, kind-hearted, but perhaps he stood in God's way of dealing with the Rebels just as thy ought to be dealt with for the good of the nation and for the good of humanity."[51] As he explained in June to a friend in England, "When the mission of Pres. Lincoln was fulfilled, God suffered him to be removed by an agency that put the finishing stroke to the last hope of compromise with the Slave Oligarchy. Mr. Lincoln was a man so intensely kind . . . that he might have been induced to leave the power of the great slaveholders unsmitten by too lenient an exercise of the pardoning power."[52]

For all of his radical virulence toward Lincoln about what the president had not done, Finney himself had accomplished comparatively little outside the safe environs of Oberlin. In fact, the approach of the Civil War (and the involvement of three Oberlin students in John Brown's raid in October 1859) sent Finney abroad on yet another of his mysteriously timed missions to England; only the word that his congregation was restlessly contemplating a division and the formation of a second Congregational church in Oberlin finally drew him back before the end of 1860. "Had it not been for this pressure, we should have remained longer in England," Finney candidly acknowledged.[53] Moreover, his memoirs (composed in 1868) contain copious details of revivals and conversions in Oberlin during the war but nary a word of the war itself. And as richly as he criticized Lincoln, he was horrified when the new president, Andrew Johnson (who was supposedly more radical in temperament), began issuing precisely the compromises and pardons Finney had expected from Lincoln. Oberlin professor James Morgan remembered hearing Finney pray aloud during one service: "And now, oh Lord," he intoned, "we pray Thee for Andrew Johnson. Wilt thou show him that he is only a man, and after all a very poor specimen of a man. But if he persists in misapprehending himself, then wilt thou *put him to bed*. Put a hook in his nose and keep him from doing this mischief."[54]

Rather than join in the Radical Republican crusade to impeach and convict Johnson and impose a severe reconstruction upon the South, Finney withdrew into a mysterious silence. "Our horrid war is over," he wrote in June 1865. "Slavery, its cause, is abolished & things are settling we trust into a desirable shape."[55] But, in fact, they were not. Reconstruction failed to reorganize the South as a repentant convert to Northern principles or to place the newly freed slaves in a secure position of political and economic equality. Instead, the victorious North gradually wearied of the effort required to occupy and rebuild the South in its own image, and with the onset of an economic depression in 1873 and the flaccid presidency of Ulysses Grant, the nation turned away from the consequences of slavery and toward a sentimental orgy of sectional reconciliation.[56] Soldiers returned from the horrors of war with less confidence in an overruling and purposeful God, and their confidence was further undermined by the impact of Charles Darwin's work (*Origin of Species,* published in 1859, had received little attention at first in the United States because of the war's distractions).[57] America's self-definition was increasingly based not on religion but on the material advancement made possible by new industrial technologies.[58] Having reached its apogee of cultural power on the eve of the Civil War, American religion in the postwar years seemed diminished rather than strengthened, as though the promise that disinterested benevolence would surely be the reward for all the suffering had simply not come true and could no longer be believed with the old certitude.

Finney stepped down as the president of Oberlin College in 1866 and as the pastor of what had become the First Congregational Church in 1872. In his last years, he did not focus on denouncing Johnson's betrayal of the sacrifices of disinterested benevolence at Shiloh, Antietam, and Gettysburg; instead he battled the shadowy evils of freemasonry. This campaign had consumed upstate New

Yorkers in the 1830s, and Finney returned to it in the 1870s partly as a substitute for the failure of religious influence in the Gilded Age and partly as one last attempt to recapture the taste of his youthful idealism. He died in 1875, suspicious at the end that even Oberlin would betray his unremitting commitment to the perfection of the will. In fact, it did: By 1910, Oberlin had swerved away from Finney's rigorous evangelicalism and moved toward a genteel and fashionable religious liberalism. The student body gradually began segregating itself in the 1880s, and not until the late 1940s did the college hire its first black faculty member. Even today, the white and black communities in Oberlin lead largely separate lives, and bigotry lurks surprisingly close beneath a more modern patina of racial harmony.

In his day, Finney embodied much of what revived American religion in the young decades of the Republic—its fierce dedication to righteousness and justice, its unrelenting self-honesty and self-abasement before God, and its never-hesitating willingness to risk all in the immediate service of God's truth. He also represented its limitations—its unrealistic expectations, its moralistic poses, and its exaggerated promises, begging for a fall. His moves from rural New York to urban New York City and then to rural Ohio track, in an eerily convenient way, the movement of American religion. From a confined private sphere, religion moved to a public place where it promised to become the principal means of molding culture in the Republic; then, in the face of challenges, it retreated back to the private sphere.

For the brief time that Protestant evangelicalism seized a public initiative, however, its role was vital in the coming of the Civil War. And even from its rural isolation, Finney's Oberlin still aspired to reform a world gone astray. "It was at Oberlin," recalled two of the college's alumni at the school's fiftieth anniversary in 1883, "that the great army of anti-slavery workers, preachers, teachers and lecturers went forth to work; it was from Oberlin that nearly one-half of the adult population marched off, when the war began to fight the rebellion. And these non-tobacco-chewing, non-whiskey-drinking, non-swearing, praying, howling, ranting 'religious fanatics,' made good soldiers, and withheld not their blood and their lives to free the Union."[59] At their head, in spirit if not in person, was Charles Grandison Finney, marching as to war.

Notes

1. Jon Butler, *Awash in a Sea of Faith: Christianizing the American People* (Cambridge, MA, 1990), 270.

2. Alfred Kazin, *God and the American Writer* (New York, 1997), 127, 132.

3. Charles Grandison Finney, *Lectures to Professing Christians, Delivered in the City of New York in the Years 1836 and 1837* (New York, 1837), 255–56.

4. Charles Grandison Finney, "Evidences of Regeneration," in Teaching Notes, Charles Grandison Finney Papers, Oberlin College Archives, Oberlin, Ohio (hereafter cited as Finney Papers).

5. Charles Grandison Finney, *Lectures on Systematic Theology*, 2 vols. (Oberlin, OH, 1846), 1:362.

6. Charles Grandison Finney, "Sinners Bound to Change Their Own Hearts," in his *Sermons on Important Subjects* (New York, 1836), 32.

7. Charles Grandison Finney, Sermon outline, 1869, in Finney Papers.

8. Charles Grandison Finney, *Lectures to Professing Christians*, 58, 84, 117.

9. Finney, "Sinners Bound to Change Their Own Hearts," 8–10, and *Lectures on Systematic Theology*, 1:260.

10. Charles Grandison Finney, *The Memoirs of Charles G. Finney: The Complete Restored Text*, ed. G. M. Rosell and R. A. G. Dupuis (Grand Rapids, MI, 1989), 354.

11. Finney, *Lectures on Systematic Theology*, 1:430, 433.

12. Finney, *Memoirs*, 362.

13. Charles Grandison Finney, "The Sinner's Natural Power and Moral Weakness," *Oberlin Evangelist*, August 13, 1856, 129.

14. Charles Grandison Finney, *The Oberlin Evangelist*, August 18, 1852, 130–31.

15. Finney, *Memoirs*, 363.

16. Ibid., 371.

17. Nat Brandt, *The Town That Started the Civil War* (New York, 1991), 47.

18. "Scraps from Letters of a Student Now Deceased, to a Classmate," in *The Oberlin Evangelist*, January 1, 1845, 5; Edward H. Fairchild, *Historical Sketch of Oberlin College* (Springfield, IL, 1868), 9.

19. Robert Samuel Fletcher, *A History of Oberlin College from Its Foundation through the Civil War* (Oberlin, OH, 1943), 89.

20. James Harris Fairchild, *Oberlin: Its Origin, Progress and Results* (Oberlin, OH, 1871), 4–5.

21. Brandt, *The Town That Started the Civil War,* 27.

22. Charles Hambrick-Stowe, *Charles G. Finney and the Spirit of American Evangelicalism* (Grand Rapids, MI, 1996), 270.

23. Fletcher, *A History of Oberlin College,* 290–92.

24. Brandt, *The Town That Started the Civil War,* 46.

25. Finney, *Lectures to Professing Christians,* 95.

26. Asa Mahan to Finney, February 26, 1832, in Finney Papers.

27. Hambrick-Stowe, *Charles G. Finney,* 148.

28. Charles Grandison Finney, "Grieving the Holy Spirit," in *The Oberlin Evangelist,* December 4, 1839, 193.

29. A. L. Shumway and C. DeW. Brower, *Oberliniana: A Jubilee Volume of Semi-Historical Anecdotes* (Cleveland, OH, 1883), 73.

30. Fletcher, *A History of Oberlin College,* 267–68.

31. Finney, *Lectures on Systematic Theology,* 1:321.

32. James David Essig, "The Lord's Free Man: Charles G. Finney and His Abolitionism," in *Civil War History* 24 (March 1978): 25–45.

33. Finney, *Memoirs,* 362–63.

34. Finney to Arthur Tappan, April 30, 1836, in Finney Papers.

35. Charles Grandison Finney, *Lectures on Revivals of Religion,* ed. W. L. McLoughlin (Cambridge, MA, 1960), 302.

36. Finney to Weld, in *Letters of Theodore Dwight Weld, Angelina Grimke, and Sarah Grimke,* ed. G. H. Barnes and D. L. Dumond, 2 vols. (New York, 1934), 1:319.

37. Finney to Arthur Tappan, April 30, 1836, in Finney Papers.

38. Fletcher, *A History of Oberlin College,* 266.

39. Charles Hodge, "Slavery," *The Biblical Repertory and Princeton Review (BRPR)* (April 1836):292, and "Abolitionism," *BRPR* (October 1844): 580–81.

40. Francis Wayland, *The Limitations of Human Responsibility* (New York, 1838), 169.

41. "The Republican Convention at Chicago," in *The Oberlin Evangelist,* May 23, 1860, 83.

42. Fletcher, *A History of Oberlin College,* 879.

43. E. A. Finney to C. G. Barlow, December 22, 1860, Finney Papers.

44. Fletcher, *A History of Oberlin College,* 876.

45. Charles Grandison Finney, Sermon outline, 1862, in Finney Papers.

46. Finney to Alice Barlow, January 8, 1862, in Finney Papers.

47. Finney to Alice Barlow, February 13, 1863, in Finney Papers.

48. Fletcher, *A History of Oberlin College,* 78–79.

49. Charles Grandison Finney, Sermon outline, 1863, in Finney Papers.

50. Ibid.

51. Fletcher, *A History of Oberlin College,* 83.

52. Finney to Alice Barlow, June 22, 1865, in Finney Papers.

53. Finney, *Memoirs,* 15.

54. Shumway and Brower, *Oberliniana,* 81.

55. Finney to C. G. Barlow, June 22, 1865, in Finney Papers.

56. James H. Moorhead, *American Apocalypse: Yankee Protestants and the Civil War, 1860–1869* (New Haven, CT, 1978), 236–44.

57. Paul A. Carter, *The Spiritual Crisis of the Gilded Age* (DeKalb, IL, 1971), 65–83.

58. Anne C. Rose, *Victorian America and the Civil War* (Cambridge, MA, 1992), 68.

59. Shumway and Brower, *Oberliniana,* 156.

12

John Sherman
Republican Senator

Roger D. Bridges

John Sherman was one of the most important Northern politicians of the Civil War and Reconstruction era. Not only a prominent U.S. senator from Ohio, he was also the brother of William Tecumseh Sherman, the highly regarded field commander. In this chapter, Roger Bridges, director of the Rutherford B. Hayes President Center in Fremont, Ohio, and coeditor of *Illinois: Its History and Legacy* (1984), recounts John Sherman's Civil War experiences, from his election to the Senate in 1861 until the assassination of Lincoln. He emphasizes Sherman's steadfast dedication to the old Hamiltonian Federalist-Whig principles of government activism and centralized power. Sherman equated the strength of the nation with the power of the central government. He believed that secession's greatest evil was its threat to that power, and in response he strove to increase the government's power to previously unknown levels.

W ill you be kind enough to Communicate in the proper way this my resignation as a member of the House of Representatives of the 37th Congress for the 15th Cong. Dist of Ohio?"[1] Nothing in this brief note from Ohio's newly elected U.S. senator John Sherman suggested either the gravity of the times or his bitter struggle, just concluded, to secure the seat recently vacated by President Abraham Lincoln's selection of Salmon P. Chase as secretary of the treasury. Chase's resignation from the Senate touched off a lengthy and sometimes acrimonious contest for the vacant seat in the midst of the nation's most severe crisis, the Civil War. Maneuvering for the position had begun long before Chase's resignation. As early as January 15, 1861, a young Ohio legislator, James A. Garfield, wrote: "If Mr. Chase goes into the Cabinet—as he probably will—we shall have another exciting contest of election of a Senator. Dennison, Sherman, Corwin, & Schenck will be prominent candidates probably."[2]

Sherman's quest for the Senate seat was extremely difficult. Lacking a sense of humor, he appeared cold and aloof to all but his most intimate associates. Moreover, Republican legislators from southern Ohio wanted a senator from that section of the state. But the most serious objection related to Sherman's role in the second session of the Thirty-sixth Congress, where the Ohioan had supported the compromise proposals of Thomas Corwin.

When the contest dragged on into mid-March, Sherman traveled from Washington to Columbus and took personal command of the struggle. Meanwhile, as the *New York Times* reported, "strong influence [was] at work in Washington for him." Sherman had asked Secretary of State William H. Seward to defer making some foreign appointments, for "two gentlemen who will be strongly pressed for these places are now working for my promotion at Columbus," and Seward promptly forwarded the note to Lincoln. Other influences were at work, as well. Two of his leading supporters turned to noted financier Jay Cooke for the funds necessary to cover Sherman's travel expenses and the banquets at which influential legislators were entertained.[3]

Sherman and his friends were successful, for on the seventy-ninth ballot the Republican caucus nominated him for the Senate. The Republican-controlled legislature followed by selecting him, and on March 23, 1861, he was sworn in as Chase's successor.

The new Ohio senator was already a seasoned politician and a recognized leader of the Republican Party although he was not quite thirty-eight years of age. He was still in the early stages of a long public career that would eventually include six years as a congressman, thirty-two years as a senator, four years as secretary of the treasury, and one year as secretary of state at the end of his career. The son of an Ohio Supreme Court justice who died when he was only six, John trained for the law by reading in the office of his oldest brother, Charles T. Sherman.

The new senator first entered public office when he was elected to Congress from a traditionally Democratic district as an anti-Nebraska Whig in 1854. In 1855 the young Ohioan took an active part in the organization of the Ohio Republican Party and presided over its first state convention. During his first congressional term, he was selected as one of a three-member House committee to investigate the difficulties in Kansas. The well-written majority report, composed primarily by Sherman, brought him additional recognition in the nation's capital. By 1859 the Ohio congressman was accounted a leader of the young Republican Party, and he became its nominee for Speaker of the House. After one of the most protracted and bitter contests in House history, Sherman finally withdrew his name from consideration for that post. His candidacy had foundered on his endorsement of a plea for funds to help distribute Hinton Helper's antislavery book, *The Impending Crisis of the South*. In return for bowing out, Sherman was named chairman of the powerful House Ways and Means Committee.

The new senator owed his electoral success in large part to the positions he had taken in the final session of the Thirty-sixth Congress. The Republican Party as a whole and Ohio's Republican legislators as well had been deeply divided over how to deal with the threatened Southern secession. Sherman supported measures that could be construed as upholding the essential positions of the Republican Party while also supporting insubstantial concessions to Southern pride.

Shortly after the 1860 election, John had written his brother, William Tecumseh Sherman, denying that the Republican Party would interfere with slavery in the states. Once passions raised by the election cooled, he said, Southerners would realize they had nothing to fear from the Republicans. But he feared anarchy if Southern hotheads rushed their states into secession: "If, by a successful revolution, they can go out of the Union, they establish a principle that will break the government into fragments. Some local disaffection or temporary excitement will lead one state after another out of the Union. We shall have the Mexican Republic over again. . . . Secession is Revolution. They seem bent upon attempting it. If so, then comes civil war, fearful subject for Americans to think of." The Ohioan insisted that the Southern states must submit willingly to Republican rule or be forced to acquiesce, for he intended to "insist on preserving the unity of the States, and all the States without exception and without regard to consequences."[4]

Although he harbored little hope, Sherman participated actively in Congress's various Union-saving schemes—to no avail. All that was agreed on was to submit a constitutional amendment forbidding Congress to interfere with slavery in the states where it was legally established. John hoped the border states would not join the states of the Deep South in the crime of secession. His willingness to compromise, however, was limited to an extension of the Missouri Compromise line and a promise not to interfere in intrastate slavery. Even this willingness was more apparent than real, though, for he believed slavery had reached its natural boundaries within the continental United States and that new states would be free. He was ready to guarantee noninterference with slavery in the states where it existed by law because he believed it was beyond the constitutional reach of the national government. Still, he recognized that war was a distinct possibility.

In retrospect, Sherman considered the interval between Lincoln's inauguration and the opening of armed conflict "the darkest one in the history of the United States." The new administration appeared indecisive while the South was rapidly organizing its national government and preparing to assert its independence by force of arms. The attack on Fort Sumter (April 12, 1861) snapped the nation out of its paralyzing lethargy and divisiveness. Citizens and leaders of the Northern states demanded that secession be put down.[5]

Sherman believed that abstract questions on the nature of the Union and the right of the Federal government to preserve itself would now be tested on the field of battle. This testing did not, however, prevent prolonged and bitter discussion in Congress, in the press, in the pulpit, and elsewhere. The results of the war would determine whether the Union was supreme and indestructible or whether it would disintegrate under the pressure of attempted secession. Whether the Constitution in 1861 "was a source of weakness . . . at best irrelevant, quaintly antique, and probably obsolete" or whether the 1861 eclipse of John C. Calhoun's dual federalism and the reemergence of national supremacy in the tradition of Hamilton and John Marshall occurred, it is clear that the event at Fort Sumter marked a significant change in the dominant concept of the nature of the Union.[6]

The nation, however, was ill prepared to fight a war with its rebellious countrymen. The treasury was bare, and many of the leading figures from the Buchanan administration sided with the seceding states. Because of his financial proclivities and genius, Sherman would play an important role in funding the war. Owing to the absence of the predominantly Democratic Southern senators and representatives when Congress reconvened in special session on July 4, 1861, Republicans had sizable majorities in both houses. Although a newcomer to the Senate, Sherman was placed second on the important Committee on Finance, chaired by William P. Fessenden of Maine. The committee's control over taxation and appropriation bills gave its members considerable influence in other matters pending before the Senate.[7]

His assignment to such a conspicuous position, at the specific request of Fessenden, reflected both Sherman's knowledge and the influence he had gained as chairman of the House Ways and Means Committee in the previous Congress. Although less glamorous than serving in the armed forces, securing the funds necessary to preserve the Union was equally important, which Sherman recognized. To do so, he supported the highest taxation possible during the Civil War, for he believed taxes would be more cheerfully paid during and after such a conflict.

Chase informed Congress that the national income was insufficient to meet the extraordinary expenses incurred by the onset of the Civil War. He recommended that $80 million be raised by taxation and approximately $240 million by loans. The secretary suggested securing the proposed amount by adjusting the tariff to raise the remainder of the needed revenue. He cautioned Congress that direct and excise taxes should be considered only if necessary. Chase noted the constitutional necessity of apportioning a direct tax among the states according to population and the difficulty of collecting it in the present disturbed condition of the nation. Nevertheless, he asserted, difficulty of collection was no argument against the constitutionality of a direct tax. Ultimately the House passed a lower than recommended tariff. To make up the difference, it also passed a bill calling for a direct tax of $30 million to be apportioned among all the states of the Union.

The Senate, under the leadership of Fessenden and Sherman, added an individual income tax. Eventually a conference committee consolidated the bills. The final measure reduced the direct tax to $20 million, imposed a 3 percent tax on incomes in excess of $800, and modestly raised the tariff features. Sherman urged the bill's passage, declaring: "If it is necessary to pass any direct tax at all, this is as mild a form as it can be in." The measure passed, and thus, the exigencies of the Civil War forced Sherman and his fellow Republicans to approve the first income tax in American history, with little constitutional quibbling.[8]

Although Sherman's most important contributions during this brief special session related to finances, he was not oblivious of the political and constitutional controversies that swirled about the effort of the Southern states to secede and create an independent nation. Two days after the opening of the special session, Sen. Henry Wilson introduced a joint resolution "to approve and confirm certain acts of the President of the United States, for suppressing insurrection and rebellion."[9] This resolution would make legitimate the actions Lincoln had taken between March 4 and July 4, including the proclamation of April 15 that called up seventy-five thousand men; the blockade proclamations of April 19 and 27; the suspension of the privilege of the writ of habeas corpus in military communications areas in the Washington and Philadelphia regions and on the Florida coast; and the proclamation of May 3 calling forty-two thousand men into the regular army for three years.

This resolution provoked numerous spirited debates in the Senate during the special session. Sherman was troubled by the Wilson resolution, for, although he believed the president's actions were justified by the Civil War crisis, he was also a conservative constitutionalist who thought Lincoln had exceeded his constitutional authority in suspending the habeas corpus privilege and increasing the size of the regular army. At the same time, he believed the president's acts were necessary and their results were beneficial. Sherman observed that if he had been president, he would have pursued the same line of action. Eventually, Congress voted a modified approval of Lincoln's extraordinary actions. Sherman, Fessenden, and Wilson managed to get a moderately worded amendment approving the president's acts tacked onto an army appropriation bill.

The suspension of the privilege of the writ of habeas corpus proved to be one of the most troublesome problems in the Civil War and Reconstruction period. The Constitution provides that "the privilege of the writ of habeas corpus shall not be suspended, unless when in cases of rebellion or invasion the public safety may require it." Lincoln's suspension of the privilege raised questions concerning the application of the constitutional provision. Who was to decide on the existence of rebellion or invasion? When was public safety menaced? Did the power to suspend the habeas corpus privilege rest with Congress, the president, or both? If the power belonged jointly to the president and Congress, could the president suspend the privilege while Congress was not in session? Could the privilege be suspended in areas not directly involved in insurrection or invasion? These problems provoked debate throughout the nation and led to one of the most celebrated civil liberties disputes arising out of the Civil War—*ex parte Merryman.*

The *Cincinnati Gazette* had harshly criticized Sherman for his opposition to the resolution approving presidential actions. If Sherman's contentions were correct and Congress could suspend the privilege, the editor argued, there would be no protection to constitutional liberties. Further, he maintained, if war broke out while Congress was not in session, how could the holding of prisoners of war be justified, since they were denied the privilege of the writ? How long and where could the privilege of the writ be suspended? The writer saw no limit to the possibilities for evil if Congress could suspend the privilege whenever the peace of the nation—as in Kansas before the war—was disturbed: A partisan Congress might well take advantage of such disturbances and suspend the habeas corpus privilege for an indefinite period of time over the whole country, leaving no way to repeal the arbitrary suspension. Finally, the editor charged: "Thus our boasted Constitutional Government has, according to Mr. SHERMAN's ideas, the largest facilities for an unlimited despotism. . . . Mr. SHERMAN has placed himself by the side of the worst enemies of the National Government on this question."[10]

John refused to back down from the position he had taken in Congress, stating that only that body had the right to authorize suspension of the writ of habeas corpus. The Ohioan informed the *Gazette*: "There are times when our executive officer must anticipate the action of Congress, but in such a case he assumes the hazard of a 'Bill of Impeachment,' or a 'Bill of Indemnity.' The President merely assumed this hazard, and in the vacancy of Congress wisely assumed a power not delegated to him by the Constitution." The sen-

ator then reiterated his approval of the president's actions and justified them on the basis that the chief executive faced a crisis in
which no other course was possible.[11]

The *Gazette* refused to accept Sherman's position and charged
that his opinion would make it impossible even to hold prisoners of
war until after Congress had suspended the privilege of the writ of
habeas corpus. The newspaper also carried Sherman's position to its
logical conclusion by arguing, "If civil law must be suspended before
our armies can hold prisoners of war, the protection of civil law to
life must be suspended before our armies can shoot the enemy in
battle, else they would be guilty of murder."[12]

From the war's outset the nation's leaders began considering
two basic theories of reconstruction. Lincoln announced one in his
July 4 message to Congress when he declared that secession was
impossible and that a state had no power outside the Constitution.
He insisted no state had ever existed except under the jurisdiction
of either the Articles of Confederation or the Constitution. Thus, in
his view, there would be no real reconstruction; states would merely
resume their proper relationship with the Federal government and
the other states of the Union. An alternative view was put forward
by Lincoln's old Illinois friend and Oregon's Republican senator
Edward Baker. He suggested: "We may have to reduce them [the
seceded states] to the condition of territories, and send from Massachusetts or from Illinois Governors to control them." This view held
that the states had forfeited their rights and reverted to some type
of territorial status.[13]

Before a reconstruction of the Union could take place, however,
the rebellion would have to be put down, and Congress had specific
ideas on how that could be done. The effort to provide measures for
suppressing the insurrection led to a discussion of war aims. When,
on July 18, Henry Wilson introduced a bill to reorganize the expanded army, a general debate of Civil War goals ensued. Was the purpose of the war to free slaves or subjugate states? Sherman believed
neither was an appropriate goal. In his view the aim of the war was
"to preserve this Union; to maintain the Constitution as it is in all
its clauses, in all its guarantees, without change or limitation." He
insisted that the language and intent of the Constitution must
remain unchanged. Yet although Sherman believed the war had not
begun with the intention of interfering with slavery, he also considered it possible that the aims of the war could change. He was, above
all, a devoted nationalist. If it became apparent that the only way to
preserve the Union was by emancipation, he would endorse it as an
avowed object of the war. Whether emancipation became an accomplished fact or not, he was adamant that the influence of the "Slave
Power on the General Government will be forever destroyed." But to

change the formal object of the war at the present time, he thought, would only strengthen the South and weaken the North by creating dissension.[14]

Sherman's views did not change even after the Union defeat at Bull Run, which had caused many in Congress to reconsider the war aims. The Ohio senator was prepared to have the rebel's rights restored when they again rendered obedience to the Constitution. With the war aims attained, the civil conflict would end. Although he continued to deny that emancipation was an object of the war, he admitted slavery might end under certain circumstances. For example, he thought a slave should be declared free if he was used to help his master commit treason by working on rebel fortifications or aiding the rebellion in any other way. Thus, he supported Illinois senator Lyman Trumbull's bill to allow the confiscation of slaves used by rebels to build fortifications or aid their cause in other respects. This bill indicated the willingness of the Republican members of both houses of Congress to strike down slavery. At the same time, it did not immediately free slaves used against the nation. Each slave owner was to be tried in a district court before he was deprived of his property. Consequently, the process would be slow and would not disturb loyal slaveholders. The bill was not directed at slavery but at disloyal Southerners.

Before this special session adjourned, the Senate also considered how it might govern territory recovered from the rebels. Trumbull introduced a bill "to suppress insurrection and sedition, and for other purposes." It raised the question of whether captured territory would be governed by Congress or the president. The bill challenged executive control through the army by proposing to place military governments on the basis of statutory law. Military commanders would be authorized to declare presidentially designated areas in a state of insurrection. They could then issue rules and regulations for governing the territory "conforming as nearly as may be to previously existing laws and regulations," and the existing civil authorities were to enforce them. If civil officials refused to cooperate, military authorities could enforce the regulations. Rebels were to be charged with treason or sedition and tried either in civil courts or in courts-martial, depending on the circumstances. Any person in an area "declared to be in a state of insurrection or war" could be required to take a loyalty oath, and those who refused were to be imprisoned until the end of the conflict. Anyone who had taken the loyalty oath and then aided the enemy was to be treated as a paroled prisoner of war who had violated his parole. All property of men opposing the U.S. government was to be confiscated and treated as if it had been "taken in war from foreign enemies." When the state of insurrection was declared to have ceased, military power in the district was to end. For crimes committed by military and related personnel, the punishment was to be the same as if no war existed.[15]

The bill anticipated that disloyal states would be subjected to a period of military government before restoration while also recognizing the validity of rebel state governments. It represented a departure from previous positions by implying that Union sentiment was not strong enough in the rebel states to restore them immediately to their prewar Federal relationship. The debate on this bill revealed three positions in the Senate: "support of military government under executive control, support of such government under congressional control, and opposition to military rule over the states in any form."[16] Sherman endorsed the position that there should be military governments under congressional supervision. Nevertheless, the Senate was so divided that it took no final action during that session or the next one, and the problem remained unsolved.

Public pressure for a speedy Union victory increased during the summer and fall of 1861. Sherman's incoming mail suggested the public temper was moving swiftly toward support of more radical measures. By late July his correspondents were warning him that because the rebellion would be difficult to subdue, the Union must muster all its resources. In overturning secessionists, however, the national government must be careful not to destroy democratic institutions. By December the tone had become more strident. One writer warned Sherman that the government could not save both the Union and slavery. The correspondent declared that if an attempt were made to preserve both intact, "either Slavery or the Republic must perish." This advice was not offered by an abolitionist, for he declared: "In the name of God, let the war go on—and let the Nigger look out for and take himself. Let Slavery take care of itself, and let's move on and do something."[17]

Sherman recognized the nation's changing mood and was reluctant to engage in "politics as usual." His dissatisfaction with politics was heightened by the reconstitution of the Republican Party. To gain bipartisan support for the Civil War, the party had moved to garner the adherence of War Democrats by adopting a different name, the Union Party. The new political coalition increased Sherman's desire to leave politics alone and become more directly involved in the war effort.[18]

The restless Ohioan decided he could best aid in the war effort by recruiting for the army, and he was convinced he could obtain recruits who were unresponsive to Ohio governor William Dennison's efforts. Because his relationship with the governor was not good as a result of the bruising senatorial election battle, Sherman wrote Secretary of War Simon Cameron and asked permission "to recruit and organize in this part of Ohio, a brigade of two regiments of infantry, one squadron of cavalry, and two companies of artillery." If the War Department would supply field officers and equip and pay the recruits, he would cover recruiting and organizational costs, subject to reimbursement in government securities.[19]

The War Department granted him permission, and by the end of September, he began recruiting two regiments of infantry and one company of cavalry. Sherman, who received a colonel's commission, asked Cameron for two West Point graduates to train the brigade. Although he himself expected to command the troops until Congress reconvened, one of the officers detailed to the force would ultimately assume command. The senator spent the remainder of the fall organizing this unit—the Sherman Brigade—for the field.

When Congress convened in December, it was evident the restoration of the Union by compromise was no longer possible, for congressional attitudes were hardening. Antislavery leaders in and out of the government were becoming impatient with the unwillingness of Congress and the president to deal with what they saw as the most important problem of the war—slavery. That, coupled with the humiliating defeat of a Union reconnaissance probe at Ball's Bluff, caused Republican senators to call for a committee to investigate not only that defeat, but all battles lost by Union troops. Sherman urged that the investigation be broadened to include the conduct of the entire war.

Still uncomfortable with Lincoln's leadership, John suggested expanding the investigation even further. Although it now appeared that slavery would be a victim of the war, he feared that Northerners would think the conflict was about slavery alone. In his opinion the eradication of slavery was not the purpose of the Civil War. He believed the nation's citizens should understand that the war was being carried on "to preserve a free government for free men, without regard to that institution [slavery] at all." The best way to do that, he said, was to convince voters that the war's real purpose was to do whatever was necessary to bring the rebels to their knees. To this end, he advocated the confiscation of their property, including slaves. He also said that those who "commit the act of rebellion, they forfeit their lives by the Constitution of the United States; they lose everything." Simultaneously, he insisted that loyal citizens should be protected in all their constitutional rights. Rebels, by contrast, should lose their constitutional rights and should be dealt with as foreign enemies. He insisted that although confiscated property should be sold to help pay for the war, it was obvious that "the Government of the United States will not sell those slaves" confiscated; therefore, they would become free.[20]

Sherman had no illusions that income from confiscation would, by itself, support the war effort, but he knew the government needed additional funds. Income derived from taxation and the sale of bonds proved insufficient to meet the constant, voracious demands of a nation at war. Additionally there was a shortage of specie—gold and silver—forcing the government to suspend specie payments late in 1861. Without gold as a circulating medium to meet the financial crisis, it was necessary to find a new medium. Chase recommended reorganizing the national banking system to provide a market for government securities and to create a national banknote currency. Because of opposition, Congress authorized Chase to issue Treasury notes as legal tender—that is, something that was money solely by virtue of the fact that people were legally required to accept it.

The Legal Tender Bill aroused considerable opposition from northeastern bankers who opposed the introduction of such fiat money. Furthermore, the secretary of the treasury was reluctant to push for the bill because he preferred hard money. Nevertheless, he recognized and stressed the need for some provision to pay the mounting government expenses. After a lengthy debate over the bill's constitutionality, the House passed the measure on February 6, 1862. Two Ohio Democrats, George H. Pendleton and Clement L. Vallandigham, led the opposition. They asserted the Federal government could not issue legal tenders because that power was not specifically granted by the Constitution.

When the bill arrived in the Senate on February 9, 1862, with a provision that the legal tender notes should be receivable for all claims and demands against the United States *"except for interest on bonds and notes; which shall be paid in coin,"* it faced intense opposition. Despite his own reservations, however, Sherman staunchly supported the measure on the grounds of financial necessity and constitutionality. He reminded fellow senators: "Such a currency is a necessary and proper means to enable the national government to exercise its expressly delegated power to borrow money, to regulate commerce, to support armies and navies." The issue of a national currency might lead to abuses, he stated, but that was no excuse to shrink from duty. Although gold and silver had long been accepted as the standards of value, Sherman saw no constitutional reason for this; therefore, Congress was not forbidden from using another standard of value.[21]

After conference committee deliberation, both houses accepted the bill for which Sherman had led the fight, and on February 25, Lincoln signed it into existence. Thus, the United States had a national paper currency—the controversial note soon designated the "greenback." Sherman viewed the Legal Tender Act as a turning point in the Civil War. Near the end of his career, he wrote that before early 1862 the Union had been "physically strong but financially weak."[22]

Sherman continued to wrestle with the political and constitutional questions raised by the Civil War, and he moved toward positions that most Americans would not have believed possible in the antebellum years. He increasingly favored policies that tore both at the rights of state governments and the control over the lives of individuals that had formerly been the province of those governments. The exigencies of the war gradually caused him and other Republican leaders to recognize that the old Southern state governments could not just lay down their arms and resume their place in the national constellation. Leading Radicals were tending toward the position that the rebelling states had committed "suicide" and thus must be completely reconstituted before they could be readmitted to the Union. Even Sherman was coming to that view. At the very least, he believed the rebel leaders must be punished, and one way to punish them was to confiscate their property. He believed that was justified by international law, and in this respect there was no doubt but that the Confederacy must be treated as a belligerent. An important aspect of this new position was Sherman's advocacy of not only confiscating the rebels' slaves but also freeing them and arming them to fight against their former masters. He reported to his brother, General Sherman: "Surely a faction that has involved us in so terrible a war ought to feel the burdens of it. Death & Confiscation to the rebels & protection & indemnity to loyal People is the only principle that will secure a permanent Peace. . . . No one cares about the Negro except that as he is the cause of the war that he be made useful in putting an end to it."[23]

A few days later, he again wrote his brother that the success of the Union depended on the support of Southern Negroes. The Ohio senator believed the disloyal white population had to be completely subjugated. He would even go so far as to give the lands of Southern white planters to the loyal blacks. No quarter was to be shown to the rebels. Sherman said his support of harsh treatment for them merely reflected the sentiments of the public, and he informed his brother: "I have been long enough in political life to conclude that a general popular sentiment is in nine cases out of ten right."[24]

The apparent shifts in Sherman's position toward the South between December 1860 and August 1862 were more conspicuous than real. Throughout the period, he was chiefly concerned with the preservation of the Union, and to that end, he had been willing to make concessions to the South that disturbed his conscience. When it became apparent that Southerners would not be satisfied with the concessions offered, Sherman turned to the only means left to save the Union—wholehearted support of more harsh measures toward the rebels than he would have sanctioned earlier. If the only way to preserve the Union and the Constitution was by using extraconstitutional means, he was willing to take those measures.

The imperatives of mobilizing the country's resources led to a nationalization of American life and institutions on an unexpected scale. The Federal government began to direct the energies of the United States in a fashion that would allow national policy to be determined in Washington without excessive centralization. Standards were established and defined that affected all Americans. But, at the same time, a new bureaucracy was not created. Rather, the leaders in Washington worked through the existing agencies, such as the federal courts, while leaving unimpaired most traditional state functions. As Americans in the North struggled to maintain the Union, they looked increasingly to the Federal government for direction and coordination of the effort to retain the dissident South without destroying traditional state functions. In large measure, their effort was strikingly successful. The result was a kind of centralized federalism in which the Federal government directed the nation's energies and supplied some regulatory legislation but little direct supervision.

Meanwhile, Sherman and his fellow citizens turned to the biennial elections in the summer and fall of 1862. Much to his dismay, the Republican Party had given up its identity to a Union Party that was an uneasy combination of Republicans and Union Democrats. In the midst of that lackluster campaign, on September 22, 1862, Lincoln issued the Preliminary Emancipation Proclamation. Sherman probably knew of it beforehand, but he did not know when it would be issued. Lincoln cited as authority for issuing the proclamation his position as commander in chief of the armed forces; the Act of March 13, 1862, prohibiting the return of fugitive slaves to rebel masters; and the Confiscation Act of July 17, 1862. Although the September 22 proclamation only declared the president's intention of issuing an emancipation proclamation if the war was not ended by January 1, 1863, it had an immediate political impact.

Sherman was forced to defend the president's action on the stump during the closing weeks of the campaign—a task he did not relish. The proclamation was not popular in the Midwest, where there was a great fear that, once freed, blacks would migrate to the North. The reluctant crusader noted "that when I expressed my approbation of the proclamation it was met with coldness and silence." Nevertheless, Sherman did defend the president's action. At Zanesville, Ohio, four days before the state election, he told an audience that the problems afflicting the nation were the direct result of the "Slave oligarchy," and he defended the proclamation as a military necessity. He attempted particularly to allay fears that emancipated blacks might overwhelm Ohio and the other border states. The senator assured the crowd that these freed men and women would no longer need to go north to escape bondage.[25]

Although he approved of the Preliminary Emancipation Proclamation, Sherman thought its release was ill timed. He was sure that its issuance at that particular point in the political campaign contributed to the Union Party's setback in Ohio and across the nation. He was also unhappy with a series of highly controversial arrests of disloyal citizens, mostly carried out by overzealous Lincoln supporters.

If Sherman was willing to defend administration policy publicly, however, privately he expressed misgivings about the president's abilities. He characterized Lincoln in a letter to his brother the general: "You think the President is honest & patriotic & so he is. But he lacks Dignity, order, & energy, without which no man can be great. He would fail in any business except pettifogging before a Jury where antics, jokes, and a plausible sincerity might win a verdict." Although a triumvirate composed of Chase, Seward, and Stanton would provide the firmness Sherman desired, he was unwilling to subvert the government in such fashion. He only wished the government might operate "in strict subordination to the constitution."[26]

Despite his misgivings about Lincoln, John continued to support him and measures to bring about a successful close to the war. Perhaps his chief contribution toward that end was taking the leading role in creating a national banking and currency system in 1863. The Ohioan had long been antagonistic toward the system of state banks and state bank currency, and he used the opportunity afforded by the Civil War to bring them both under closer regulation. Indeed, Sherman preferred that state banks and state bank currency should cease to exist. Early in life, he became convinced "the whole system of state banks . . . was both unconstitutional and inexpedient and that it ought to be overthrown." Thus, he was prepared to do all he could to destroy the state banks.[27]

At Secretary of the Treasury Chase's request, Sherman introduced a bill providing for the organization of federally chartered private banks. These institutions would deposit government bonds with the comptroller of the currency and receive government-imprinted banknotes, which they would then issue under the stamp of the national bank. The currency issued would be distributed on a formula allocating $150 million according to the population of each state and territory. The remainder was to be distributed on the basis of business and resource needs.

Although the policy of imposing a federal monetary system was appealing to Sherman, Treasury Secretary Chase, and a few Republican senators, many prominent Americans were not so sanguine.

Used to the freedom allowed by state laws, western bankers did not want to be forced to reform their practices. Those states with sound banking practices, such as New York, were also opposed to the new system because the proposed currency would compete with their own already well-established and profitable practices. Greenback supporter Thaddeus Stevens opposed and blocked the bank bill in the House for months; he considered it a device of money monopolists and was disappointed at the general lack of federal regulations. Hugh McCulloch, later comptroller of the currency and secretary of the treasury, lobbied against the currency bill on behalf of the State Bank of Indiana. Thus, opposition to the bill was varied and formidable.

When the Senate began consideration of the national currency bill, Sherman presented a vigorous defense of the measure. The question at issue, he said, was not so much whether the Federal government had the right to establish national banks and give them the privilege of issuing a uniform currency but whether it was expedient and safe to put so much power in Washington's hands. Sherman insisted it was.

Additionally, the Ohio senator believed there were other, more important reasons for adopting the measure. In good Hamiltonian fashion, he argued that the national currency bill would create "a community of interest between the stockholders of banks, the people, and the Government." If national banks had been established throughout the country as agents of the government, he added, "they would have done very much indeed to maintain the Federal Government and to prevent the crime of secession." There was, however, a still more important reason to support the bill (and here Sherman broke with many of his more conservative friends):

It will promote a sentiment of nationality. There can be no doubt of it. The policy of this country ought to be to make everything national as far as possible; to nationalize our country, so that we shall love our country. If we are Dependent on the United States for a currency and a medium of exchange, we shall have a broader and a more generous nationality. The want of such nationality, I believe, is one of the great evils of the times. This doctrine of State rights, which substitutes a local community—for, after all, the most powerful State is but a local community—instead of the United States of America, has been the evil of the times; and it has been that principle of State rights, that bad sentiment that has elevated State authority above the great national authority, that has been the main instrument by which our Government is sought to be overthrown.

The establishment of a national currency, Sherman declared, was the most important measure before Congress. Concerning the national currency bill, he stated unequivocally:

It is more important than the loss of a battle. In comparison with this, the fate of three million negroes held as slaves in the southern States is utterly insignificant. I would see them slaves for life as their fathers were before them, if only we could maintain our nationality. I would see them free, disenthralled, enfranchised, on their way to the country from which they came, or settled in our own land in a climate to which they are adapted, or transported anywhere else, rather than to see our nationality overthrown. I regard all those questions as entirely subordinate to this. Sir, we cannot maintain our nationality unless we establish a sound and stable financial system; and as the basis of it we must have a uniform national currency.[28]

The bill narrowly passed by a vote of twenty-three to twenty-one. Later, Sherman wrote that it was only after he and Chase had a private discussion with Senator Henry Brown Anthony of Rhode Island, stressing the national importance of the measure, that the senator agreed to forget local interests and support the bill.

The House approved the national currency bill with little discussion. The question of centralized versus decentralized banking had long been one of the dividing issues between the Hamilton-Clay followers and the Jefferson-Jackson followers. The Federalists and Whigs had championed a federally chartered national bank to stabilize the American economy. The Federalist-Whig wing of the young Republican Party triumphed in the passage of the act. Even so, it is doubtful that the bill would have been passed at that particular time had it not been for the exigencies created by the Civil War. John admitted to his wife that he himself could support it only after becoming convinced there was no other way to sell government bonds than to make them the basis of a national banking system.

Sherman vigorously supported other legislation that increasingly backed national prerogatives at the expense of states' rights. He did this, however, with an increasing sense of despair over what he thought was the incompetence of Lincoln. He informed his brother: "Lincoln is a man who excites my contempt more than any person with whom I have been brought into contact. It is a fearful dispensation of Providence, or the folly of party Leaders that he is President while our Country is passing through this ordeal. . . . If we save our institutions it will be because of their inherent strength."[29]

The close of the congressional session and Sherman's return to Mansfield did not alter his opinion of the president. Sherman wished that

Lincoln was out of the way. . . . Anybody could do better. I was among the first of his political friends to acknowledge how fearfully we were mistaken in him. He has not a single quality befitting his place. . . . He is unstable as water, afraid of a child & yet sometimes stubborn as a mule. I never shall cease to regret the part I took in his election and am willing to pay a heavy penance for this sin. This error I fear will be a fatal one as he is unfit to control events and it is fearful to think what may come during his time. What he will do now it is impossible to say. He is subject to the deepest of spirits amounting to Monomania.

In the same letter, the Ohio senator declared there was little chance of ending the war until a new president was elected. Even a War Democrat would be better "than our monkey President."[30]

Sherman's opinion of the president continued to decline, and by midsummer 1863, he considered Lincoln little more than "an honest clown." The chief executive was subverting the Republic by arbitrary arrests, he said, asserting that the Preliminary Emancipation Proclamation was issued without congressional authority and was a sign of weakness and folly. Even worse than Lincoln's unwise actions was the lack of a presidential policy. Sherman despaired of the coming election, for, with the South not voting, it was conceivable no one would receive a majority in the electoral college. "The war has done a great deal to shake that implicit obedience to law which has been the great conservative element of our Government," he observed, "but the Administration has done a great deal more." Sherman denounced Lincoln again in October but expressed confidence that the republican form of government could withstand another Lincoln administration if necessary.[31]

While Sherman prepared for the opening of the Thirty-eighth Congress, set to convene in December 1863, he was aware that the nationalization of American life had to be accompanied by a parallel nationalization of responsibilities. He believed the American people were capable of meeting the challenge. Shortly after the close of the session, Americans would have an opportunity to express their judgment of the government's course in congressional and presidential elections. Sherman was sure that if Washington maintained its present course, its actions would be endorsed. He had a profound faith in republican government, which represented the will of the people. Nevertheless, he was unhappy that the electorate would probably have to choose between Lincoln and a Democrat in the coming election. Sherman did not think the chief executive had been energetic enough in enforcing national policy; he preferred that the nominee be Chase or "a good military commander." He also believed the president had displayed too many inconsistencies in handling the war effort against the South and in arbitrary arrests in the North to rally national sentiment. Presumably, Chase or a military figure could rectify these inconsistencies.[32]

Among the problems with which Sherman expected Congress to grapple during the 1863–1864 session were the reconstruction of the Union, the enforcement of the draft, and the raising of sufficient revenue to maintain the army. But he did not think questions relating to African Americans or slavery would be raised in any meaningful fashion during the coming session. In fact, Sherman preferred that Congress leave the "Negro question" alone and allow the demise of slavery to be settled by the course of the war and state action. The national government should not even touch the issue of slavery, he thought, except as a result of the war powers on which the president's Emancipation Proclamation rested.

The previous summer and early fall of 1863 likely represented the nadir of Sherman's attitude toward the president. But he recognized that the forces tending to create a stronger national government were probably in the ascendancy and that Lincoln would be swept along. By this time many Northerners had accepted the fact that African Americans would have to participate in the war and that some concessions would have to be made to enlist their support. Sherman now not only supported emancipation but also urged that blacks be encouraged to enlist. In addition, he believed they should be subject to the unpopular draft. Indeed, he linked emancipation to both enlistment and conscription. He insisted it was the duty of Congress, therefore, to see that the African American, who was risking his life for his freedom and his country, should be secured in freedom by Congress: Justice demanded emancipation for the black soldier. "The slaveowner only robs him of his wages; they only take from him the sweat of his brow," Sherman declared, "but if you take his life and then do not secure to him and to his children their freedom, you do him a still greater wrong." Furthermore, neither Congress nor the president had the power to emancipate the slaves during peacetime, he said: Slavery was exempt from congressional interference because it was a state institution, and even an insurrection would not justify emancipating slaves. In Sherman's mind, however, there was no question but that the present conflict was a civil war rather than an insurrection. He believed civil war existed when insurrection had grown to the point where marshals and constables could no longer put down the disturbance and where two organized armies, representing established governments, opposed each other in the field.[33]

It was now clear to Sherman and many other leaders that the Civil War had destroyed any reason to preserve slavery: "The time has arrived when we should reap the great fruit which springs out of this civil war when we may make our institutions more harmonious, when we may remove from our Government that feature which has been obnoxious to every just mind from its foundation;

that feature which was denounced by all the framers of the Government." If slavery was ended by the Civil War, Sherman believed the cost of that conflict would be "money wisely spent and lives nobly sacrificed." He was quick to note that when the war commenced he had no thought of interfering with slavery, but since the South started the war, he was ready and willing to end slavery by constitutional amendment. He also gave a hint of his attitude toward the position the Confederate states would take in the reconstructed Union. He said a constitutional amendment would receive the requisite three-fourths majority when ratified by all the new states that would enter the Union, whether from the territories or the disloyal states of the South.[34]

By late March, Sherman had his chance to demonstrate his commitment to emancipation, and he was eager to do so. He therefore urged that other business be set aside and that the Senate begin to consider a constitutional amendment to abolish slavery. He took the position that slavery could only be legally abolished by constitutional amendment, but he wanted to make a distinction between the slaves of rebels and those of loyal owners. He insisted that loyal owners should receive compensation for the labor their slaves owed them. At the same time, although he insisted on freedom and equality for all African Americans, he pointedly noted that the Thirteenth Amendment, when adopted, would not confer on them the right to vote. That was a privilege, he said, that could only be granted by the state in which the citizen lived.

Senators faced a second, equally difficult problem as they contemplated the ratification of the Thirteenth Amendment because eleven states were in rebellion. A constitutional amendment requires the ratification of three-fourths of the states of the nation, so it was necessary to reach some understanding as to how many and which states were needed for ratification. Should states in rebellion be counted in the total needed? If so, then it was apparent that the Thirteenth Amendment could not possibly become a part of the basic law of the land. But, if only the loyal states had to ratify the amendment, the number of states required would be greatly reduced, and it would not be necessary to have the war ended before the amendment could be adopted. Did the states persist after the rebellion had begun? Or did they cease to exist? The problem was not settled then, and, in fact, it has never been settled.

Sherman believed that the rebellious states were out of the Union. But, at the same time, he held that they remained states in certain respects. On March 7, 1864, he introduced resolutions that supported the theory that states somehow continued to exist as political entities. The first resolution declared that a quorum of the Senate should consist of a majority of senators actually chosen.

Other resolutions declared that if a presidential candidate received a majority of the electoral votes cast by "duly appointed and qualified" electors, he would be president. Similarly, a majority vote by states represented in the House should elect the president if no one received a majority of electoral votes. The significance of this move by Sherman was that it enabled him to maintain his position that for some purposes, states might be considered out of the Union, but for other purposes, they could be considered as *in* the Union.

The status of the rebel states within a reconstructed nation received the most consideration in the Wade-Davis Bill, which was called up for discussion by Ohio senator Benjamin F. Wade. The bill had been considered by the House at length, and its subject matter had been explored in the Thirty-seventh Congress. Sherman had considered the reconstruction problem for some time; indeed, much of the wartime legislation had implications for postwar reconstruction. The Wade-Davis Bill coalesced with Sherman's pragmatic view that the states, as a result of the Civil War, must be considered as being both within and without the Union. It treated the states as continuing political entities, while prescribing that new governments be organized and that the states had to be readmitted to the Union at the pleasure of Congress. It assumed that the state governments had been usurped or overthrown. Entitled "An Act to guarantee to certain States whose governments have been usurped or overthrown a republican form of government," the bill was based on the constitutional guarantee of a republican form of government. Although Lincoln pocket vetoed the bill, Sherman thought it was the best basis on which to rebuild the nation after the close of the war.

Before passage of the Wade-Davis Bill, the Republican National Convention met and nominated Lincoln. Sherman, who had been a Chase supporter and participated in an ill-fated attempt to displace Lincoln, acquiesced in the nomination. The Ohio senator had, in fact, endorsed Lincoln shortly before the Baltimore convention.[35] Despite an earlier expressed preference for Chase, he stumped Ohio, Indiana, and Iowa in support of the Lincoln-Johnson ticket and Union-Republican candidates for the House. Although he campaigned actively, beginning with a speech in Washington before the close of Congress, Sherman had little enthusiasm for the election.[36] In his words, Lincoln was "the incarnation of the popular will." It was important, therefore, that he be able to finish the work he had begun. He would "preserve the Union and the Constitution."[37]

A month later, Sherman defended the president's course during the preceding four years. He pointed out that Lincoln had moved with the people, neither too fast nor too slow. The senator reluctantly admitted he often differed with the president but noted that when

Lincoln's measures were critically examined, "they have been found wise and successful." The Ohioan added: "There is not a single act of Mr. Lincoln that I can recall but has been justified by events, unless it has been his desire to conciliate his political adversaries by undue favor and partiality."[38]

Sherman's speeches were more than bland eulogies of the president. In them, he also voiced his conception of the nature of the Union and the beneficial results to be gained from the testing fires of the Civil War. American institutions were being purified by the war, he said. Human freedom was becoming a reality, and the Declaration of Independence had real meaning in the United States for the first time. Sherman spoke in evangelistic terms as he declared: "Let us preserve the Union, and if the Constitution, in passing through the terrible fire kindled by rebellion shall be purified of the stain of slavery, it will be for a glorious resurrection and a better life." "Slavery," the Ohio Senator intoned, "was the curse of our system, which the framers of the Constitution were ashamed to name." He spoke of delivering four million blacks from a condition "worse than Egyptian bondage" and of leading them in "a grand march forward in civilization and humanity." The natural rights of man, which Thomas Jefferson had hoped to secure for blacks by emancipation in Virginia, were now to be realized across the land.[39]

Sherman said the war was tending "to nationalize, harmonize, and blend into one great system all the elements of our system, without disturbing the home functions of our State and municipalities."[40] He was not speaking of an erosion of power to Washington but referring to institutions that would bind the people together with a common sentiment. Loyalty should be national, not given to a particular state or section. The Ohio and Mississippi Rivers should be great arteries of commerce and transportation tying states together. Mountain chains were not to divide but to be traversed by railroads bringing distant states to one another. Forests and mines were to serve all Americans in providing the resources to build homes and industries. Should the rebellion succeed and disunion result, Sherman warned, the consequences would be worse than the Civil War itself. Cities would decay, and property would be unprotected. "There is no safety for this country," declared the Ohioan, "except by establishing the supremacy of laws."[41]

When the second session of the Thirty-eighth Congress assembled late in 1864, the issue of a reconstruction was more pressing than it had been previously. The end of the war was in sight, for Gen. William Tecumseh Sherman had taken Atlanta and was headed for Savannah, and Grant continued to hammer away at Richmond. The Confederacy was so desperate that its leaders were considering the arming of slaves.

Although Lincoln rejected the Wade-Davis Bill, he agreed that any state that chose to accept the stipulations laid down in the measure might comply and be readmitted to the Union. His pocket veto had left the administration in control of Reconstruction, and the president proceeded along lines already laid down in Louisiana, Tennessee, and Arkansas. His program rested on the premise that the states were still in the Union once the rebellion was suppressed and the inhabitants returned to loyalty to the federal government.

Even though Ohio's junior senator was extremely busy as the new chairman of the Senate Finance Committee, he did give some thought to the problems of reconstructing the Union. The status of presidentially reorganized states came up early in the session, when two Louisiana senators-elect sought admission to the Senate. The question of admission quickly became entangled with the related question of whether electoral votes from states organized under Lincoln's direction should be counted in the presidential election. The entire problem revolved about the locus of authority for reestablishing state governments in the South. Republicans generally agreed that governments in the Southern states would have to be organized by the national government, but they disagreed on the source of authority. Who was responsible for providing republican Southern state governments? If the president was, there was no alternative to counting the votes of Louisiana, Tennessee, and Arkansas, which had presidentially organized state governments. However, if Congress was responsible for ensuring republican governments, it was that body's job to decide whether the state governments in question were entitled to be represented in Congress and their citizens entitled to select presidential electors.

The Senate first took up the electoral problem when it began consideration of a House joint resolution to exclude the votes of states in armed rebellion against the Union. Sherman thought the issue was clear: These states had been declared insurrectionary by presidential proclamation, and they had no representation in either house of Congress. As far as he was concerned, the question was not whether Louisiana was a state within the Union but whether it could vote in the electoral college. He thought it obvious that the state was in rebellion; the loyal and legal authority there was overthrown and not yet reestablished. The state had been ruled by military governors, and it was still under a provisional governor. Although Sherman said he recognized Louisiana as a state within the Union, he would never agree to having its electoral votes counted until its new government was approved by both houses of Congress. He declared he was not passing judgment on the right of Louisiana to be represented by R. King Cutler and Charles Smith; he was merely withholding judgment on that score until the merits of the problem were discussed on the Senate floor.

Although Sherman specifically repudiated Massachusetts senator Charles Sumner's theory of "state suicide" (whereby seceding states extinguished their own existence by so doing and could then be re-created or not at the pleasure of the Federal government), he still sometimes spoke as if that was, in fact, the case. For example, he spoke of "the admission of Louisiana." He also said that Louisiana's attempt to vote in the electoral college "before her condition is fixed by Congress . . . is wrong." Again, however, he mentioned the necessity "to found and reorganize or reestablish the State government overthrown by the insurrection." Thus, he settled on a pragmatic position, later expounded with greater clarity by Ohio congressman Samuel Shellabarger—the "forfeited rights" theory.[42]

By postponing the Louisiana question, the Senate avoided responsibility in settling the constitutional issues involved in restoring Southern states to the Union. The president would be given a free hand in developing a reconstruction program during the lengthy interval between congresses, unless he chose to call the Thirty-ninth Congress into session early. Fully aware that Congress had failed to meet its constitutional responsibility, the Ohio senator was willing to allow the chief executive to deal with those portions of the rebellious states that should come under Federal control before December. Nevertheless, Sherman was not conceding full responsibility to the president, the army, or the courts. Earlier in the session, when discussing the Louisiana Union government, he announced that it was Congress's responsibility to decide when a state was entitled to representation and restoration to a normal relationship with Washington.

Taking the view that Congress was responsible for the final restoration of the nation, Sherman determined to inform himself on Southern conditions. Therefore, he accepted with alacrity an invitation by Secretary of War Edwin M. Stanton to take a Southern excursion aboard the steamer *Baltic* shortly after Congress adjourned. This trip, which took him to Charleston, Beaufort, Savannah, and other Southern points, doubtless influenced his early attitude toward the South and the problems of Reconstruction. He recognized that the South would require a great deal of aid in its effort to rebuild and saw that the problem of restoration or reconstruction would require considerable effort.

The senator had a second opportunity to visit the upper South when he was invited by his brother, the general, to visit his camp in North Carolina. With Edwin Stanton Jr., eldest son of the secretary of war, Sherman journeyed to Goldsboro, North Carolina, where he had an opportunity to observe firsthand some of the closing maneuvers of the war. While visiting with his brother, Sherman learned of Lincoln's plans for ending the war. The president's terms were lenient and aimed at securing a cessation of hostilities as rapidly as possible. Lincoln had suggested to Generals Sherman and Grant that the Confederate troops be disbanded and sent home to work their farms as soon as was feasible. He had also suggested, indirectly, that Davis and his Confederate government might be allowed to escape. When Sherman heard of these terms, he was dismayed; as he later remembered, "I did not at the time agree with the generous policy pro-posed by Mr. Lincoln."[43] The senator remained with his brother until April 1, during which time they doubtless discussed the postwar possibilities for the nation.

Shortly after Senator Sherman's return to Washington, the tempo of events quickened. On April 9, 1865, Lee surrendered to Grant at Appomattox. John Sherman exulted: "The news from Grant is so glorious that the whole nation is wild with joy." In response to Appomattox, he was invited to Columbus, Ohio, where he delivered an address celebrating Grant's victory. But while the senator addressed the festive mass meeting, tragedy struck in Washington as Lincoln fell victim to an assassin's bullet. Sherman received the news early the next morning when his close friend and political confidante Rush R. Sloane awakened him with the news of the tragedy. He later recalled that "the change from joy to mourning that day [April 15, 1865] in Columbus was marked and impressive. No event of my life created a more painful impression than this news following the rejoicings of the day before." This succession of joy and tragedy probably destroyed any chance that might have existed for an easy, quick, amicable restoration of the American Union. Sloane informed Sherman that on the death of Lincoln, "the whole feeling of the people appears to be changed, men who up to that time were hoping for peace no matter hardly how obtained, now swear for vengeance." Not only was a great leader removed from the political scene and replaced with a man of lesser ability but the mood of the nation also was radically altered. Sherman left immediately for Washington, where he attended Lincoln's funeral and then accompanied the slain leader's body through Ohio on its way to Illinois.[44]

Close on the heels of Lincoln's assassination, Gen. Joseph E. Johnston surrendered the last major Confederate army in the East to General Sherman. The terms of the Sherman-Johnston Convention that followed raised a furor that profoundly involved the Ohio senator's relation with the new administration. Although the surrender of Johnston's forces virtually ended the war, the conditions granted to the Confederates were unacceptable to many Republicans, who believed General Sherman had exceeded his authority in coming to terms with Johnston. In addition to providing for the surrender of all remaining rebel forces, the general had promised that existing state governments would be recognized when their officers swore allegiance to the national authority. The convention also provided that where there were conflicting state governments, rival claims would be presented to the U.S. Supreme Court for adjudication. Moreover, federal courts were to be established, Southern political and property rights were to be guaranteed, no further action was to be taken by the national government against the rebels, and there was to be a general amnesty.

The administration's reaction was quick and decisive. In contrast to Grant's terms at Appomattox, which had provided only for a termination of hostilities, General Sherman had virtually negotiated a peace treaty. If accepted, his terms would have put in question the legitimacy of Union state governments established in Virginia, Louisiana, Arkansas, and elsewhere. The convention would gravely jeopardize the legitimacy of West Virginia. The possibility of paying the Confederate war debt was left open, and property rights in slaves conceivably might be recognized. Thus, in a hastily called cabinet meeting at which Grant also was present, President Johnson and his advisers repudiated the convention. Stanton was told to notify General Sherman that hostilities should be resumed after giving the stipulated forty-eight-hours' notice, and Grant was dispatched to Raleigh to inform the general of the administration's action. Stanton then announced the terms of the Sherman-Johnston Convention and the administration's repudiation of them to the press. In addition, he gave the reasons for the repudiation and came close to accusing General Sherman of disloyalty.

Senator Sherman was "distressed beyond measure at the terms granted General Johnston by General S." and wrote to Secretary Stanton expressing his displeasure. In his view, the rebels should have been forced to surrender unconditionally, and the leaders of the rebellion, along with those who participated in it, should have been indelibly branded "with infamy." In fact, rebellion should have been made so odious that, for a generation at least, no one would dare to justify or defend it. Nevertheless, in defense of his brother, Sherman declared the general should not be judged too harshly: He had granted terms that were far too liberal but not by design, and they were only slightly more liberal than those granted by Grant, which had been applauded by Lincoln. He contended that General Sherman had not understood the difference between his terms and those Grant had given Lee at Appomattox; he had viewed the contest as purely military and had not understood the political considerations. John Sherman further defended his brother's actions by saying: "He thought the disbanding of their armies the end of the war, while we know that to arm them with the elective franchise and state organizations is to renew the war." He expressed much the same view in a letter to his brother a few days later, pointing out that on at least two counts, the original agreement had been unsatisfactory to Northerners. The first such count was the proviso guaranteeing Southerners that their property was being construed by many to include slaves, which was "an impossible condition after we had induced them to enter our service by promise of freedom." The second unsatisfactory provision dealt with recognizing existing state governments in the South. Such a concession, Sherman lectured, was unjust to Union friends in the South, "especially in the border states, and would inevitably lead to a renewal of the war."[45]

For all intents and purposes, the Civil War was over when John Sherman returned to his hometown and eulogized the late president. He praised Lincoln as a man and as a leader, asserting that he had demonstrated remarkable wisdom in directing the energies of the Union during the four years of crisis. He had acted with a sense of timing that had united, rather than divided, the nation. He had not called for emancipation until he knew that his views would be sustained by public sentiment. And throughout the war, he had held steadfastly to his goal of national reunification. Sherman related that in his last discussion with the president, Lincoln had spoken "about the mode of bringing back [the] rebellious States into harmonious relations to the Union." The president had hoped to restore the states to their "full constitutional power, subject only to such changes as would secure the freedom promised to the slaves." Sherman said he accepted this goal but wanted more. The rebellion had to be stamped with infamy if the nation was to be secure. The doctrine that held secession a legitimate recourse for the disaffected had to be forever repudiated in the interest of "national security." The Union could not be restored until measures were taken to guarantee rebellion would never again rear its ugly head in the United States. In the meantime, he added, the South was at the mercy of the new president and "must submit to such terms as he grants them."[46]

Notes

1. John Sherman to William Dennison, Washington, DC, March 23, 1861, Vertical File Material, Ohio Historical Society Library, Columbus. Unless otherwise specified, all references to Sherman are to John Sherman.

2. James A. Garfield to Burke A. Hinsdale, Columbus, January 15, 1861, in *Garfield-Hinsdale Letters: Correspondence between James Abram Garfield and Burke Aaron Hinsdale,* ed. Mary L. Hinsdale (Ann Arbor: University of Michigan Press, 1949), 56.

3. James A. Garfield to his wife, Columbus, March 19, 1861, in Theodore Clark Smith, *The Life and Letters of James Abram Garfield,* 2 vols. (New

Haven, CT: Yale University Press, 1925), 1:156; *New York Times*, March 16 and 18, 1861; Sherman to William H. Seward, Washington, DC, March 1861, Robert Todd Lincoln Collection of the Abraham Lincoln Papers, Manuscripts Division, Library of Congress, Washington, DC (Presidential Papers Microfilm).

4. Sherman to W. T. Sherman, Mansfield, Ohio, November 26, 1860, in Sherman, *John Sherman's Recollections of Forty Years in the House, Senate and Cabinet: An Autobiography,* 2 vols. (Chicago: Werner, 1895), 1:235–37.

5. Sherman, *Recollections,* 1:242–43.

6. Quoting Harold M. Hyman, "Reconstruction and the Political-Constitutional Institutions: The Popular Expression," in *New Frontiers of the American Reconstruction*, ed. Harold M. Hyman (Urbana: University of Illinois Press, 1966), 12.

7. Curry, *Blueprint*, 10–11.

8. *Congressional Globe*, 37th Cong., 1st sess., 398 (August 2, 1861).

9. *Congressional Globe,* 37th Cong., 2d sess., 16 (July 6, 1861).

10. *Cincinnati Gazette*, August 8, 1861.

11. Sherman to the editors of the *Cincinnati Gazette,* Mansfield, Ohio, August 12, 1861, in *Cincinnati Gazette*, August 20, 1861.

12. *Cincinnati Gazette,* August 20, 1861.

13. *Congressional Globe*, 37th Cong., 1st sess., 45 (July 10, 1861).

14. Sherman to M. J. Thomas, Washington, DC, July 21, 1861, John Sherman Papers, Manuscript Division, Library of Congress, Washington, DC (hereafter cited as Sherman Papers).

15. *Congressional Globe,* 37th Cong., 1st sess., 336–37 (July 30, 1861).

16. Herman Belz, *Reconstructing the Union: Theory and Policy during the Civil War* (Ithaca, NY: Cornell University Press, 1969), 35.

17. Lorenzo Sherwood to Sherman, New York, July 27, 1861, C. Sprat to Sherman, New York, July 26, 1861, and J. H. Jordan to Sherman, Cincinnati, December 22, 1861, Sherman Papers.

18. Sherman to W. T. Sherman, Mansfield, Ohio, September 12, 1861, in Rachel Sherman Thorndike, ed., *The Sherman Letters: Correspondence between General and Senator Sherman from 1837 to 1891* (New York, 1894; reprinted in 1969, New York, Da Capo); Sherman to [George A. Benedict], Washington, DC, June 24, 1862, Sherman Papers.

19. Sherman to W. T. Sherman, Mansfield, Ohio, September 12, 1861, in Thorndike, *The Sherman Letters,* 129–30; Sherman to Simon Cameron, Mansfield, Ohio, September 24, 1861, Sherman to Salmon P. Chase, Mansfield, Ohio, September 24, 1861, in Sherman, *Recollections,* 1:262–63.

20. *Congressional Globe*, 37th Cong., 2d sess., 31–32 (December 9, 1861).

21. John Sherman, *Selected Speeches and Reports on Finance and Taxation from 1859 to 1878* (New York, 1879), 23–32, quotes on pp. 27, 32.

22. Sherman, *Recollections,* 1:280–81.

23. Sherman to W. T. Sherman, Mansfield, Ohio, August 8, 1861, William Tecumseh Sherman Papers, Library of Congress, Washington, DC (hereafter cited as WTS Papers).

24. Sherman to W. T. Sherman, Mansfield, Ohio, August 24, 1862, WTS Papers.

25. Sherman, *Recollections,* 1:330.

26. Sherman to W. T. Sherman, Washington, DC, January 2, 1863, WTS Papers. The quoted passages are deleted from the copy in Thorndike, *The Sherman Letters,* 177–78.

27. Sherman, *Recollections,* 1:282–85; Ben: Perley Poore, *The Life and Public Services of John Sherman* (Cincinnati, 1880), 27; Theodore F. Burton, *John Sherman* (Boston: Houghton Mifflin, 1906), 134; Sherman to W. T. Sherman, Washington, DC, November 16, 1862, WTS Papers.

28. *Congressional Globe,* 37th Cong., 3d sess., 820–26 (February 9, 1863), 840–46 (February 10, 1863); the speeches are also in Sherman, *Selected Speeches,* 51–79.

29. Sherman to W. T. Sherman, Washington, DC, February 16, 1863, WTS Papers.

30. Ibid.; Sherman to W. T. Sherman, Washington, DC, February 26, 1863, WTS Papers.

31. Sherman to W. T. Sherman, Mansfield, Ohio, July 18, 1863, WTS Papers; cf. Thorndike, *The Sherman Letters,* 206–8; Sherman to W. T. Sherman, Mansfield, Ohio, October 18, 1863, WTS Papers.

32. Sherman to W. T. Sherman, Mansfield, Ohio, October 18, 1863, WTS Papers; Sherman to Salmon P. Chase, Mansfield, Ohio, September 9, 1862, Salmon P. Chase Papers, Historical Society of Pennsylvania, Philadelphia, Pennsylvania.

33. *Congressional Globe,* 38th Cong., 1st sess., 438–45 (February 2, 1864).

34. *Congressional Globe,* 38th Cong., 1st sess., 541–42 (February 4, 1864).

35. Sherman to unnamed convention delegate, Washington, DC, June 5, 1864, reprinted in the *Baltimore American and Commercial Advertiser,* June 7, 1864.

36. Sherman to W. T. Sherman, Mansfield, Ohio, July 24, 1864, WTS Papers; Sherman to W. T. Sherman, Mansfield, Ohio, September 4, 1864, WTS Papers; *Cincinnati Gazette,* October 6, 1864; *Chicago Tribune,* October 25, 1864; Robert Todd Lincoln Collection of the Abraham Lincoln Papers, Manuscripts Division, Library of Congress, Washington, DC (Presidential Papers Microfilm).

37. Speech to the Ohio Club, Washington, DC, June 18, 1864, *Washington Chronicle,* quoted in *Cincinnati Commercial,* June 22, 1864.

38. *Cincinnati Commercial,* July 18, 1864.

39. Speech to the Ohio Club, Washington, DC, June 18, 1864, *Washington Chronicle,* quoted in *Cincinnati Commercial,* June 22, 1864.

40. Ibid.

41. Speech at Cincinnati, Ohio, July 16, 1864, quoted in *Cincinnati Commercial,* July 18, 1864.

42. *Congressional Globe,* 38th Cong., 2d sess., 578–79, 582, 594 (February 3, 1865).

43. Sherman to A. K. McClure, January 29, 1862, reprinted in A. K. McClure, *Abraham Lincoln and Men of War-Times* (Philadelphia: Winston Company, 1892), 237–38.

44. Sherman to W. T. Sherman, Washington, DC, April 11, 1865, in Thorndike, *The Sherman Letters*, 246; Sherman, *Recollections,* 1:354; Sherman to W. T. Sherman, Mansfield, Ohio, May 2, 1865, WTS Papers; Rush R. Sloane to Sherman, Sandusky, April 17, 1865, Sherman Papers. On the reaction to Lincoln's death, see Roy F. Nichols, *The Stakes of Power, 1845–1877* (New York: Hill and Wang, 1961), 158–59; Eric L. McKitrick, *Andrew Johnson and Reconstruction* (Chicago: University of Chicago Press, 1960), 18; Charles J. Stewart, "Lincoln's Assassination and the Protestant Clergy of the North," *Journal of the Illinois State Historical Society,* 54 (Autumn 1961): 268–93.

45. Sherman to Edwin M. Stanton, April 27, 1865, quoted in George C. Gorham, *Life and Public Services of Edwin M. Stanton,* 2 vols. (Boston: Houghton Mifflin, 1899), 2:195; Sherman to W. T. Sherman, Mansfield, Ohio, May 2, 1865, WTS Papers; Sherman to W. T. Sherman, Mansfield, Ohio, May 16, 1865, WTS Papers.

46. This eulogy was delivered on May 6, 1865, and printed the same day in the *Mansfield (Ohio) Herald.*

13

Robert Smalls
"I Stand Here the Equal of Any Man"

Richard Zuczek

At the epicenter of the Civil War stood 3.5 million blacks, the slaves who were the South's chief capital investment and whose labor powered Southern agriculture. To assure that those blacks would always remain slaves, the South had bolted the Union and started the war. Yet the slaves themselves were not always mere passive observers of the events around them; some took an active part in helping to gain their freedom and that of their race. For many, such a part entailed supplying information to advancing blue-clad armies or aiding Federal soldiers who had escaped from Confederate captivity and were trying to make their way to Union lines. Many more slaves took the opportunity offered by a passing blue-coated column to get away from their plantations, "stealing themselves," as the saying went, and reducing the domain of slavery that much more with each departure. For more than one hundred thousand black men, taking an active part in gaining their freedom meant enlisting in the Union army, in which many of them saw action before the war was over.

Robert Smalls, a man of rare talent and daring, made even greater contributions to the cause of freedom, both during and after the war. His story, though an extreme case, is in some sense representative of the many Southern blacks who resisted slavery in every way that opportunity presented and wit could contrive.

Richard Zuczek, author of *State of Rebellion: Reconstruction in South Carolina* (1997), teaches history at the U.S. Coast Guard Academy in New Haven, Connecticut.

The Civil War settled many of the political, economic, and constitutional issues that had plagued Americans, but it also created others. Controversies about slavery were replaced by questions concerning the status of 3.5 million freedpeople. The black experience during the Civil War and Reconstruction defies generalizations. Although most blacks, North and South, became Republicans, rarely was their allegiance to party blind. Even the term "black" itself is inadequate in this context, for there were freeborn blacks, former slaves, Northern-born blacks who went South after the war, and both mulattoes and purebloods. But despite their countless differences, one goal unified them all: the desire for *equality* and the same rights and opportunities enjoyed by white Americans. This is the story of a man who won his own freedom and went on to fight for his people, demonstrating for an entire nation the potential and capacity of all black Americans.

Robert Smalls was born into slavery in 1839 in Beaufort, South Carolina.[1] He was not a full-blood African but a mulatto; his mother was Lydia, a slave, and his father—or so it is believed—was John McKee, her white owner and a Beaufort planter. This mix was more common than many whites wanted to admit. Robert served as a house slave and personal valet for McKee's son Henry, but his mother wanted him to understand fully the harshness of slavery. So when Robert was not tending horses or accompanying the McKees hunting, Lydia would take him to the jail to watch slaves being whipped or send him to the fields to help other slaves toil.[2]

In 1851, after the death of John McKee, Henry sold the Beaufort property and moved to a plantation outside Charleston, where he began hiring Robert out. For some time, Smalls worked as a waiter and then a lamplighter, with his earnings going to Henry McKee, his new owner. Before long, Henry found Smalls work around the Charleston waterfront. He unloaded ships before landing a position repairing sails and fixing rigging.[3]

By about 1857, Smalls's future—perhaps his destiny—began to take shape. First, his harbor work expanded to include sailing, and soon he was operating boats with notable skill. Also, he convinced McKee to allow him to hire himself out, and pay McKee a flat fifteen dollars per month. Smalls kept any money in excess of that. He needed the extra cash, for he had just married Hannah Jones and had offered to pay her owner seven dollars a month for her freedom. Their relationship became more complicated in 1858 with the birth of their daughter, Elizabeth Lydia. Hannah's (and therefore also the daughter's) owner, Samuel Kinginan, agreed to release both mother and child from slavery for a flat fee of eight hundred dollars. Despite overwhelming odds, Smalls's opportunism and intelligence marked him as a man destined for success: by 1861, he had accumulated seven hundred dollars for the "purchase" of his wife and daughter.[4]

After the Civil War broke out in 1861, Robert's sailing abilities did not escape notice in the Confederacy, and he found service as pilot of the *Planter*, transporting supplies and munitions between Charleston's harbor forts.

On May 12, 1862, Smalls's courage and cunning were put to the test. Along with eight other black crewmen, he had decided to escape from slavery and the Confederacy by sailing the *Planter* out of Charleston harbor and up to the blockading U.S. fleet. The plan was crafted carefully: Smalls chose a night when the white officers were ashore, learned the whistle signals needed to pass the forts, and prepared a white sheet for surrendering to Federal vessels. Nonetheless, the risk was great because capture meant death; the men had decided to blow up the ship if they were stopped "since they knew they would have no mercy."[5] There was also no guarantee the Federal ships would not open fire as Robert and his crew approached. But the operation proceeded flawlessly, and the *Planter* slipped out of the harbor, picked up Smalls's wife, daughter, and several other women and children, and sailed past Fort Johnson. With the Confederate and state colors flying, the proper signal given, and Smalls walking the deck in the captain's clothes (taken from the officer's stateroom), the ship glided out of Confederate waters.[6] By the morning of May 13 the *Planter* proceeded past Fort Sumter, heading toward the Federal fleet. A crewman replaced the flags with a white sheet of surrender, and the USS *Onward* took possession of the *Planter*'s crew and cargo.[7]

The U.S. Navy and government were nearly as jubilant as the refugees, for they gained a ship, several cannon, and a man with an intimate knowledge of the Charleston harbor defenses and waters—Robert Smalls. In return, Smalls not only gained freedom for himself and his family—and a fifteen-hundred-dollar bounty for the ship—he also became a national hero. Missionary groups and even the U.S. Army were soon using Smalls as a spokesman for the famous Sea Island experiment on South Carolina's coast. In Philadelphia in 1864, when the hero was evicted from a city streetcar, an uproar resulted that led to the integration of the city's public transportation system. Smalls was even made a delegate to the National Union Convention in 1864, but he could not attend.

Most of his first three years after the escape to freedom were spent around the South Carolina coast, piloting vessels (including, at times, the *Planter*) and operating ships in attacks on Confederate forts. Several naval officers commented on his courage under fire, and it appears that by December 1863 he had been promoted to captain (although bureaucratic errors complicated his attempt to get a pension after the war). If that history is correct, then Smalls was the highest-ranking South Carolina black in the Civil War.[8]

At war's end, however, it did not seem likely that other Southern blacks were to share in Smalls's triumphs. After the Confederacy collapsed in the spring of 1865, Andrew Johnson, who became president following the death of Lincoln, began his policy of presidential reconstruction. Slavery was abolished under the new Thirteenth Amendment, but Johnson placed former Confederates in power in Southern states, and they established "black codes" that severely restricted freedpeoples' rights. Blacks could not sue in court, for example, or hold any job besides farming without a license. They also could not own firearms, vote, or hold office. Consequently,

Smalls was again caught between worlds, just as he had been before and during the war.

When many blacks were forced to work under former masters, Smalls was insulated by being an employee of the Federal military. He held special status and lived fairly well, continuing to operate his transport into 1866 and accumulating a fair amount of savings in the process. He apparently spent some of his money on private tutors; barely literate (he may have learned some reading skills in the North and in the military), he was intent on improving his education. With the decommissioning of the *Planter* in late 1866, Smalls returned to Beaufort, where he opened a store (using the bounty money awarded earlier) and moved into a house he had bought at a government auction—the very house he was born in, which had belonged to John McKee. It was fitting that Smalls should possess his master's home, and his fame, connections, and experience would lead him into other formerly white areas as well.[9]

What those areas might be became evident soon enough. The obstinance of the Southern states—which had passed black codes, rejected the Fourteenth Amendment, and ignored violence against the freedpeople—drove Congress to embark on a new reconstruction program. Determined to protect blacks in the South and expand the Republican Party there, Radical Republicans in Congress passed the Military Reconstruction Acts in 1867. In South Carolina and nine other former Confederate states (Tennessee had already been readmitted to the Union), the U.S. Army supervised the voting registration of black men and the holding of state conventions that would create new state constitutions. Then another election would select a new governor and a new legislature to replace the governments President Johnson had established.

Through the summer and fall of 1867, South Carolina's black population prepared for the November election of delegates to the state convention. One candidate from Beaufort was Robert Smalls, who established his own Beaufort Republican Club. The November vote resulted in a Republican landslide, since Democrats—mostly native whites—boycotted the election. Blacks held 76 of the 124 seats, and Smalls was one of 5 blacks in the 7-man Beaufort contingent. So began a political career that would last, including appointments, until 1913.

Smalls did not stand out at the state constitutional convention of 1868, although a witness called him one of the "more distinguished" delegates.[10] He was a member of the Committee on Finance—quite an honor for a former slave—but his chief interest was education, and he supported a sweeping provision that included compulsory school attendance. Once the constitution was completed, he returned to Beaufort to stand for election again, this time for state representative in the new South Carolina government.

With the new black Republicans outnumbering white Democrats, the election of 1868 resulted in a predominantly Republican general assembly, which (unlike that of any other Southern state) had a majority of blacks in the lower house. Among these was Robert Smalls, who had already begun to consolidate his power in Beaufort County. His election was no surprise: Despite his slave background, he was rapidly becoming a man of means through his postwar business and continued purchases of federally confiscated properties. Most important, he was a slave turned hero in an overwhelmingly black district, and, as one observer put it, "The voters of Beaufort had less confidence in white people than in Negroes."[11] He spent the next seven years in the South Carolina General Assembly, first as Beaufort representative (1868–1870) and then as state senator (1870–1875). Smalls so dominated local politics that one newspaper called him "the King of Beaufort County."[12]

In the legislature, Smalls divided his attention along several lines: direct help for his local constituency, general support and protection for his race's newfound rights, and self-preservation, both in terms of election success and financial status. His experience illustrated the difficulties of Reconstruction, including the problems facing the freedmen, the challenges facing the new government, and the temptations facing the new politicians.

Eager to help his constituents get back on their feet, Smalls tried to improve the economic condition of the Beaufort area. As a representative, he demanded the U.S. government release confiscated property in his district, property that could be put to good use. Knowing access to transportation would benefit the local economy, he supported the state-assisted building of a railroad connection from the Port Royal–Beaufort area to the Charleston and Savannah Railroad line. Other measures he pressed for included a special levy to rebuild the county courthouse and jail and a bill granting a monopoly to two companies that mined phosphates from the state's rivers. (These companies employed hundreds of blacks and provided supplemental income for farmers in the low country.) Understanding political rights as well as economic needs, the fledgling politician advocated the use of Federal soldiers to protect black voters, for during the election of 1868 the Ku Klux Klan had terrorized, attacked, and murdered white and black Republicans.[13]

White violence was only one problem the Republican Party faced. Another dilemma came from within and dominated the headlines after Smalls moved to the state senate in 1870. Republican Reconstruction governments became legendary for their scandals, and South Carolina's was the worst. The inexperience of the politicians, the greed of some adventurers, and the demands and challenges of the period came together to foster an environment ripe for corruption. Facing a ruined economy, the legislature plunged into dubious schemes involving mining, railroad development, bond sales, and land investments in an effort to raise cash and bring in external investment. Most of these ventures failed due to economic conditions, poor strategy, or internal fraud.[14]

Despite the pervasive nature of government malfeasance—legislators, cabinet members, and even the governors were involved—Robert Smalls stood apart. In fact, his drive for fiscal responsibility alienated some fellow Republicans even as it impressed white Democrats. He supported cutting judges' and attorneys' salaries, opposed per diem accounts for legislative travel, disbanded investigative committees that had ceased functioning, suggested reduced pay for short "special sessions" of the legislature, and called for investigations of the phosphate companies when their payments were in arrears. Playing on his wartime exploits, Smalls told an audience in 1871 that he intended to "guide the ship of state . . . past the rocks, torpedoes and hostile guns of ignorance, immorality and dishonesty."[15]

Typically, Smalls based his stance on practical reasons as well as moral ones. Corruption divided the party and damaged its reputation in the North. Further, although a loyal party member and true to his race, Smalls understood the need to cultivate connections to Carolina's whites, even Democratic ones. One example of this was his assistance to his former owner's family. Legend has it that he opened his home to his former master's widow and allowed her the use of his horses and carriage.[16] One English traveler found Smalls "not unpopular among the white people. He behaved well toward his former master's family and assisted them." This traveler, Sir George Campbell, also commented on the state of racial affairs in Smalls's district, where "black rule has been most complete and lasted longest." Whites complained of this "black paradise," but Campbell was surprised to find "exactly the contrary. At no place that I have seen are the relations of the two races better and more peaceable . . . white girls go about as freely and pleasantly as if no black had ever been in power."[17]

Robert Smalls could not, however, escape the taint of Republican dishonesty. One Democratic complaint revolved around his position in the "black militia." By the early 1870s, Smalls was a general in the state militia, which was largely black because whites refused to serve with blacks. As a general, Smalls received an extra paycheck and further patronage power, and he could appoint men to certain positions under him. Whites bridled at this whole system, but the only official charge of misconduct came by way of his role on the state senate's Committee on Printing, to which he was appointed after his reelection in 1872; even so, evidence indicates that the charges were unfounded and politically motivated. As for Small's followers in Beaufort, Sir George Campbell observed that Robert "seems to have their unlimited confidence."[18]

This confidence carried him from the state legislature to the national one, and in 1874, he was elected to the U.S. House of Representatives for the first of five terms. In December 1875, he arrived in Washington accompanied by his daughter, Elizabeth Lydia, who served as his private secretary. Even though he faced a Democratic House—the first in eighteen years—the freshman dived head first into his new role. As always, the needs of his constituents were not far from his mind. The Port Royal naval station received added appropriations for improvements, he sponsored a bill for the relief of his former master's family, and he fought, albeit unsuccessfully, for racially integrated army units.[19]

The central issue of his first term, however, was the ending of Reconstruction. The program was in its twilight when he went to Washington, for Northern interest had declined and Southern Democratic violence had intensified. State after state in the old Confederacy returned to Democratic control, and the legal and political rights blacks had struggled for were swept away. Nowhere was this more evident than in South Carolina, the last Southern state held by the Republican Party. The 1876 campaign between the Republican incumbent, Daniel H. Chamberlain, and the Democratic challenger, former Confederate general Wade Hampton, was marred by rampant violence and fraud. Democratic "gun clubs" terrorized black and white Republicans in an effort to overcome a black majority. One incident that attracted national attention was the murder of a number of black militiamen in the town of Hamburg in early July. Using the assault as evidence, Smalls made an impassioned plea in Congress for the retention of Federal troops in his state. Samuel Cox, a Democrat from New York, challenged the reliability of Smalls's sources and even asked who vouched for Smalls. "A majority of 13,000," Robert replied, to the cheers of fellow Republicans. He even defended South Carolina Republicans; when Cox complained of their corruption, Smalls turned the tables and remarked upon the infamous abuses of New York's Boss Tweed ring. Seasoned politicians found an able rival in this former slave, described by one contemporary as "excellent in repartee."[20]

His wit could not help his state through the election, though, so Smalls ventured back and took an active role in campaigning. Although up for reelection himself, he spent most of his time speaking on behalf of incumbent Daniel Chamberlain. In 1876, Smalls took his life in his hands on the stump, and at least two rallies in Edgefield County had the governor and congressmen fleeing for their lives.[21] Smalls described how Democrats planned to win the election by "the killing of colored men; making threats of personal violence . . . riding armed through the country, by day and night; by firing into the houses of Republicans; by breaking up Republican mass-meetings."[22]

The election of 1876 ended Reconstruction in South Carolina and in the nation. Violence and fraud brought Democrats back to power and so complicated the 1876 presidential election that many historians maintain a deal occurred, the so-called compromise of 1877. According to the terms of the alleged compromise, Republicans traded the South for the presidency: Republican Rutherford B. Hayes was chosen president by special commission and agreed to cease interfering in Southern affairs. In other words, Federal soldiers and marshals would no longer supervise elections or protect voters in the South.[23] Economic power, especially land ownership, had long been in white hands, and now political power would reside there as well. In an address to Congress, Smalls criticized whites for "securing by fraud and murder what could not be obtained by honorable means" and thereby forcing blacks "into a condition of political dependence upon the former slaveholders." Understanding how the legacy of terror would reflect on the South, he predicted that "the blood of innocent freedmen, shed by Southern Democrats would in the future prove one of the dark spots upon the fair name of the American Republic."[24]

An immediate result of the Democratic victory in South Carolina was an attack on one of Reconstruction's remaining symbols— Robert Smalls. Even though Democrats seized the legislature and the governorship, Smalls continued to dominate coastal politics and had won reelection to Congress. With his constituency still loyal, Democrats needed another way to remove him from political affairs. When the new government began investigating prominent Republican politicians, hoping to discredit the party and convict its members of corruption committed earlier, one of the chief targets was Smalls, whom Democrats charged with accepting a bribe for awarding a printing contract in 1872 while on the state's printing committee. The Democrats' goal was simple: to threaten Smalls with trial in a Democratic-controlled court to convince him to resign his seat and avoid conviction. Robert remembered a conversation he had held with the chair of the investigating committee, who told him that "these men have the court, they have got the jury, and an indictment is a conviction."[25] One newspaper editor even offered that "if you will vacate your office we will pay you $10,000 for your two years' salary." Smalls replied that if Democrats could "get the people who elected me to pass resolutions requiring me to resign, then you can have the office without a penny." Otherwise, he declared, "I would suffer myself to go to the Penitentiary and rot before I would resign an office I was elected to."[26] Knowing his people needed a voice in Congress, Robert, displaying his usual fortitude, refused to buckle under pressure.

As predicted, the trials, held in late 1877, resulted in convictions for several leading state Republicans, including Smalls. Evidence in his case was flimsy, and his sole accuser had been convicted of stealing hundreds of thousands of dollars before fleeing the state; he returned and was pardoned in exchange for turning state's witness. Even the state attorney general and lieutenant governor admitted that the charges could not stand up to legal scrutiny.[27] But Congress refused to let the state ruling interfere with the "privilege of a sitting member of Congress," and so Smalls retained his seat. He went about his business for the rest of his term, and the petitions he presented included one for upkeep of the Port Royal naval base and another in favor of women's suffrage.[28]

When Smalls ran again in 1878, the Democrats focused on destroying him directly; according to Laura Towne, a teacher on the Sea Islands, Governor Hampton said "there was but one man he thought ought to be out of the way, and that was Robert Smalls."[29] Robert's speaking engagements drew hundreds of armed whites, who harassed him and the listeners. He was shot at, chased, and even hunted like an animal. Towne said that if Smalls was elected, "I do not think his life would be worth a button."[30] In the end, he was not elected, and he attributed his defeat, according to Sir George Campbell, "entirely to fraud and intimidation."[31] Evidently, Republican voters did also, for Laura Towne noted that "the people are greatly grieved about it, and are not reconciled to the result."[32]

With Smalls out of office, Carolina Democrats had the opportunity to wiggle out of another jam. In a new deal with the Federal government, state authorities freed themselves from more residue of Reconstruction. State Democrats agreed to drop charges against Republicans, and, in exchange, the Justice Department would not prosecute Democrats accused of voting violations in the 1876 election. In 1879 the new governor, William D. Simpson, pardoned Robert Smalls and several other Republicans, but none of those suspected of atrocities in the 1876 campaign were ever brought to trial.[33]

Robert Smalls prepared to return to Congress. His decision demonstrated courage and conviction, for Reconstruction had ended and the struggle for black rights was unpopular, even within his own party. With Southern whites manipulating elections, each year saw fewer and fewer blacks in the state and federal governments. In addition, the nation's attention had moved on from the divisive subjects of black rights and Civil War. With each session, Smalls became more anachronistic, a leftover from an earlier struggle. As the nation looked to industrialization, economic expansion, and a final confrontation with Native Americans in the West, Smalls watched helplessly as disfranchisement, racial violence, and segregation reduced blacks to a situation little better than slavery.

Undaunted, he ran and was reelected to Congress in 1880 and again in 1884. His actions were meager but sincere as he stood fast for the people and issues that had always driven him. He opposed a bill allowing railroad companies to provide "separate" accommodations for blacks and whites, and he presented an amendment to another bill, calling for equal access to "eating-houses" and similar establishments in the District of Columbia. He sponsored a number of relief bills for constituents, requested funds for naval facilities in his district, and won a pay raise for black servants at the United States Naval Academy. He introduced a pension bill for Maria Hunter, widow of David Hunter, an "abolitionist" general who, without authority, emancipated slaves and enlisted black soldiers. Smalls called Hunter one of "freedom's pioneers," a man whose actions were "so far advanced" that Lincoln invalidated them. Blacks would not forget "the Moses who led us out of the land of bondage," he said. Allowing his frustration with racial relations to get the better of him, Smalls warned the president, Democrat Grover Cleveland, that a veto of the pension would expose "the hypocrisy of the assurances for the colored man by striking a blow at the nation's brave defenders and the colored man's best friend." Maria Hunter received her pension.[34]

Like the race he represented, Smalls's time on the national stage was at an end. In 1886, he lost his last campaign for Congress in a close race with former Confederate colonel William Elliott.[35] Before Smalls left Washington, he laid the groundwork for his new career as a collector of customs at the port of Beaufort. Robert's national fame, state service, and many Civil War connections prompted Republican president Benjamin Harrison to nominate him to that post, and the Senate confirmed him in 1890. Such positions were patronage assignments handed out to party men as rewards; Smalls held the post, with one four-year exception, until 1913.

His last great public appearance in defense of his race came in 1895 during the state's constitutional convention. White Carolinians, led by governor Benjamin "Pitchfork Ben" Tillman, decided to revamp the state's constitution to disfranchise blacks legally. The Fifteenth Amendment, ratified in 1870, prohibited voting discrimination based on race, so whites planned to make land ownership, poll taxes, literacy, and a knowledge of the U.S. Constitution requirements for suffrage. Since blacks trailed far behind whites in educational level and economic circumstances, these qualifications would effectively eliminate much of the black vote.

Outnumbered at the convention 154 to 6, Smalls and his black colleagues knew opposition was futile. Yet in his last public role as defender of American constitutional guarantees, Smalls was at his best. One observer called his arguments "masterpieces of impregnable logic, consecutive reasoning, biting sarcasm. . . . His arguments were simply unanswerable, and the keenness of his wit [showed whites] that the negro's capacity for intelligence, courage, and manhood was not inferior to the bluest blood in the old Palmetto State."[36] When Benjamin Tillman dared him to explain why blacks deserved to vote, Smalls countered, "My race needs no special defense, for the past history of them in this country proves them to be the equal of any people anywhere. All they need is an equal chance in the battle of life." When Tillman turned his attack on Smalls, Robert replied, "I stand here the equal of any man. I started out in the war with the Confederates; they threatened to punish me and I left them. I went to the Union army. I fought in seventeen battles to make glorious and perpetuate the flag that some of you trampled under your feet [and] no act of yours can in any way blur the record that I have made at home and abroad."[37]

Smalls's principles and logic were no match for the force of numbers and the power of racism. The new state constitution, with its stringent qualifications for voting, became law in December 1895. When Robert refused to sign the finished product, the assembly presented a resolution denying travel reimbursement to him; in response, a witness reported, "Smalls said he would rather walk home than sign the instrument."[38] Nonetheless, most South Carolina blacks ceased to play a role in state politics. When legal segregation—the Jim Crow laws—appeared in the state in 1898, the two races became more separate than ever before.

In his final years, Smalls was frustrated and depressed, for he was helpless to change the racist political, social, and economic structure that was now in place in South Carolina. He continued as a customs collector until 1913, when he was removed by the Democratic Wilson administration. By then his health had deteriorated, his political career had ended, and he was a widower twice over; his first wife, Hannah, died in 1883, and his second, Annie Elizabeth Wigg, passed away in 1895.[39] Once out of office, his drive seemed to dissipate, and his rheumatism, diabetes, and lingering ailments from wartime malaria became intolerable. He died in Beaufort on February 23, 1915.

Two years earlier, writing to black leader Booker T. Washington, Smalls expressed the hope that "I have succeeded to so manage affairs that when I leave . . . I will do so with credit to myself, my family, and my Race."[40] Although he was discussing the collectorship, his statement was an eloquent comment on his life. He was, indeed, the equal of any man—and perhaps a great deal more.

Notes

1. Before the war, he was apparently called "Robert Small," but during the war, "Smalls" became the accepted usage. Edward A. Miller Jr., *Gullah Statesman: Robert Smalls from Slavery to Congress, 1839–1915* (Columbia: University of South Carolina Press, 1995), 7.

2. Okon Edet Uya, *From Slavery to Public Service: Robert Smalls, 1839–1915* (New York: Oxford University Press, 1971), 3–4.

3. Ibid., 5–6.

4. Miller, *Gullah Statesman,* 8–9; Uya, *From Slavery to Public Service,* 7.

5. Elizabeth Ware Pearson, ed., *Letters from Port Royal, 1862–1868* (New York: Arno Press and the *New York Times,* 1969), 47.

6. Joel Williamson, *After Slavery: The Negro in South Carolina during Reconstruction, 1861–1877* (Chapel Hill: University of North Carolina Press, 1965), 7.

7. Miller, *Gullah Statesman,* 1–3.

8. Ibid., 18–24; Uya, *From Slavery to Public Service,* 20–23, 26–27.

9. Uya, *From Slavery to Public Service,* 36–37.

10. Miller, *Gullah Statesman,* 49.

11. Ibid., 66.

12. Uya, *From Slavery to Public Service,* 60.

13. Miller, *Gullah Statesman,* 54–55, 58; Uya, *From Slavery to Public Service,* 64–65, 70, 72–73.

14. The most comprehensive treatment of the Republican scandals is found in the Democrats' investigations, which, although heavy on political verbiage, contain a great deal of useful testimony. See General Assembly of the State of South Carolina, *Report of the Joint Investigating Committee on Public Frauds and Election of the Hon. J. J. Patterson to the United States Senate Made to the General Assembly of the State of South Carolina, at the Regular Session of 1877–1878* (Columbia, SC: Calvo and Patton, 1878).

15. Uya, *From Slavery to Public Service,* 70–76; *Beaufort County Republican,* January 4, 1872, quoted in Miller, *Gullah Statesman,* 64.

16. George Tindall Brown, *South Carolina Negroes, 1877–1900* (Columbia: University of South Carolina Press, 1952), 56; Miller, *Gullah Statesman,* 127; Uya, *From Slavery to Public Service,* 59.

17. Sir George Campbell, MP, *White and Black: The Outcome of a Visit to the United States, or "A Bird's-Eye View of the United States," Being the Substance of a Series of Addresses Delivered in Scotland in February, 1879* (New York: R. Worthington, 1879), 176–77, 332.

18. Ibid., 345.

19. *Congressional Record,* 44th Cong., 1st sess., 442, 1484, 3272–75, 3457–68, 3757, 4161.

20. *Congressional Record,* 44th Cong., 1st sess., 4641–43; Miller, *Gullah Statesman,* 102.

21. Miller, *Gullah Statesman,* 103; Uya, *From Slavery to Public Service,* 100–2.

22. *Congressional Record*, 44th Cong., 2d sess., appendix, 125.

23. For accounts of this "compromise," see C. Vann Woodward, *Reunion and Reaction: The Compromise of 1877 and the End of Reconstruction* (Boston: Little, Brown, 1951); Allan Peskin, "Was There a Compromise of 1877?" *Journal of American History* 60 (1973): 63–75; and Vincent P. DeSantis, "Rutherford B. Hayes and the Removal of the Troops and the End of Reconstruction," in *Region, Race, and Reconstruction: Essays in Honor of C. Vann Woodward*, ed. J. Morgan Kousser and James M. McPherson (New York: Oxford University Press, 1982), 417–50.

24. *Congressional Record*, 44th Cong., 2d sess., appendix, 123.

25. Miller, *Gullah Statesman,* 115; Uya, *From Slavery to Public Service*, 85.

26. Miller, *Gullah Statesman*, 115–19; Uya, *From Slavery to Public Service,* 85.

27. Uya, *From Slavery to Public Service,* 83; Williamson, *After Slavery*, 414–15.

28. *Congressional Record*, 45th Cong., 2d sess., 323, 372, 1805, 2706, 4034.

29. Rupert Sargent Holland, ed., *Letters and Diary of Laura M. Towne, Written from the Sea Islands of South Carolina, 1862–1884* (Cambridge, MA: The Riverside Press, 1912; reprint ed., New York: Negro Universities Press, 1969), 289–91.

30. Holland, *Letters and Diary,* 291.

31. Campbell, *White and Black,* 341.

32. Holland, *Letters and Diary,* 292–93.

33. Miller, *Gullah Statesman,* 130.

34. Ibid., 155–56; *Congressional Record*, 48th Cong., 2d sess., 316, 2057; *Congressional Record*, 49th Cong., 1st sess., appendix, 319–20.

35. Miller, *Gullah Statesman,* 158–70.

36. Uya, *From Slavery to Public Service,* 148.

37. *Journal of the Constitutional Convention of South Carolina Begun to Be Holden at Columbia, S.C., on Tuesday, the Tenth Day of September Anno Domini Eighteen Hundred and Ninety-Five* (Columbia, SC: Charles A. Calvo Jr., 1895), 474–76.

38. Miller, *Gullah Statesman,* 214.

39. Ibid., 191–213.

40. Robert Smalls to Booker T. Washington, April 22, 1913, Washington Papers, Library of Congress, Washington, DC, quoted in Miller, *Gullah Statesman,* 244.

14

Willis Augustus Hodges
"We Are Now Coming to New Things"

Richard Lowe

The black experience in the Civil War and Reconstruction era was as varied as the members of the African American population themselves. And that population showed as broad a variety of occupations and levels of education as white society did. Some Southern blacks were not even slaves, and the free black often were among the most highly educated of their race. As such, many of them, including Willis Augustus Hodges, were well prepared to assume leadership roles when the end of the Civil War brought many new things to what had been the Old South.

Richard Lowe, Regents Professor of History at the University of North Texas, Denton, Texas, first became interested in Hodges while writing *Republicans and Reconstruction in Virginia, 1856–1870* (1991). He is also the author of *Planters and Plain Folk: Agriculture in Antebellum Texas* (1987). In recounting the story of Hodges's life, Lowe explores the challenges faced by blacks during the period known as Reconstruction, as well as the ways in which many of them responded.

One of the most persistent myths about the era of the Civil War and Reconstruction is that the millions of African Americans freed from slavery were all or nearly all illiterate and ignorant field hands, totally unprepared for citizenship and leadership. Many Southern and even some Northern white observers estimated that black Americans would require a generation or two before they could be trusted with the rights to vote and hold public office. Stemming from that myth was a widespread assumption among many white Americans, North and South, that African Americans would have to be shown the way to literacy and good citizenship and that they had no ideas, leaders, or initiatives of their own. They were like clay to be molded, according to this view, not actors in the great drama of the Civil War and Reconstruction.

Historians who have studied this period understand that these attitudes were wrongheaded. Courageous and intelligent black men such as Robert Smalls of South Carolina were natural leaders who only needed an opportunity to develop their talents and political skills. While Smalls spent his early years as a slave in Charleston, another black American some 350 miles to the north—Willis

Augustus Hodges—led a very different life as a freeborn and educated African American from a prosperous family in southeastern Virginia. Although they came from different backgrounds, Hodges and Smalls both demonstrated that black Americans were capable of thinking for themselves, developing their own leaders, and participating in their own elevation from slavery and second-class status.

Willis Augustus Hodges, the son of free mulatto parents and the grandson of a Revolutionary War veteran, was born a few weeks after the end of the War of 1812, on February 12, 1815. His birthplace, Princess Anne County in the southeastern corner of Virginia, was home to about three hundred free African Americans. The number of free blacks in the county was increasing at the time of his birth, doubtless due to the growing numbers of manumissions in the wake of the American Revolution. Flourishing in numbers, free black Virginians in Princess Anne County were also able to acquire land and become property-holding taxpayers. At the time of Willis's birth, his father, Charles Augustus Hodges, owned a fifty-acre farm, where Willis and his two older brothers and three older sisters played the usual children's games and romped around the family home. By the time Willis reached his midtwenties, his father had bought still more land, nearly two hundred acres in all, and the Hodges farm produced large crops of corn and other vegetables for sale in the nearby cities of Portsmouth and Norfolk. The hardworking and prosperous family also produced lumber, hogs, and other livestock for the markets of southeast Virginia.

During Willis's youth his family enjoyed cordial relations with their neighbors, both black and white. The family, eventually including twelve children, attended Sunday religious services along with whites in the neighborhood Baptist church, albeit sitting in a segregated corner. Willis and his older brother William played in the woods and fields with their cousins and with the sons of a nearby white family. The Hodges boys were unrestricted by the kinds of regulations that would later bedevil black Virginians.

Willis's father was not only prosperous; he was also ambitious for his children. He arranged for them to receive a proper education at a time when many white Virginia children had no schooling at all. He hired a white woman to tutor his children in the rudiments of reading, writing, and arithmetic. He later employed an Englishman to teach his sons and daughters in the home, and one of his white neighbors sent his own children to sit beside Willis and his siblings to learn the three Rs. Charles Hodges was determined that his children would have as many of the benefits of freedom as the times permitted. He kept a gun in his house and used it on several occasions to scare off hostile, harassing whites. He also sued a white man who had attempted to intimidate him into paying a fraudulent bill. His wife, Julia, was equal to her husband in her determination to resist second-class status and the indignities that many African Americans, slave and free, faced in antebellum America.

Willis's older brother William inherited his parents' pride and hatred for slavery—and then some. He became a preacher and had the courage to speak out against slavery and racial discrimination even to the white people in Princess Anne County. Soon, rumors began creeping through southeastern Virginia that William was doing more than preaching, that he was, in fact, forging documents to show that particular slaves were free, thus enabling those fugitives to make their escape from bondage. His outspoken sermons and rumored involvement in antislavery activities eventually landed him in a Norfolk jail, along with one of his cousins. In April 1829, shortly after a trial and conviction, William, his cousin, and four other black men made a daring escape from the jail. Eluding the posses on their trail, Hodges and his cousin fled all the way to Canada.

The prominent and prosperous family now became the target of hostile white vigilantes, who blamed their troubles on "uppity" black preachers like William. On one occasion a white mob searching for the fugitive brother invaded the Hodges house and knocked Willis's mother to the floor, and one of the crowd held a pistol to young Willis's head, threatening to blow out his brains if he did not reveal his brother's whereabouts. "I saw him cock his pistol and place it at my head," he recalled. "I then shut my eyes expecting to open them in eternity. I heard the report [of the gun] and thought I was shot until I heard our dog that was by my side howl out. I looked and saw that he had received the contents of the would-be murderer's pistol instead of myself." Incidents like this outraged Willis, and he soon became, in the eyes of local whites, "a very proud and saucy young fellow."[1]

Before this series of assaults and threats completely subsided in Princess Anne County, white Virginians in general, terrified by the famous Nat Turner slave uprising in nearby Southampton County, turned on the entire class of free blacks in the Old Dominion. The state legislature passed laws to prohibit black men from acting as preachers, and old laws that no one had bothered to enforce before were now revived to suppress free African Americans such as the Hodges family. Slave patrols crisscrossed the county, searching for black people who could not show proper authorization to travel about the countryside. Free black men were now required to show "free papers," documents proving their free status. And white mobs forced their way into the Hodges' home, carrying off "books, papers, bibles, dresses and many small and useful articles."[2] They arrested the family's English tutor for consorting with black folk and generally terrorized the black neighborhoods in Princess Anne County.

These and similar events in the late 1820s and early 1830s convinced Charles Hodges that his family was no longer safe in the land of their birth. He moved his wife and children to New York City, where they joined William, who had become a resident of the city after leaving his refuge in Canada. Although most of the family returned to Virginia after the Nat Turner hysteria subsided, the path between Princess Anne County and New York would be worn smooth over the next few decades as one or another of them moved back and forth between Virginia and the great metropolis on the Hudson River. Willis stayed behind to care for the farm when the family first relocated, but by early 1836, disgusted with the treatment of black workers in the South, he, too, went north to join his brother and an older sister in New York.

When Willis left Virginia at age twenty-one, he was required to have his "free papers" with him to prove his status as a free man. This document described him as "a light complexion free negro man, with bushy hair, with scar over his right eye, five feet six inches and a half high."[3] For the next twenty-five years, Willis occasionally visited his Princess Anne home, but the important events of his life took place in the North. A completely new and exciting era opened for him when he relocated to New York. At his sister's insistence, he improved his reading and writing and changed his countrified way of dressing and speaking. He got a job in a city store, joined the Abyssinian Baptist Church, began reading antislavery newspapers, and blended into the crowds at abolitionist meetings. No longer an innocent young rustic, he was now merging into the exhilarating city life of Northern free African Americans.

Willis Hodges later described his years in antebellum New York City as "some of the happiest days of my life."[4] He worked at various jobs—clerk, stevedore, painter, grocer—to support himself, plunged headlong into the public life of the city, and soon established himself as one of the leaders of New York's black community. He mobilized the residents of his neighborhood to start a school for black children, organized a temperance society to fight against alcohol abuse, joined the movement for equal suffrage rights for African Americans in the state of New York, attended abolition meetings, and frequently spoke up to remind his Northern friends of the plight of Southern slaves and free blacks.

When Hodges was in his early thirties, he joined with another free African American in New York to establish a newspaper that would advance the antislavery cause. Hodges and his partner (a locally prominent restaurateur named Thomas Van Rensselaer), hoping to knock down the walls of slavery, called their weekly paper

The Ram's Horn, recalling the biblical story of Joshua and his army using rams' horns to bring down the walls of an enemy city. In his role as editor and publisher of the newspaper, Hodges soon became friendly with a man he called "a good and noble-hearted Christian gentleman who has always been a friend to the poor and oppressed."[5] This man was John Brown, the white antislavery crusader who later became famous for his assault on Harpers Ferry, Virginia.

Willis Hodges and John Brown held some ideas in common, especially their conviction that mere words and long-winded prayers were not enough to bring down the institution of slavery. His attendance at countless abolition meetings had convinced Hodges that some of his Northern comrades were more interested in attracting attention to themselves with flowery speeches than in taking direct action on behalf of the South's persecuted blacks. They were, in his words, "more men of words than deeds."[6] Hodges had seen antiblack violence firsthand, and he and Brown reinforced each other's determination to do something more than talk. As the years passed, the two men cooperated on various projects, including the newspaper and an attempt to settle black families on farmland in upstate New York.

During the winter of 1848–1849, while he was still in his early thirties, Hodges wrote his autobiography. This document described his early years in Princess Anne County, the harassment of his family by local whites in the aftermath of his brother's escape from jail, his own move to New York, and his transformation from a country boy into an outspoken leader for black rights in New York City. His purpose in writing the autobiography, Hodges wrote, was to tell the world of "the wrongs and sufferings, the free people of color in the southern states have undergone, and are still undergoing." He did not intend to distract attention from the growing crusade against slavery. Rather, he said, he would "present them [slaves and free blacks] as one man of sorrow worthy of your aid and attention." Adhering closely to his belief that words alone could not end slavery, Hodges included in his autobiography a stirring declaration: "I further hold and truly believe that blood is the only thing that can wash the stain of slavery from this land."[7]

While Willis continued his antislavery activities in New York during the 1850s, his friend John Brown followed through on their shared belief that direct action was needed to erase the sin of slavery. In October 1859, he led eighteen followers into Harpers Ferry, Virginia, to arm the slaves and begin active resistance to the bondage of black men. It is very probable that Brown had discussed his idea for an invasion of Virginia with Hodges. If they did discuss the plan, Willis doubtless gave his wholehearted support to the project. However, the raid failed almost immediately, and Brown and his men were captured and put on trial for treason, incitement of slave rebellion, and murder. On his way to the gallows after his conviction, John Brown echoed the earlier call to action made by his friend Hodges in eerily similar language: "I John Brown am now quite *certain* that the crimes of this *guilty land* will never be purged *away* but with Blood."[8]

Brown's raid on Harpers Ferry was one of the events that catapulted the United States into a civil war in 1861. Willis Hodges, forty-six when the first shots were fired, was too old to serve in the Union army once it began enlisting African Americans two years later. But early in the war, he seized the opportunity to take direct action against the Confederate regime in his home state. In May 1862, shortly after Confederate forces evacuated Norfolk near his family home in Princess Anne County, Hodges acted as a scout for Union army patrols in the old neighborhood. With his intimate knowledge of the woods and roads of southeastern Virginia, he was doubtless an invaluable resource for Federal units stationed around Norfolk. On frequent occasions from 1862 onward, the Federal army sent columns into the countryside to ferret out Confederate bands hiding in the forests and swamps of Princess Anne County. The services of local African American guides such as Willis Hodges made life miserable for some of the same men who had persecuted his family when he was a teenager.

Hodges did not confine his wartime activities to scouting for the Union army, however. In the summer of 1864, acting on behalf of charitable organizations in New York City, he investigated charges that the free blacks and recently freed slaves of southeastern Virginia were being cheated and mistreated by the Federal occupying forces around Norfolk. After traveling around the farms and fields of Princess Anne and other nearby counties, he discovered that "there were a lot of speculators" who were selling the food and clothing sent by relief agencies in New York.[9] Instead of providing relief for poor black families, these supplies were being sold to line the pockets of some army personnel. When Hodges brought these activities to light and arranged for a public meeting in Norfolk to protest the situation, military officers ordered him out of town. Willis demanded justice, not only from Southern whites but also from the U.S. Army.

Even before the Confederacy finally collapsed in the spring of 1865, Willis and three of his brothers moved back to Virginia from New York. Almost immediately, they began organizing and agitating among the black residents of southeastern Virginia. Now that slavery was breathing its last, many black Virginians expected to enjoy full rights as citizens, including the rights to vote and hold public office. On April 4, five days before Robert E. Lee's army surrendered at Appomattox, older brother William presided at a public meeting of black Norfolk residents. William and the other African Americans at that meeting demanded that they be allowed to participate in the election of a new government for Norfolk. He—and doubtless his brothers—also helped to organize a black club to demand full political rights in the new age of freedom.

William, the long-ago fugitive from a Norfolk jail, also organized a school for the black people of southeastern Virginia. His high visibility finally landed him back in jail when local whites dusted off the charges first filed against him nearly forty years earlier. In 1866, he was sentenced to five years in prison for his activities in 1829. Willis, well known in abolitionist circles, immediately came to the rescue of his brother. He quickly secured an appointment to see Gen. Oliver O. Howard, the chief of the national Freedmen's Bureau, at his Washington office. At Willis's urging, General Howard convinced the Unionist governor of Virginia, Francis H. Pierpont, to pardon William. Nevertheless, the conservative white press in southeastern Virginia began referring to the Hodges brothers as criminals, often confusing William and Willis in their denunciations.

Undeterred by these public defamations, the brothers continued to organize the black people around Norfolk. When Congress initiated a more radical plan of Reconstruction in 1867—a plan that included black voting and officeholding—they redoubled their efforts around Norfolk and Princess Anne County. They addressed large crowds of African Americans, urging them to participate in the political process for the first time. They also traveled throughout the region, organizing voter-registration drives and urging blacks to elect their own representatives to a new state constitutional convention scheduled for late 1867.

Their past political experience in New York and their widely recognized names in Princess Anne and Norfolk Counties made Willis and his brother natural candidates for seats in the constitutional convention, now scheduled to meet in Richmond in December 1867. On election day in October, William was defeated for the seat from Norfolk County, but Willis—with 807 black votes and not a single white vote—was elected over two white candidates in Princess Anne County. All his years of attending meetings, making speeches, writing newspaper columns, and agitating for black rights had paid off and put him at the center of political power in his home state. The frightened young boy who had been threatened with a pistol in 1829 was now a popular leader among his people and an important political figure in Virginia.

The constitutional convention that assembled in Richmond in December 1867 was unlike any public meeting ever seen in the long history of the Old Dominion. This meeting had not been initiated by local citizens or institutions; it was mandated by Congress's new plan of Reconstruction. And the membership of the new assembly was completely different from those of earlier constitutional conventions. Northern-born immigrants (the so-called carpet-baggers), native whites who had joined the Northern-dominated Republican Party (the so-called scalawags), and especially black delegates—some former slaves but mostly African Americans free before the war—outnumbered the native white element that had always governed and written constitutions in the past. A new era had obviously dawned in old Virginia, and Willis Hodges had helped to bring it about.

The white conservative newspapers of Virginia, especially those in Richmond, were disgusted to see former slaves and other black men sworn into high public office, and they blistered Hodges and his fellow African Americans with scornful editorials and reporting. The *Richmond Whig and Advertiser*, among the more moderate journals to report on the convention, ridiculed Hodges by describing him as a "bacon colored son of Ham." The *Whig*'s reporter, like most white observers, dismissed him as a man out of his depth: "He is a field hand, but appears in the convention clad in his Sunday clothes, wears enormous brass-rimmed spectacles, and boasts a suit of glossy, well greased hair." The newspaper made no mention of Hodges's experience as a newspaper publisher, his antebellum political activities in New York, or his background as a public speaker. The white press instead had enormous fun at his expense, referring to him as "Specs" or "Uncle Specs" or "the Hon. Spectacles Hodges," alluding to his large eyeglasses. At times, the Richmond newspapers reported the comments of Hodges and other African American delegates in slave dialect, all to demonstrate how unfit these men were for their lofty positions.[10]

Hodges was a favorite target of such derision primarily because he took a leading role in the convention's proceedings and voted a straight Radical Republican line. He voted for a white Radical Republican as the convention's chairman, against a proposal to exclude blacks from voting in state elections, for an amendment to exclude most former Confederate military officers from the franchise, for an amendment to disfranchise those whites who had voted for secessionist delegates to the secession convention of 1861, for a proposal to exclude from public office any white Virginians who had supported the Confederacy, and for a provision that required racial integration in Virginia's public schools. No delegate to the convention was more determined to root up the old Virginia and replace it with a new, racially integrated, and forward-looking society. Willis Hodges had seen the old Virginia, and he did everything in his power to change it. "I hope we will soon be able to re-organize Old Virginia, or New Virginia, as it will then be," he said. "The old one has passed away with a great noise, and we are now coming to new things."[11]

He demanded that the convention adopt policies that would protect "the poor but loyal laboring men" of Virginia "who have been distressed and intimidated on account of their voting and supporting the Union Republican ticket." These men "were not only thrown out of employment, but were at once thrust forth from their homes" by former Confederate employers and landlords. Hodges also took a swipe at the editors and reporters who ridiculed the African American delegates in Richmond: "These are the men who are found in every community and may be likened unto the unclean bird which is found all over our State, and which has two z's in its name, that turns from everything clean, wholesome and healthy to feast upon filth and corruption."[12]

Hodges found it particularly ironic that white conservatives should be so scornful of the more modest educational levels of former slaves and free blacks. "They have made it unlawful for us to read, to preach, or in any way to elevate ourselves. They have kept us down with a brutal and a cruel hand. The degradation, the ignorance which they presume to despise in us, is all the work of their own hands."[13] In this and many other matters before the convention, he demonstrated that a supposedly dull-witted and ignorant "field hand" was quite capable of detecting inconsistency and deceit among his political foes.

He objected to every attempt by other delegates—black or white—to inject racial categories into the new constitution. There should be no racial references at all in the new Virginia, according to Hodges. The state should be totally color blind in all its business, including the education of its children. On this matter, he proved to be more radical even than some of his black colleagues, for the measure requiring racially integrated schools was defeated by a vote of 67 to 21, with 10 black delegates opposing the measure and 12 favoring it. He was more successful in another attempt to equalize the burdens and benefits of citizenship. Hodges proposed that the state's tax system be restructured by dropping the regressive taxes on individuals and replacing them with taxes on real and personal property. The final version of the new constitution incorporated these ideas, to the great benefit of the lower and middle classes in Virginia.

After months of debate and voting, the convention finally completed its work in April 1868. The constitution written by Hodges and his fellow Republicans provided Virginians with their first system of public education, distributed the tax burden more equally among the various classes, enacted suffrage and office-holding for African American males for the first time, prohibited racial discrimination in jury selection, made more public offices elective, and gave debtors additional opportunities to escape bankruptcy and ruin. For a convention dominated by men described in the newspapers as ignorant field hands and greedy carpetbaggers and scalawags, it had managed to produce one of the best constitutions in the state's history, and Willis Augustus Hodges had been one of the leading figures in the proceedings.

Hodges's role in the constitutional convention of 1867–1868 was the peak of his public career. He failed to win a seat in the state senate in 1869, but he continued to be active in Republican party politics and local government after the constitutional convention. He served in various county and local posts in Princess Anne County, and three of his brothers held state and county offices in the early 1870s. Within a few years, however, the Hodges brothers were, one by one, removed from office and relegated to the political sidelines, either by more moderate white Republicans or by old conservative enemies.

Out of office and out of public life, Willis eventually returned to New York City in 1881, but the old soil called him back to Princess Anne County a few years later. Now in his seventies, he spent his last years working as a plasterer and serving as a minister to black Virginians around Norfolk. On September 24, 1890, at age seventy-five, Willis Hodges died at his home near Norfolk, not far from the scenes of his boyhood romps with his brothers and sisters, his scouts for the Union army during the Civil War, and his speeches demanding justice and equality for all Virginians. It had been a good life.

The private and public careers of Willis Hodges contradicted the popular perception, then and later, that the African Americans who emerged from the Civil War had few if any intelligent and experienced leaders. Raised in a free, tight-knit, and prosperous family, he learned to read and write while still a child. Later, he took part in various reform movements in New York and published an abolitionist newspaper. He formed a friendship with John Brown and guided Union army columns through the backcountry of southeast Virginia. And after the Civil War, he served his people as a local and county official. He organized former slaves for their new roles as voters and officeholders and took a leading part in drafting a new constitution for Virginia. His life was marked by courage, intelligence, persistence, and a vision—far ahead of its time—of a new America based on equality for all its citizens.

Notes

1. Willis Augustus Hodges, *Free Man of Color: The Autobiography of Willis Augustus Hodges*, ed. Willard B. Gatewood (Knoxville: University of Tennessee Press, 1982), 17, 29.
   2. Ibid., xxvii.

3. Ibid., 43.

4. Ibid., 53.

5. Ibid., 78.

6. Ibid., 1–11.

7. Ibid., 4, 56.

8. Quoted in James M. McPherson, *Ordeal by Fire: The Civil War and Reconstruction*, 2d ed. (New York: McGraw-Hill, 1992), 120.

9. *The Debates and Proceedings of the Constitutional Convention of the State of Virginia, Assembled at the City of Richmond, Tuesday, December 3, 1867* (Richmond, VA: Office of the New Nation, 1868), 163.

10. *Richmond Whig and Advertiser,* December 10, 1867, and January 7, March 2, March 28, April 8, and April 17, 1868.

11. *The Debates and Proceedings,* 164.

12. Ibid., 60, 61, 62.

13. Ibid., 62.

Suggestions for Further Reading

Those who wish to further explore the lives of the fourteen subjects of this book or various topics raised by their stories have much good reading material available to them.

For further information about Peter Welsh, see Lawrence Frederick Kohl and Margaret Cosse Richard, eds., *Irish Green and Union Blue: The Civil War Letters of Peter Welsh, Color Sergeant, 28th Regiment Massachusetts Volunteers* (New York: Fordham University Press, 1986). For more about the common Union soldiers, see Earl J. Hess, *The Union Soldier in Battle* (Lawrence: University Press of Kansas, 1996); Gerald F. Linderman, *Embattled Courage: The Experience of Combat in the American Civil War* (New York: Free Press, 1987); James M. McPherson, *What They Fought For* (Baton Rouge: Louisiana State University Press, 1994) and *For Country, Cause, and Comrades: Why Men Fought in the Civil War* (New York: Oxford University Press, 1997); Reid Mitchell, *Civil War Soldiers: Their Expectations and Their Experiences* (New York: Viking, 1988), and *The Vacant Chair: The Northern Soldier Leaves Home* (New York: Oxford University Press, 1993); James I. Robertson Jr., *Soldiers Blue and Gray* (New York: Warner Books, 1988); and Bell I. Wiley, *The Life of Billy Yank: The Common Soldier of the Union* (Baton Rouge: Louisiana State University Press, 1952). On the topic of foreign-born troops in the Union ranks, see William L. Burton, *Melting Pot Soldiers: The Union's Ethnic Regiments* (Ames: Iowa State University Press, 1988).

On Winfield Scott Hancock, see Glenn Tucker, *Hancock the Superb* (Indianapolis, IN: Bobbs-Merrill, 1960). On Richard Ewell, see Donald Pfanz's biography of that remarkable Confederate general, *Richard S. Ewell: A Soldier's Life* (Chapel Hill: University of North Carolina Press, 1997).

On Raphael Semmes, see Spencer C. Tucker, *Raphael Semmes and the* Alabama (Abilene, TX: McWhiney Foundation Press, 1996); John M. Taylor, *Confederate Raider: Raphael Semmes of the* Alabama (Washington, DC: Brassey's, 1995); and Edward Boykin, *Ghost Ship of the Confederacy: The Story of the* Alabama *and Her Captain, Raphael Semmes* (New York: Funk and Wagnalls, 1957).

Charles Henry Foster has no biography, but those who wish to learn more about the struggle within eastern North Carolina during the Civil War can read Wayne K. Durrill, *War of Another Kind: A*

Southern Community in the Great Rebellion (New York: Oxford University Press, 1990).

On Francis T. Nicholls, see Evans J. Casso, *Francis T. Nicholls: A Biographical Tribute* (Thibodaux, LA: Nicholls College Foundation, 1987).

For more about Anna Dickinson, see Wendy Hamand Venet, *Neither Ballots nor Bullets: Women Abolitionists and the Civil War* (Charlottesville: University of Virginia Press, 1991). On LaSalle Pickett, see Lesley J. Gordon, *General George E. Pickett in Life and Legend* (Chapel Hill: University of North Carolina Press, 1998).

On the remarkable Prince and Princess Salm-Salm, see the princess's own memoir, *Ten Years of My Life,* 2 vols. (London: Richard Bentley and Son, 1876).

Lucy Virginia French has no biography, but on the general topic of women in the Confederacy, see Catherine Clinton and Nina Silber, eds., *Divided Houses: Gender and the Civil War* (New York: Oxford University Press, 1992), and George C. Rable, *Civil Wars: Women and the Crisis of Southern Nationalism* (Urbana: University of Illinois Press, 1989).

Those interested in reading more about Charles G. Finney and the issues raised by his career can consult James H. Moorhead, *American Apocalypse: Yankee Protestants and the Civil War, 1860–1869* (New Haven: Yale University Press, 1978). To learn more about John Sherman, see his autobiography, *John Sherman's Recollections of Forty Years in the House, Senate, and Cabinet* (Chicago: Werner, 1895).

On Robert Smalls, see Edward A. Miller Jr., *Gullah Statesman: Robert Smalls from Slavery to Congress, 1839–1915* (Columbia: University of South Carolina Press, 1995). On Willis Augustus Hodges, see his own *Free Man of Color: The Autobiography of Willis Augustus Hodges,* ed. Willard B. Gatewood (Knoxville: University of Tennessee Press, 1982).

Index

Abolitionists, 6, 16, 54, 61, 65, 95, 96, 98, 102, 104, 156, 208, 216
Acklen, Adelicia Franklin (Lide), 148–49
Adams, Charles Francis, Jr., 128
Adams, John Quincy, 43, 128
African Brigade, 72
Agrippina (Confederate navy ship), 46, 48, 49
Alabama (Confederate navy ship), 43, 46–56: battle with *Kearsarge,* 55–56; crew and officers, 46, 47, 48–49, 52; sinking of, 56; steam and sail power, 46, 52; weapons, 46
Alexander, Edward Porter, 37
Allan, William, 38
Amalgamation church, 157
American Anti-Slavery Society, 96, 98, 99, 157
Andersonville (GA) Confederate prison, 72
"Anna E. Dickinson and the Gynekokracy" (editorial), 107–8
Anthony, Henry Brown, 184
Anthony, Susan B., 104: *History of Woman Suffrage,* 103
Antietam, Battle of (1862), 4, 18, 84
Anti-immigration sentiment, 2
Antiseptic knowledge, 11, 83
Anti-Slavery Society. *See* American Anti-Slavery Society
Appomattox surrender of Lee to Grant (1865), 192, 193
Ariel (U.S. steamer), 49
Arkansas, 190

Armfield, John, 147, 148
Armistead, Lewis, 14
Army of Northern Virginia (Confederate), 34, 37, 84, 85
Army of Tennessee (Confederate), 141, 147, 149, 150
Army of the Potomac (Union), 4, 6, 9, 16, 22, 127: command, 18, 19, 20, 124; reorganization, 21; review by Lincoln, 129
Army of the Valley (Confederate), 82
Army of Virginia (Union), 126
Azores, 45

Bahama (Confederate navy ship), 46
Baker, Edward, 175
"Baldy." *See* Smith, William F.
Ball's Bluff, Battle of (1861), 198
Baltic (steamer), 191
Banks, 182–83
Baptists, 153, 161, 216
Barcelona. See Enrica
Beaufort (SC) Republican Club, 202
Beauregard, Pierre G. T., 89
Beecher, Henry Ward, 102, 154
Beersheba Springs (TN), 146, 147
Bell, Henry H., 50
Bell, John, 137
Bennett, James Gordon, 130
Bennett, James Gordon, Jr., 130
"Black codes," 201, 202
Blackmore, Bettie Ridley, 148
"Black Republicanism," 62–63